The Woodbine Chronicles

The Woodbine Chronicles:

A Neighborhood Love Story

Suzanne O Stelling

The Woodbine Chronicles: A Neighborhood Love Story
Copyright © 2023 by Suzanne O Stelling

Disclaimer: The events in this book are my memories from my perspective. The names of my former neighbors have been changed to protect their identities.

ISBN 9798386920678
Printed in the United States of America

Follow @suzannestelling on Instagram for more glimpses into life on Woodbine Avenue.

Front Cover: Photo Example of Gentrification, © Suzanne Stelling, 2019
Oxford Languages defines *gentrification* as "the process whereby the character of a poor urban area is changed by wealthier people moving in, improving housing, and attracting new businesses, typically displacing current inhabitants in the process." According to public record, this 1890s Barber house in our neighborhood was sold in March of 2017, costing $51,000 at $20/sq ft. It then sat for quite a while. Here and there we would see trucks coming by briefly. Work began in earnest in late 2021. It was listed in January, 2022, for $599,500 on Zillow.com, $230/sq ft, a 1,075.5% increase.

This book is based on actual people:
beautiful, God-created people in complex situations.
Please honor their lives as I do: with respect.
I have changed their names, and as of publication,
all but two have moved off of my block.

To my Woodbine people: I love you.
God has used you to open my eyes and bless me,
to challenge and wreck me, and to love me.
I miss your close proximity, your complicated lives, your laughter,
your moods, and your styles.
The porch swing is still up any time you can get by.

To Jean Thompson, Jane Morrow, and my Handsome:
Oh my goodness, thank you for refining this book.
Without your efforts, it would be a lesser creation.

Main Character Reference List

Suzanne Standing: nicknamed the Babe and Suzy, married to Handsome, co-owner of the Woodbine House

Grant Standing: nicknamed Handsome, married to The Babe, co-owner of the Woodbine House

Marlie and Lu: Grant and Suzanne's daughters

Cinco, nicknamed Sync: beloved, Vol-crazy neighbor boy

Reyana, nicknamed Reys: singing, bubbly neighbor girl

Beels: Cinco's half-sister

Thunderbolt & Freddy: tempestuous, treasured biracial couple

Ray-Mee: cherished neighbor, mother to Cinco.

Collins: House guest at the same time as Njalla. Tall, slim, white male photographer with OCD issues.

Njalla: House guest at the same time as Collins. Black, fierce, homeless young woman with substance issues.

Bryant, Barb, Nona, Maria, Shelton: conversational friends

Table of Contents

Please note:
Quotations from the Bible are in Bold Times New Roman.
Journal excerpts are in Palatino bold italic.

In Closing: Beyond Woodbine

Appendices

iii

Preface

Glaciers tell a story of transformation, of reshaping the landscape as they slowly scrape and push and decimate and move, gradually, titanic inches at a time.

A mathematical certainty appears: pressure, mass, and time combine, and a terrain is reconfigured. The old dies and the new is reborn.

Such happened to me; I name my glacier Woodbine Avenue.

"Every single thing that happened to you is yours, and you get to tell it … in your own voice. That's why you were born." Anne Lamott, in her TED Talk, "12 truths I learned from life and writing," gave me permission to take a year and a half of my life to write this story. It's both for me and for you, Dear Reader.

This book is an invitation to climb onto the glacier that resurfaced my heart and peer into what it looked like for us to intentionally move into an urban minority neighborhood.

We came as learners, which was paramount. Our teachers were heavyweights:
Racism cataloged harsh lesson plans and was often Pass/Fail, no grace.
Classism constantly carried a ruler, measuring any sense of false security or pointing out subtle snobbery in my thinking.
Gentrification kept ripping pages out of the textbook of how I thought I would love my neighbor.

But there was also instruction that came with hope.
Love ferreted out any hardness of heart, any preconceptions or assumptions.
Laughter came with the children, who just want to be loved and seen.
Patience helped me calm down and try again.
Prayer channeled my growing affection, even ferocity, heavenward.
Failure said gently, "Try again, my dear."

We're still learning.

Join us.

Chapter One: Getting to Woodbine, Fall 2016

I AM IN THE GREEN WATER, buoyant, surrounded by sheep-like hills furry with every hue of green. A minnow nibbles at my toe and I startle, splashing myself as I sit upright on the float. I hear my rowdy brother and his friends coming down the path, ready to slalom. I join in, claiming my spot at the front of the boat where I can sing in anonymity while I watch for stray submerged logs. The quest for the afternoon: who can get their elbow to the water as they cut away from the wake?

After a swim, I walk the steep path to the cabin, naming the flowers and insects I observe, noting every move in the tall grass, counting the piliated woodpecker drills, wondering why the wrens are upset. Deer scat is piled in brown pebbles to the side of the walkway. Except for a streak draining from my long hair, I'm almost dry when I reach the front door. A line of red rims my bikini — shoot, another place I missed with the sunscreen. That will peel.

My father is full of mischief this Saturday, gathering all of the lunch leftovers, a few vegetables, and a bucket of water. As the boys come up the hill, the battle ensues: my Nordic, sturdy, brilliant father acting my age, 15 years old, pelting the boys with old tomatoes, spent coffee, and a carton of eggs. They scatter, yelling, creating a revenge plan as they near the house. I smile. This was home: summer set in forest and water, pinks and play; nights reading and playing Spoons, or counting shooting stars from the rooftop, all other sound drowned by cicadas.

Enfolded in affection, my childhood was surrounded by the joy and curiosity of discovery. Global cultural exposure began when I was barely in double digits with a trip to Spain and Portugal: I could've sat at the feet of a flamenco dancer for the rest of my life. On the way to Tanzania and Kenya, our plane was boarded at a refueling stop in Uganda. Idi Amin had just come to power, and the world was holding its collective breath: would he be a brutal dictator, a constructive builder of his nation, or a laissez-faire leader? Our answer came as his soldiers took every passport. We had to wait in the plane, seatbelts fastened, for hours. Even at age 11 I knew the large guns slung across their backs could ravage each of us in a moment, killing us all, yet somehow I could not fathom that they would do it. Ah, I was young.

My father educated African doctors about his new invention, the flexible sigmoidoscope, then joined us for safaris. Africa became like an IV bag, dripping the love of dirt and fire and wild animals and black faces into my blood, the lifeline of future affections.

I did not know what to do with the poor, carved-out faces rows deep by the train stations. I asked my father, who had told me to walk briskly by, why he would not give them money. See their broken limbs? See those scars? See their sores? Couldn't we help? He could not explain to me the systems of slavery and the brutal networks of begging-as-business; I could not comprehend a government that allowed such a shameful, pitiful existence. Were such hellish predators actually alive who would do horrible things to the helpless? He felt I was too young, too naive with my privileged background to have such conversations. I would have to learn on my own time.

We tracked with the Great Migration of zebras, wildebeests, and elephants, always learning from our guides. We gained nicknames: my father, at 6'4", was *Twiga*, Swahili for giraffe. My brother called me the Swahili word for wart hog. Siblings: What can you do?

I felt alive in the natural world of East Africa, but also in other unique, glorious spaces: Austria as an exchange student, with its precipitous mountains and (of course) the songs of Julie Andrews. Egypt, so hot, people thick like bees at the hive on buses and in tiny, bumping, honking cars. Japan, with me an awkward almost-tall blond. Jordan and Israel with their ancient histories, mysteries, and religious strife. European countries with their ornate cathedrals, high fashion, and rationality. Canadian and American national parks with all things snow, blue, and cold. Everywhere was wonder and discovery. Natural beauty filled me with the joy of living.

I flourished in a place where cars had names like Lola Lexus and Prissy Prius, and boats had clever references to my father's vocation as a gastroenterologist: Sea Scope, MicroScope, and RiverScope. Science and medicine were in my veins even when I was unaware of their presence, impulses and ideas flowing along axons, igniting life and thought.

At fifteen I was pursued by a boy whose pathologies were twin cancers: lying and manipulation. The sweetness of my family nest had not prepared me well for such a deceitful stalker. When he attempted suicide at our breakup, I cried out in wordless despair to the God of my childhood songs:

"Jesus loves me, this I know, for the Bible tells me so.
Little ones to Him belong, we are weak but He is strong.
Yes, Jesus loves me, yes, Jesus loves me.
Yes, Jesus loves me! The Bible tells me so."

That night, lying on the floor of a friend's house and shivering with tears in my sleeping bag, I heard God's reply, Spirit to awakening spirit, brimming Person to broken person: "I love you." Three days later, the same firm voice in my spirit: "I am enough." And my life was forever changed.

God began His gentle reordering of my heart that summer. I pored over the Bible, shocked with the relevancy of Proverbs, tenderized by the full story of Jesus, and warned from the rise and fall of God's people in ancient times. I was numinous before God: all my wonder and delight was focused on Him. His affection simultaneously stopped me cold like a dirty peasant before a resplendent King, and made me twirl like a little girl in pink tulle and sequins, lost in joy. I craved His affection, writing love notes to Him on the pages of my lab notes and textbooks. At my family lakeside cabin, I felt the call of God in the trees, the lake, the sunsets, the hills. As I sang love songs to my Father, I was truly lit from within.

~elllee~

I entered my junior year of high school re-made, a new creation, internal atoms re-charged with a spiritual electricity. My classmates noticed changes within me with curiosity. "Why are you so happy?" I had to convince them I was not on speed: "No, really, it's *Jesus*. I had no idea He loves me so much! And He loves you too! He's amazing. Do you know about Him? I'm completely changed by His love." I had no tact, no sense of "witnessing" or "testimony" or doing some religious duty by speaking about my faith. Love just burst out, genuinely and joyfully. I could not get over Jesus.

During my senior year, school took a lonely turn. Senioritis infected my friends, and they fled from faith (temporarily) to experiment with the wilder side. They did not want me near. I would walk into my school's most coveted space, the Senior Lounge, and the girls would look at me with disdain and saunter out. Solitude drove me deep into my heavenly Father's heart, where He made space to nurture me. My roots in Him gained grit and traction.

I found my people at Vanderbilt where college years were warm and formative. I sang my way into God's Presence, acting in community theater as I developed the skills of research and study. My roommates were deep-water women, and they swam the ocean of faith, boys, and academics. I learned with a thrill that you actually could eat Oreo ice cream for breakfast. Gasp.

I met and married a professional athlete who introduced me to love and betrayal. As we traveled the world for his sport, I noted with sadness the frightful emptiness and malaise of the wealthy and the constant attempts to fill a spirit with physical satisfactions. There were always fangirls in the lobby waiting to see who they could bed for the night. Week after week, city after city, they were always there, always the same: pretty, sexy, long hair, great legs, hungry for a famous penis and sexual stamina. Bright faces and B-cups. I was sickened and grieved.

At Year 12 of my marriage, I faced a similar debacle. Our frail scaffolding of fractures and failures could not be overcome. Fourteen years, one daughter, two homes, multiple miscarriages, over a dozen countries, and one unyielding requirement: full fidelity or divorce. I could not force him — anyone — to love me, to choose me. I hoped, shaking, in total vulnerability. His answer became clear, and I filed. Three months later, I reverted to my maiden name.

Divorce forced its way into my body and soul and broke me into pieces, shattering my confidence and silencing my joy. For a time, yes, for a time. I gasped for breath, tried to care for our daughter, and felt God call me into strength: "Backbone, girl. Warrior up. Shards will come; you've got to grow strong enough to stand. This is your reality, but remember, I am here. Don't run from the pain; just fall into Me. This will hurt, but I am at work. Trust Me."

Trusting — trusting *anyone* — felt like raw fear, like balancing on a high-wire over the Grand Canyon on a breezy day, like branching out onto thin ice in the middle of a lake, like jumping out of a plane with or without a parachute. I inched along, slower, more thoughtful, more quiet, tentative and speculative and protective. My parents were a haven for me and 5-year-old Marlie.

Over time, I was renovated into a single working mama. My father gave me a stable job as a lab assistant, and my mind reawakened from the fog of emotional trauma. I used lasers as a diagnostic tool on skin lesions. My job was to create an algorithm to identify the status of a lesion: was it normal, did it have levels of low or high dysplasia, or was it cancerous? The work felt concrete, measurable, assessable — so different from my interior life.

"Better," I analyzed, "to be a teacher. Then I will be on my daughter's schedule." An intense master's degree later, I worked in my local middle school bringing scientific wonder into my students' lives. The cell — *the cell!* What could be more remarkable? The kingdoms of creation, classification, DNA, Punnett Squares, the basics of anatomy and physiology, dissecting fish and pig hearts, looking at pond water under the microscope ... I was alive again, biological life breathing personal life back into me. I poured love into my adolescent students, and they responded with their own awkward, beloved, moose-like, middle school attempts at affection.

A complex-minded philosopher, Grant Standing, mowed my grass, headset on and mind working to comprehend God. His life had been dulled by drugs for a decade, but the sturdy Christian bones of his upbringing were rattling back to life. He cried two weeks of repentant tears, and re-emerged, a new man.

4

I brought him water and fresh sourdough bread.

More than once, when my child was securely at a friend's house, I would go into my steep suburban backyard and weep over my dead marriage and obscure future. My sobs would be interrupted by the sound of his lawnmower coming around the bend of my yard, and there he was, green chlorophyll spattered below the knee on his rough, baggy jeans, bits of blades of grass in his beard, melanin strong on his forearms. He would see me and stop. A few paces away, he would simply sit. Near, but not close.

After a few minutes, when my tears had slowed: "You gonna be okay?"
"Yes. Thanks."
I would go inside; he would resume his mowing.

The fourth year after my divorce he asked me to the mountains, to the Sinks in the Smokies. I remember it still: a cool day for July. Sun and light filtered through the trees gently but with energy. I heard bubbling water and the happy squeals of swimming children. I looked for salamanders and crawdads under rocks along the stream's edge. After rock-hopping for hours, he turned my chin to him and kissed me gently. I never went out with another man. Till the day one of us must scatter ashes, I will call him Handsome and he will call me The Babe.

One afternoon in early 2004 I happened to course down a gravel road that dead-ended into a field with a hand-made sign: "For sale. 6.6 acres." It was nestled behind a 100-acre horse farm in West Knoxville, creating the illusion of a much greater expanse of property. Amidst the massive oaks, the shy deer, the curious raccoons, and the native ginger, we became a family of four in April 2004: his and hers daughters, both the hormonal age of 12. We built a house I drew on a napkin, each daughter getting their own bathroom in case teen fireworks exploded between them. The girls became a team at home, both glad to not be "onlys," happy to face their newly blended parents with a proposal or demand as a pair.

Over the next decade Handsome, a landscaper, did his magic on the 6.6, timing flowers to bloom from snow-spring's yellow and purple crocuses to fall's scarlet and crimson maples. He etched out a stream in front of our house, loading it with purple and yellow irises, accenting dark evergreen laurels with ground-hugging, deep purple ajuga. Pink spirea shared space with a three-story, five-caned crepe myrtle. Ornamental grasses reseeded here and there along the stream, waving and congratulating each other on their fine position. A Contorted Filbert twisted and turned by the second pond, making an excellent perch for the finches who raided the seeds of the nearby purple coneflowers.

Our front porch was broad, made for rockers and leisurely conversations and reminders to slow down. There were always fresh flowers on our hand-me-down caned porch furniture. We used his company's skid-steer and our John Deere to place a massive stone as a bridge over the stream to the porch. Crossing that stone was like walking over into peace. The world *out there* was rough; *here* was rest.

On that porch, I chose a new job; prayed for my family; watched our girls grow up into fashionable beauties; refreshed my soul in the silence; and nurtured my love of learning. I studied to the sound of flowing water and worshiped to the tune of spring peepers and bullfrogs. Spotting deer in the field became sport; feeding marshmallows to the raccoons on the back porch, a thrill. Two large koi swam in the deepest pond — the cranes couldn't get their large frames into their throats, as they had every other fish. Cats and dogs brought us a sense of play and seemed to fill out our limited human senses of sight and smell. Handsome and I whooped at the occasional fox sighting, and howled along with the coyotes at night when they communally celebrated their kills.

I believed in Biblical Eden: in the stories of its divinely planted beauty and purpose, of Almighty God having conversation with earthy Adam and the innocent woman, of the treachery of scintillating Satan, of the fall of mankind. The woman had chosen to eat the forbidden fruit; why? It was lovely. It was nourishing. It would make her wise. I, too, was an Eve, enjoying beautiful things, wanting to eat healthfully and nourish others, and deeply desiring to be wise. Wasn't that almost every woman I knew? Eve's sin, independence. Going after right things in the wrong way. Oh, how well I related to her. And the man, unmoved, failing to protect, failing to intercede: "Wait, let's go to our Father! He said not to do this thing. Stop, beloved, and let's go talk to Him about it." Adam's sin, immobility. Not taking action when action was needed.

Since that fall from God, I believe we are all instinctively searching for our own Edens. Handsome and I created ours on the 6.6 in field and flower and woods and home. "Come, cross the stone and sit awhile," I would tell friends. "Listen to the wind speak the love and beauty of God Almighty. Really. His peace is here."

⁓

Handsome, my masculine, strong-minded poet, strummed his guitar on our porch. "Is this really what God wants for us?" He looked around at the four-story white and red oaks, the pencil-straight pines. His brow furrowed in its familiar way. "Babe, I think we've built our own kingdom here. Do you feel it? For over a decade we've populated this area with fragrant bushes, flowering trees, perennials, and specimen plants. We've created a physically usable, visually lovely sanctuary, a refuge. We've made this place — this beautiful place — and honored it as God's gift. But I'm restless." He looked at me, eyes serious

6

and penetrating. Ah, my philosopher, constantly asking and thinking. I stayed silent, waiting for him to gather words.

"Are you restless, Babe? I'm fitted for challenge, for difficulty, for the poor, for the limited, for the person who's been dealt a raw hand, and here I am in luxury and natural beauty beyond what I ever dreamed of. But rather than being thankful and comfortable and relieved, I'm awkward and ...."

He took a thoughtful breath, the kind that cued me to know something weighty was about to be said. I didn't know whether to lean in or to run.

"Babe, I don't think we need to live here anymore. I think we need to move into the city. Into the battle. Where people are hurting. When I read about Jesus' lifestyle, it doesn't look like this. This isn't the Christian life I read about and respect. Where's the sacrifice? Where's the cost? Where's the suffering? Where are the poor, the hurting, the sick, the homeless, the helpless? Where's the risk and the inconvenience and the love that actually requires something of us? How are we 'losing our lives to find them'? We've got everything we need and more."

There was no guilt in his tone; there was *urgency,* there was purpose: following Jesus. Choosing a sacrificial lifestyle because of Jesus, not guilt. But while his words rang true, I resisted them. I talked to God about it: I've kept a journal since I was a girl, and for some reason, apart from the clarity of Scripture and the sheer goodness of being in a forest, writing out my prayers is how I hear God best. I write about whatever is on my mind, and then I pause, waiting for some type of response that aligns with what I know of God through the Bible. I know this is foreign to some Christians (like my husband) who perceive God in other ways. This is just what opens Him for me; I sense His invitation when I write.

"Father, I'll miss the creek and the sound of the water."
He answered, "I am your living water."
"I'll miss the fire."
"I will light a fire within you."
"I'll miss this house."
"I am your home."
"I'll miss all the wildness — the deer, the raccoons, the coyotes and their songs."
"Trust Me, Child. I will bring you wild creatures beyond your imagination."

God challenged me, not sparing my feelings. His directness caught my attention:

"Daughter, you are sick with safety;
condemned by your comfort;
and weakened by your wealth."

Oh dang.

I trusted this, because even though the words stung, they had a tone of love ... perhaps even rescue? It felt like I was hearing the more feral side of God, the untamed One who allows His people to suffer, the truth that makes following folk uncomfortable. The One who directs us to take up our cross and to lose our lives to find them. The One who plays outside conventional boundaries and safe doctrines.

Alliteration is my love language, which God knows: "sick with safety...." Although safety was what I wanted, it was not always what God promised Jesus' disciples.

I *was* comfortable; I *was* wealthy. It was all true. I had seen the world; my parents had paid for my elite education. I had enjoyed the privileges of dance, exercise clubs, lessons, class trips, safaris, adventures, and amusements. I had traveled to soft-sand beaches, foreign cities, mountain ranges far from home, dunes, tropical rain forests, deserts, and glaciers.

All this while seeing the poor in Egypt, Mozambique, Kenya, Jamaica, Costa Rica, China, and Haiti. Their sunken, dark eyes; their hopeless begging; their incalculable thinness; it all deeply distressed me. I will never forget a small girl in Egypt, her crackly arms frozen in an upheld posture, her dress loose around her bent knees, her eyes closed ... asleep ... while begging. What chance did she have? How could I help her? What could I do? Most people said to sponsor a child or invest in trustworthy organizations, but to not look for answers from governments. Government corruption made me rail with anger. How could a government rob its own people? How could they be so selfish as to let supplies rot in a ship off the coast when their own people were starving? Where were their systems of education? How could their own engineers and farmers save their people?

I only knew the American poor from a distance or from reading, and had no personal experience with the factors that swelled like consecutive waves against them. Why was my life's bucket continually full of good things, and their buckets always seemed to drain so quickly, rarely refilling without intervention?

Grant and I heard the cry of a world — our world, on our watch — aching under the weight of harm: racism, injustice, fear, classism, abuses, usury, alienation, drugs, violence, crime, theft, kidnapping, brutality, gang wars, political scandals, carbon footprints, global warming, extinction. We felt the need to get into battle.

How? Neither of us knew, exactly. It felt as if we were standing on the apex of the continental divide, one foot on each side, watching the raindrops fall and flow toward the Pacific or Atlantic. It seemed that God was asking us to leave one side and commit to the other: to leave our home of refuge and safety and wealth and security and beauty and quiet and solitude and deer and raccoons and peepers and peace. And we knew we had to go.

I felt the sorrowful ache of giving up the space I loved. I wrote in my journal, *Your hand is here, churning up the norm, calling us to leave, to get into the battle, to let go of our pretty lives, and go die. I've read in the Gospels for decades how I must lose my life to find it; why is that just now making sense to me in the context of where I live?*

While Handsome and I did not experience guilt and shame as a strong motivator in this conversation, we knew we needed true-north guides. Who could help us understand race and class? We began reading in earnest to see what we could not see. *Strangers at My Door. The Insanity of God. Interrupted. Jesus and the Disinherited. Children of Fire. Half the Sky. I'm Still Here. Restavec. Same Kind of Different as Me. Tattoos on the Heart. The Color of Compromise. The Beautiful Community. The Lost Letters of Pergamum. The Space Between Us. Tightrope. Waking Up White. White Awake. The Gospel of Matthew,* listening with attention specifically given to race, class, and culture. *Deuteronomy, Leviticus, Philemon, Amos, Micah* in the Old and New Testaments.

We launched with personal questions: Jesus mentioned the 'deceitfulness of wealth' in His parable about the soils (Matthew 13:1-23). What did that phrase mean? How was I being deceived by wealth? What were my blind spots? Was it the illusion that the order and beauty I experienced seemed universal? That I could be a Christian and be complacent toward the poor, giving while keeping a safe distance? That I could live a self-centered life and still give my tithe? That I didn't even consider the poor or those with less options or networking opportunities, because I'd never personally experienced those as problems? How were my advantages and opportunities keeping me blind?

From the Bible, I knew the Kingdom of God was racially and economically diverse, yet Handsome and I lived in a white world in privileged, bubble-like West Knoxville. Our networks were white; our jobs were white; our government was white; our church was white; our opportunities were white; our neighborhood was white. "God," I whispered, "forgive us for our racial divisions. Why are we so segmented and partitioned, like oil and vinegar? Why are we not more mixed in every way? Your Kingdom will be rich with variety, *from every tribe and tongue and nation* (Revelation 7:9). Grant and I want to start practicing now."

As I mulled over these questions, I seemed to hear Jesus say,

"I did not give up My wealth and heavenly riches to make you rich and smugly comfortable. I gave up My glory to set an example before you: leave these riches and go give your life away. Then your riches will be great in heaven. Don't worry, My Child: I've got an abundant life for you. My wealth will flow into you as you keep the flow of abundance moving to others."
Even as I answered, *Yes, Lord*, I wondered, What does it mean to give my life away? Will this question define the next phase of my life?

"Unless a grain of wheat falls into the earth and dies, it remains alone; but if it dies, it bears much fruit. He who loves his life loses it, but he who hates his life in this world will keep it for eternal life. If anyone serves Me, he must follow Me; and where I am, there shall My servant be also; if anyone serves Me, the Father will honor him."

In thinking through that passage (John 12:24,25), I wrote it thus as if Jesus was speaking to me:
Daughter, put a seed in your hand. Unimpressive, small, and odd, is it not? Yet the potential for productive life within that seed is vast. You, my dear Child, are like that seed. I'm asking that you bury yourself in My purposes for you. Leave the 6.6; your fruitfulness here is at an end. It is time for you to bear fruit elsewhere. I know to you it feels like dying to give all this up; do it anyway. It is time for this refuge to go to someone else who will steward it well. Daughter, follow Me, and stay close at My heels. I am taking you to a different place, and you will bear fruit there that will last into eternity. I will not leave you or forsake you, beloved Daughter; I Am right there with you. I await your arrival. Come and experience abundant life, for there is more that My Father and I wish to show you. The Holy Spirit will help you.

Summer of 2016

I love the rain. Every thunderstorm, I run to the front porch, hold my breath as lightning flashes, squeal with awe as the thunder sends compression waves through me. And the rain—oh! Pouring, slashing, blowing; then easing, falling, flowing. I love it all. As our gutters fill, the dry creek beds begin to flow, and my senses thrive and I'm overwhelmed with life. I will deeply miss this. But I am beginning to trust that You will send the rain no matter where we go.

My Handsome let go of having his Shop on the 6.6. The shop was a 40'x40' structure that was crammed to the exposed rafters with pine straw bales, rock on pallets, a mobile work bench, a tractor, three work trucks, composted dirt, saws, plants pulled from clients' yards to throw away, thriving plants destined to be planted in clients' landscapes, two kayaks, and tools, tools, tools. It was literally

10

my man's happy place. My male relatives would walk into his Shop and emerge hours later, sawdust in their hair, dirt under their nails, smiles on their faces, and a completed project in hand.

In one week — one week! — he found a dilapidated house to become his new office. The renovation was complete in about six months and gave us some experience of *vision*. How did he walk into a house that was so full of fleas that he left bitten all over his ankles; how did he see beyond the moldy cabinets, the unspeakable smell, the repugnant refrigerator? He just *knew*. That house became the new location for his specialized landscaping company, a living parable.

We began to think through and pray about where to live. We were both drawn to zip code 37917. It wasn't magic; it was a feeling, an attraction that we paid attention to. That area seemed to be more diverse racially and financially, two of our driving priorities.

We took a few Sundays after church and drove around 37917. We started where Handsome had been playing basketball with lawless and crazy high school boys at Mr. Monty's old brick church. There was a beautiful house nearby that needed renovating, and I got excited. A possibility! It was large enough for us to have people live with us, which had become part of our vision for our future, but the house was built in a way that we could still have privacy. Perhaps this one could work?

We discovered *city-data.com*. Through that site we explored the racial, ethnic, and financial makeup of streets and neighborhoods within 37917. The area we had seen was all white, majority poor. That was a No. Next step: we saw a few houses with our agent and friend Realtor Tom. Nope. Too sketchy, too nice. Too small, too stinky, too smoky, too neglected.

We began to drive on Washington, Jefferson, and Woodbine Avenues. We saw white and black faces, and some waved as we drove by. Grant was drawn to Woodbine like a magnet; I was impartial, willing to be led. Done.

A restored house came on the market on a Friday; we met there with Realtor Tom the next morning at 9 AM. I watched as my husband warmed to the place, relaxed underneath the tin roof of the back porch, and dreamed of being a neighbor. I was moved with love for him. He's wild. Brave. Doesn't need much. And ... he loves God more than he loves me, in the best of ways. Crucial.

After a bidding war, final offers, and a bank debacle, on precisely the 103rd day after our initial offer, Handsome and The Babe moved to 2330 Woodbine Avenue in East Knoxville, Tennessee. We claimed this space for love.

A friend of mine wrote us a house blessing:

In this home
dry bones will come alive
women will find rest
men will meet their Father
and children will dance …
to the everlasting song
of God's heart.
Welcome home, Standings. You are loved beyond measure.

~elles~

For decades, I recorded my prayer conversations with God 'speaking' in my journals. When we moved to Woodbine, I listened to God (note the capitalized pronouns) as He guided me:

Beloved one. How I love you! I'm so glad you have come to Me, for I am the source of all goodness and grace. Deepen your trust in Me. Fix your eyes on Me, for I am the author and perfecter of your faith, the first and the last, and I will see you through to the end of your earthly days. I will never leave you or forsake you. I invite you to lean on Me; I will not fail you.

As you and I journey together, I will meet your every need. I will be your source of joy, love, peace, patience, and self-control. Your gentleness, kindness, and goodness will be evident to all because of My Spirit within you. Do not lean on your own understanding; acknowledge Me, instead. Check in with Me at all times. Stay present to Me. This will take practice; do not be discouraged when you wander. Instead, remember My love for you and quickly return your attention to Me.

Trials will come; do not be surprised. This does not mean I have left you; it means I am alive and working. You may not understand My ways; they are higher than yours. But Child, I Am trustworthy! Great and marvelous are My deeds, even when those deeds include the death of My people, My Son.

I will allow you to be refined; I will discipline you with a good father's touch. Picture a silversmith, heating the unrefined rock to lava flow, until the impurities rise for him to skim them off. When the silver is ready, he can see a perfect reflection of himself in the liquid silver. This is a picture of us: I, the refiner, will cause your life to 'heat up'. Your

12

sin-dross will melt away, and I will skim it off, and you will become more like Me. It's not pleasant, but it is sacred, beautiful, beneficial. Then, as you move through this earthly time, you will be like Me — bringing life, spreading love, a helper and healer, a mover of mountains. You will appear in politics and police stations, in homes and hospitals, in farms and financial institutions, to bring My light. You will challenge the darkness with My light, the corrupt with My incorruption, the haughty with humility, the powerful with meekness.

Though beautiful and holy, it will cost you, just as it cost My Son. Seek My approval, not others'. What the world exalts, I often despise, so keep your eyes on Me.

Now: spend time with Me. Rest in Me. Find your strength in My presence. Then, prepared by who I Am, go love in My Name. Cheers, my Beloved Daughter.

2016: Woodbine

My entire white, wonderful life led me to brown, wrestling Woodbine.

Woodbine, to the human eye, is a long, paved road near the heart of downtown. It is not extraordinary. It has small, medium, and large homes, most between sixty and one hundred years old, some of which are falling down, and some, restored. The yards are mostly mowed. Dogs bark, kids bike, cars come and go. The people are brown and black and white, but mostly black. The music is loud, the cars thump, the adults yell, and the porches are full of watchers.

But to the spiritual eye, Woodbine is more like a river than a street, a river flowing with pure, clean, life-giving Kingdom values of love, peace, patience, and goodness. Yet it is littered with prostitution, drugs, alcohol, addiction, domestic unrest, and violence. So you have to choose how to see Woodbine: is it filled with the devil's delights, or is it God's place that needs His loving reform? Is it hopeless and scary or is it ripe with Kingdom potential? I had to pray for eyes to see. I knew from my times around the streams and waters of the world that there is one consistent truth about water and obstacles: obstacles don't stop water. They reveal its force. Was the force of God's living water in me strong enough to wash over the rocks of Woodbine?

God moved us to Woodbine for the sole purpose of being a good neighbor. It was not about being a 501(c)3, not about the nonprofit approach of coming on afternoons to do child care or feed the homeless; it was not about accolades or recognition or atta-girls. It was about simply living here, being here, knowing names, and stepping into the Woodbine river. It was about getting wet, getting bumped by the litter of addiction and violence as the river flowed. It was about seeing the corruption in the water and being willing to wade in and do our small part to replace harm with love. It was about staring down the evils here in the Name of Jesus, standing in their path, blocking their flow, and saying "no" quietly and firmly. It was about dreaming of the glory of God resting on my neighborhood.

Didn't Jesus do that for us? Absolutely. He left heaven, glory, honor, and privilege and came down to earth freshly clothed in olive-toned skin. He worked to support a family; He interacted with everyday people. He didn't just wade into the river of humanity; He dove in, heart and soul. He gave up The Best to give us His best. Through Him, our waters can run cleanly again.

～⁓⁓

When I reflect on the path of my life, I would not call myself a hypocrite; I would call myself a learner. Yes, I enjoyed all the privileges being white had to offer in my day. That was my context when I was young, and as I learn about race and class, I move away from toxic parts of that context. Moving from one framework to another is unsettling. After moving to Woodbine, I was disoriented, out of sync, confused, in the tensions of two worlds. Now the words flow easily for me, a sequence:
Orientation, disorientation, reorientation.
Connection, disconnection, reconnection.
Integration, disintegration, reintegration.

I imagine this sequence was relevant for Jacob when he wrestled with the Lord in Genesis 32:

22 That night Jacob got up and took his two wives, his two female servants and his eleven sons and crossed the ford of the Jabbok. 23 After he had sent them across the stream, he sent over all his possessions. 24 So Jacob was left alone, and a man wrestled with him till daybreak. 25 When the man saw that he could not overpower him, he touched the socket of Jacob's hip so that his hip was wrenched as he wrestled with the man. 26 Then the man said, "Let me go, for it is daybreak." But Jacob replied, "I will not let you go unless you bless me." 27 The man asked him, "What is your name?" "Jacob," he answered. 28 Then the man said, "Your name will no longer be Jacob, but Israel, because you have struggled with God and with humans and have overcome." 29 Jacob said, "Please tell me your name." But he replied, "Why do you ask my name?" Then he blessed him there. 30 So Jacob called the place Peniel [the Face of God], saying, "It is because I saw God face to face, and yet my life was spared." 31 The sun rose above him as he passed Peniel, and he was limping because of his hip.

Jacob's framework from his family of origin left him in a deeply personal, relational, generational, emotional, familial crash-and-burn scenario: It was time to confront his history with his brother and parents. Jacob had been involved in a multi-generational tangle of lying, favoritism, and strife between brothers before he fled the family. When he humbled himself after 20 years of being estranged, he found out his brother was powerful, assumed his brother still hated him, and would likely do him harm. Jacob spoke to him as if Esau still held the birthright. He feared greatly for the safety of his family, his goods, and his own life, so he hatched an escape plan. Jacob tried to appease Esau, resorting to old habits of trying to manipulate to preserve his own skin. Even while Jacob was trying to fix the problem with complimentary language and lavish gifts and shows of prosperity and humility, underneath, his faith crisis poured out in prayer ("*You* told me to go").

What is God's answer to Jacob's prayer during his disorientation, disconnection, and disintegration? I believe God sends pre-New Testament Jesus, flesh and bone and muscle, to wrestle Jacob in the dark night of no answers. During that night of dread, fear, anguish, uncertainty, self-doubt, separation, and disappointment, Jesus didn't give Jacob additional light or understanding or supernatural peace or even a good night's sleep. They wrestled; *all night*. They could not have been physically closer on this night of distress: this was a clash. God brought additional fatigue and physical pain to Jacob, as if He was saying to Jacob, "Above all else, what you need is an encounter with *Me*. Feel Me, literally, wrestling you in the darkness. I'm not giving you answers. I'm colliding with you, not comforting you. This is not a soft explanation; this is an explosive wrestling match."

Many people in the world are wrestling with God about race and class, colliding with God over racial norms and attitudes they learned from former generations, societal laws, law enforcement, power networks, job availability, social norms, myriad types of injustice … the list is long.

From Jacob we learn that wrestling with God is an intimate part of devotion. It's part of life with God. So are wounds and sweat and tears and delayed relief and no answers and fresh starts and new days. This is something we can work to accept about the life of faith. There is room in the life of faith for struggle, disorientation, grief, loss, frailty, suffering, disappointment and uncertainty. Wrestling is an invitation into deeper intimacy. Wrestling is an invitation into deeper faith.

During disorientation, something must shift: a misunderstanding of God, an expectation, a way of life, a way of thinking, a way of relating. It must be re-made: a new, accurate understanding of God. A new way of relating or thinking or living. A pathway opens to a new humility, fresh fruit of the Spirit, a gentleness toward the broken, a tenderness toward the living.

And as Jacob begins the process of reorientation, he does a beautiful thing: he refuses to let go of Jesus. Wrestle and rage, Dear Reader, but await the blessing — refuse to let go till He blesses you.

For me, as I lived on Woodbine and my life was reoriented, the Kingdom of God came into clearer view through my rusty trust and weariness and delightful encounters with children. God did not baby me, but called me — shoved me? — into disorientation and reorientation. By God's grace I shifted and am still shifting. I am like a sunflower, constantly reorienting myself to wherever the sun is, learning a new pathways, following fresh light. I have so much to learn.

Disorientation was not a time to lose faith, although I think that's one path from the devastation we feel during disorientation. It was a time to be carried ... by friends, family, authors, whoever would be gentle with me in this process of breaking down and rebuilding. You will meet many of my teachers in this book; know that they still come through my door, over my airwaves, and on every page I turn, into my heart.

Finally, Jacob received a reconstructed life in the form of two gifts: a new name and a lingering wound. Jacob meant *trickster, deceiver*; Israel meant *he wrestles with God and man and prevails*. A new name symbolized a new phase of life. As Jacob walked — limped — into the dawn, he was changed. He never walked the same. Their encounter existed in every step until the day he stopped walking. He moved with physical weakness, but oh, how Jesus shines in our weaknesses!

Jacob's final act in the story is to name the place of his re-formation. Peniel = the face of God. There is value in naming and remembering the places and events that form us. My daily journal was quickly dubbed "The Woodbine Chronicles."

I imagine this: "Granddaddy Jacob, why do you walk like that?"
"Oh child, let me tell you the story. I saw the face of God ... in a wrestling match ... in the dark! I have been re-made by God's own hand. Let me explain."
And I experienced this: "Suzanne, why do you live on Woodbine Avenue?"
"Oh friend, let me tell you the story. I see the face of God ... on my street ... in the homeless and poor and stable and unstable and black and brown and white. I have been re-made by God's own hand. Let me explain."

I only wish I'd learned what I know now much sooner. I have many "I wish" thoughts, but I lift those to the Lord and ask Him to keep moving in me, keep changing me, keep re-forming and reconstructing me. One of my mentors says there will always be things left unfinished. But my most sincere, most persistent "I wish":

I wish to be like Jesus:
olive-skinned,
racially mindful,
culturally aware,
loving,
socially wise,
insightful,
compassionate,
humble,
truth-talking,
grace-giving,
meek,
sacrificial,
Jesus.

Only God can create such a transformation.

Because of His radical love, I believe He will persist in pouring out His grace and truth within me until the day I die. As I go through the dailies of life, I will be imperfect, but I will also be increasingly empowered to do and say whatever He asks of me to bring His Kingdom. And ah!, His Kingdom!

Yes, may there be more light, more love, more joy and peace and patience! May there be more kindness, more goodness and faithfulness, more gentleness and self-control!
May the people of God — a messy people, a flawed people, like me — stand up for the good of others.
May we be like Jesus, humble and meek, willing to sacrifice power, prestige, public opinion, position, and privilege. May we lift others up.

Or of course, You can just come now, Lord Jesus, and settle this. I'm so ready. Please.

Chapter Two: Our Block, Early 2017

IN MY DREAM, I was walking through a tall forest, a climax community: the tall, old trees had added their shed leaves as floor fertilizer for decades — centuries? — and deer, raccoons, quail, grouse, and possums roamed the ground. Foxes and bobcats, alert to every movement, waited to move until the eagles focused on the lake at the bottom of the hill. I saw an owl pellet on the ground and poked it with a stick: miniature scapula bones and skulls. An eagle pellet laid on the path's edge: flashing scales and fish bones. Who could number the squirrels, voles, chipmunks, moles, and mice in this plush, fertile world? Even the dirt seemed to be in motion with worms, spiders, ants, caterpillars, and untold species of beetles. Lightning bugs rested on tree leaves near stink bugs, praying mantis, and dragonflies. Flocks of turkeys picked and plucked their way through the undergrowth, which provided all they needed. Squads of starlings played and fed, weaving their way through the trees like hand shuttles, releasing a mighty *whirrrr* when they took a wood-bound murmuration flight. Blue-tailed skink lizards decorated the trees while turtles' hexagon shells told stories of long age. Sound waves carried the drum beat of the pileated woodpecker, the song of the wren, and the high pitch of the diving hummingbird. Occasionally, a lone bear lumbered past, looking for honey and grubs. I was at peace there, full of a calm delight, resting in the dappled sunbeams competing for land, feeling the cool breezes seasoned with honeysuckle scents.

Then the trees began to change, expanding at the trunk, and doors appeared in them, and they joined together to create buildings, yet high branches remained green and waving at the overstory. The animals moved away, but at their own pace, not frightened or offended, but not willing to remain.

I watched the trees, awed, and windows appeared in them, and then people in bright clothing were opening the windows and greeting each other. "Isn't it a lovely day today?" they called. And the cushioned, composted loam beneath my feet became a sidewalk, and a car drove past, and the street was lined with other cars. A black boy, smiling and concentrating, dribbled past with a bright orange basketball.

I heard the drumbeat of the woodpecker become the drumbeat of a song, and a car with shimmering rims rhythmically boomed past me, a black man waving and nodding to the music. I smiled and gave him a peace sign back, but then turned to my last sighting of the bear and wept.

～ello～

In 2022, Australia re-opened its borders for travel, so Marlie flew the 26 hours home. Lu flew down from Brooklyn: my girls. They had just turned 30. Sitting on the porch swing, they asked me about my 5.5 years on Woodbine, and how Woodbine was shaping me. Pointing to each house, I explained who had lived where and how I knew them. It shook me that, with the exception of two homes, every single dwelling had changed hands; gentrification had greatly modified our street. Even as I spoke of the original occupants, feelings of love and tenderness welled up within me. Truly those relationships had moved over and into me, glacier-like, shifting the ground of my understanding.

"Girls, when we moved onto Woodbine in 2016, our little section of the long avenue was like a multi-colored tapestry of race, personality, class, and situation, an ever-changing microcosm of our country. On one end of our block there was a house of women who looked worn to weariness, and it was quickly explained to me that we were not supposed to know that theirs was a halfway house. But it was obvious, and we were so glad to support them in any way we could. The manager was named Big Mama, an enormous black woman with un-did hair, tent dresses, and a kind heart, and we would always greet her and whoever else was smoking on the porch."

I pointed right: "Reyana, K'mia, and various other family folk were in the next concrete block and vinyl siding house, a gray square with a workable front porch populated with wrappers and baby toys and an unraveling chair. Their black 4-door had a 'Baby up in this Bitch' bumper sticker — that always made me chuckle. Between the sidewalk and the street, the grass was always worn bare from drivers parking up off the road. (I missed having a garage, girls. And my poor Honda showed the wear of being outdoors all the time.) There was a vacant house with high weeds being upgraded by a Hispanic team one house down. Next came Freddy and Thunderbolt, a black and white couple. Thunderbolt earned her nickname because of her lightning-fast temper and thunderous, profane yelling. She looked like she was in her late 60s, but was actually younger than I. They were next to Ray-Mee and Henry, another unmarried, poor, mixed-race couple, with their strikingly gorgeous children, whom we came to dearly love. The girls had creamy skin, not brown but not white; well-appointed lips, lively dark hair, and somewhat shy personalities. Summer mosquitos pierced their legs with alarming frequency. You should have seen those raised red blotches. I felt so sorry for them. Thank God for screens.

"Next there was a single white woman in her 30s who was dating a policeman; then a rental house and MeLissa directly across the street; then Rev Rena and her husband, steady black professionals and a force in Knoxville's black

19

community. Rev Rena had grown up in that house. Then another quiet black family, then a rental nicknamed "the Loud House" (long before the media series), a magnet for rowdy renters. Then a vacant house, a single black dad with a high-paying manufacturing job, and two more vacant houses.

"On our side of the street there was a glorious old home similar to ours that was slowly becoming blighted — literally falling in on itself. An older white couple lives there to this day, and we almost never see them outdoors. I'm very concerned about them. Their home looks like a fairy tale gone wrong, with patches of roofing gone and a dead tree threatening to topple the entire back section of the house. The front porch is caving in and there is detritus piling up here and there. Within the weeds the landscaping has beautiful bones: azaleas, daffodils, tulips, and purple-blue grape hyacinths.

"Next to them were three white families hovering in the economic in-between of the working poor. All rented and all were in run-down houses. The children were social, playful, and glad to have a chat on our porch swing. They also loved cats and grieved with me when our Ninja Bear Kitty died.

"Then there was Miz Janet, a black woman in her 60s who was well-visited by her children and grands. She made the best fried okra! We were truly friends. I wept when she had a stroke, and was happy to fold her laundry as she recovered. Next, leap-frog our home to the former orphanage next door to us on the other side. I've seen a picture of 32 children seated in front of that grand old house, not a smile to be seen.

"Another blighted house, an empty lot, then two remodels (both became very upscale and appealing), and finally, a barn-style home that was recently painted purple. I love how our neighborhood, Parkridge, has colorful houses. One of the remodels belonged to a gay white couple who had the same type of car, two dogs of the same breed, and similar professional jobs. When they broke up, one of the men quietly moved out, and the other remained in the house. It became too much for him; too many sad memories. He made his fresh start in another part of the city about two years later."

I took a breath, considering the larger picture of Woodbine: At the far end of the avenue is our entertaining city zoo, a delightful home for tigers and tortoises, gibbons and gorillas (Handsome's favorites), baboons and beavers. The opposite end of Woodbine hosts a dilapidated knitting mill (famous for making underwear in its wartime heyday) with blown-out, jagged windows, a peeled and dried rind of a former life. It is a spooky place with whispers of past prosperity and work-based friendships and a thriving community. After the business died, the building held on for a while, until now, decades later, it is a shivering shell that invites drug addicts, the homeless, and the trafficked to live shadow-lives in its hull. When the time comes for a business or the city to breathe life into it again, it must be done well, for the sake of Parkridge.

Tucked beside the knitting mill was a surprise: a community farm. One early blue morning I volunteered there, and who did I meet?

1. A Scandanavian-looking gay young man with a strong Biblical name, Caleb, and his short, brown, effusive partner. They were eager to help and jump right in, ready to engage the vision of the farm. I've never enjoyed pulling weeds so much as I did that day with them.

2. A minority Councilwoman who was standing strong against establishment bias and the old boy network. She was so tough; I did not grow up with such verve. I respected her instantly, even as we disagreed on certain issues.

3. A white man in his 40s whose business "creates pathways out of poverty for young adults through job readiness training, while equipping communities with environmental literacy skills." Impressive vision, and it was working.

4. A few homeless folks who crowded their valuables into a grocery cart and some backpacks, then littered as they walked by.

5. To my joy, six or seven hens.

"Even with just a handful of us there, what diversity! But the farm, too, is gone, now growing weeds and dented cans and the trash left by homeless folks. This is our Woodbine."

The girls listened patiently, then pointed out that most of those people were no longer on the block, but were still somewhere in Knoxville.

"You're right. That's part of the story of the poor here: they were disposable when the tsunami of gentrification swept through Parkridge. Within two months every person on our block who received government housing assistance was gone, both black and white. Very few renters survived the post-COVID inflation swell. It was so sad. We had come to Parkridge to be among the poor, to be a racial minority for the first time in our lives, and to mix classes. Gentrification narrowed the colorful stratification we first experienced — varied incomes, distinct perspectives on politics, differing patterns of viewing the world, assorted interpretations of beauty and wealth — all in one block. We became more homogenous. It was a devastating blow. We even wondered if we should move."
"But you didn't, Mama — why did you stay?"
"We had created a home here, and we were serious about our commitment to stay at least a decade in order to know and love our neighbors. Let me tell you few stories." We fluffed our pillows and settled in.

Here We Go: 12/2/16

We moved into our 100-year-old home on December 2, 2016. I prized the photos the builder had left for us: the pink-cheeked first homebuilder in a bowler hat; the ruin the house had become before it was rehabbed; the reconstruction process of jacking up the cellar ceiling. There is something glorious about returning a home to living conditions, taking a space from dark to light, from desolate to breathing, from cold walls to warm windows. It seems, in the light of eternity, an important thing to do: create a welcoming haven of hope and play, an intermission from the demand of the dailies. A place to know and be known, to see others as they are and lovingly choose them.

How does a person create a home? At that time, I thought a home should be filled with heartfelt affection, animated voices, deep conversations, and an appreciation of beauty. Silence should be chosen — not from neglect — and balanced with music. There should be space for friends to gather, for celebrations to cheer the ordinary, and for much-needed peaceful rest. We completed our house with healthy food, worn quilts, art supplies, outdoor gear, a cat and dog, and toll house cookies. The house gained a heartbeat.

"Here we go," I thought, and dove into boxes and paper, kitchen first, bedroom second, and bathroom third.

"What was unexpected about the house?" asked Lu.

"There were challenges. Our bedroom had no closets. My pretty work clothes temporarily went into another room and I ordered an old-fashioned, heavy-duty garment rack. We had some sheers and roller shades, but no heavy curtains (anyone could see into our family room). All but three of the roller shades were torn or had holes in them; I hadn't noticed that before. In the bathrooms, there was no place for our wet towels. The odd oven would not go above 350 degrees. It leaked heat, and I thought I could see sheetrock through the oven cavity … could that possibly be safe? Could I really cook without burning the house down?

"As we thought about placing pictures and hooks, we realized some of the walls were very old plaster and others were painted sheetrock. I was scared to drill a hole anywhere. And where was all the water pressure? The entire kitchen sink swayed with the movement of an over-sized faucet. Not one of our main-floor windows had a decent, secure lock."

I remembered clearly the late afternoon on that first day. Grant, affectionately known to me as Handsome, had driven to a nearby Ace Hardware to get supplies while I stayed to work on populating the guest bedroom with linens, pictures, and lamps. Shots began to ring out, and they were *close!* I instinctively lowered my body and moved away from the window.

I was raised knowing how to load and shoot a gun and was a decent shot when I was younger. We grew up with limits on guns: we shot sophisticated targets like soda cans, tree stumps, or old bottles, and we practiced far away from the city, people, or animals. We liked the skill and competition. My brother went on to become a bird sharp-shooter, valuing any life that he took; no one can cook duck as well as Scotto can!

I felt my senses go hyper-alert. "God, this is why we've come. This is why we are here! Thank You!" I marveled that during the first shooting Grant was not with me; I could not run to him. It was me and God and the immediate situation. In my bones I knew He was with me and was pleased that I was there, right there in the midst of gun violence.

My attention diverted back from the flood of memories to Marlie and Lu. "Girls, I never saw the shooters, but I did feel the power and encouragement of God. That was enough for me. Pause for a moment and marvel with me: *I was not afraid.* I was exactly where God wanted me to be, exactly at the time He wanted me to be there. He was with me. My heart was at rest."

~elleo

Hello, are there any friends out there?

One of my whispered prayers was, "God, would You please bring me a friend on Woodbine?" And there she was, right across the street. It just took us a minute.

Our first December came and went with very little relational warmth on the street. I felt disconsolate. As 2017 rolled in I reverted to a former habit: baking bread. In my mid-twenties to mid-thirties, I baked two loaves of sourdough each week. I kept one for my family and gave away the other.

After getting starter from a friend, I began. Add the starch, white sugar for the yeast to eat, and warm water to jumpstart the process; swish and swirl the jar. Watch for bubbles, listen for the phzzzzzz sound when you open the lid. Fine organic wheat bread flour, white bread flour, and a finish of ground flax; my dad's honey, a cup of starter, a pinch of salt; shape into loaves, let them rise. Bake till golden brown like a fading sunset. Serve with softened butter and/or Daddy's honey. The entire house smelled like heaven.

I took a deep breath, realizing I had to initiate friendship on Woodbine. No one was bringing me a welcome pie or handing me their cell number on a sticky note just in case I needed to know where the nearest grocery store was. This was not comfortable. It was a risk, and I felt like I was back at the first day of school, the first day on a job, the first time I was naked with my husband, all the firsts: *Here I am. Will you like me? Will you let me in?*

I walked across the street in a warm coat with hot bread. "Excuse me, I'm your new neighbor. I bake our bread … two loaves at a time … and wondered if you'd like the extra loaf?" No one on the street ever turned down that honey-laced, butter-browned, celestial-smelling bread. It was like hospitality in a loaf of wheat, an invitation to open your door.

"I'm MeLissa. Thank you! That's so kind!" Her brown eyes were bright and honest. "God bless you for this!" That was my cue. Conversation started from there, instantly warmed by our Christian sisterhood. We met several times during the next month, and I could sense her authenticity.

We prayed together. Listening to MeLissa pray was an exercise in glory. I sat in rapt attention, eyes wide open, watching my neighbor, learning about her culture and faith with every hand-raising, eye-clenching, voice-booming request. Her polished and studded nails lifted into the air. Tears sometimes rolled down her brown cheeks. I felt schooled. My prayers were so tame, so proper, so matter-of-fact, so less emotional, so Presbyterian. MeLissa's prayers came from her heart, unguarded; mine, from my head, measured. She begged for God to move; I was already solving my own problems as I prayed, not relying on God at all.

For the cold weeks of January and February, we rarely saw people unless they were walking to the bus stop or corner store, JC's. Some were walking their dogs; it seemed that almost every house had a dog. Thankfully, when the sun came out, so did the people, as long as it was at least 60 degrees. As springtime blossomed, I began to meet my adult neighbors: Miz Janet, kind and loud and so at home in her almost wrinkle-free, 60-something brown skin. Erika, with her long, fitfully-colored hair and nails, a Hispanic beauty. Dinho, her dog, a playful and energetic escape artist who bounded over as often as he could get out of his fence. Angela, with her love of purple irises. Henry, father to Misi-ell, teaching him how to play football and use his burliness to block. Kent, remodeling a massive former orphanage next door. Rev Rena, dressed impeccably, professional and quick to say hello. Her husband, tending to their lawn and vehicles.

⁓·

"Y'all, I don't have a closet."

"What? What did you say?"

My friends from West Knox were aghast. These were capable world-shakers, strong women, well-heeled, effective professionals.

"How can you not have a closet?"

Maria volunteered, "Is there another room in the house you could convert to a his/hers walk-in closet? I'll design it with you: a wall for shoes, his side, your side, and you need a place for your hats."

"Well, I'm thinking of doing something completely different. We want to keep our rooms open for guests, for people to live with us if they need some love. So I've started practicing a version of a *capsule wardrobe*: a minimum of select pieces that mix and match functionally for work and home. So far, I love it. As I intentionally lighten my wardrobe, I feel lighter too. I started a Pinterest board to help me learn and track my ideas. Please look — it's cute! I find that I gravitate toward the simple basics of white, cream, taupe, and denim; then add strong bright corals and pinks and reds; brown in the fall, black in the winter; and random greens, to match my eyes. These colors seem to describe my soul: browns and greens for my love of the mountains and the outdoors; pinks and reds for my sense of joy and bright life; denim for my sturdy work ethic and love of good dirt; white for a fresh start and a clean soul."

The women were sitting back in their upscale seats, staring at me. There were questions:
"Why limit yourself when you don't have to?"
"Are you judging *my* closet?"
"I don't want anything to do with a capsule wardrobe. But I love your color palette."
"Okay, I'm going to get on your Pinterest board and check it out."
I wanted them to be with me in this — they felt so much farther away now that I had moved."Better yet, y'all, come over! I'd love for you to see the house."
Nona and Maria said they'd love to come … but the others just took sip of sweet tea.

Nona and Maria came together, confessing to dividing up the 25-minute trek thus: one navigating and looking out for hoodlums, the other driving. They did not know my part of town at all, but they knew its reputation: *bad*. Crime. Drugs. The national news had reported a horrific atrocity just miles from us: The Christian-Newsom murders. They were genuinely scared when they pulled up.

"Should we park on the street? Is this okay?"
"Absolutely fine! Come in!"
I could see them relax when they saw our broad porch, daffodils pushing up toward the sun, and our dog.

We surveyed the house, my bedroom, the lack of closets, the backless oven, the low lighting in the dining room, the two raised bed gardens, the fenced-in back yard. They kept using the word "potential." I could feel the divergence of our ideals as we dreamed about how to proceed with the house. Make an entire room a closet? No. Put those beautiful blinds in every room? Too expensive. Change the electrical in the dining room? Not going to happen. Build out a closet in our bathroom? Wouldn't work. It was all too extravagant and contradictory, knowing some of my neighbors were on food stamps. Such up-scaling felt cacophonous, out of tune with my street.

I had been in the expansive phase of life when my daughters were young; this was a contraction. 6.6 acres down to .33 acres. Less yard, less mowing, less cleaning, less time caring for *things*. I wanted this to apply to my clothes too.

"I am responsible for my time on this earth. This is our watch. How am I being a good proprietor on the earth? How am I watching my waste, my recycling, my carbon, my emissions? How much is enough? When should I draw the line on spending money? When is a good bargain really translating into a harsh supply chain? There are women around the world with just a few options for clothing; my capsule wardrobe would be extravagant to them, yet to us, this is minimalistic. We researched companies that took good care of their suppliers, right down to the seamstresses, hours worked, factory conditions — and Patagonia won our hearts." I paused and shrugged. "But big picture aside, I still have to figure out how to handle my clothes."

Before they left I showed them what I had ordered: an industrial, old-fashioned garment rack that fit in with the 1920s vibe of the house. They raised their eyebrows and tried to like it, for my sake.

As they left I thought about 1 Corinthians 7:30,31: **"From now on those who buy something should live as if it were not theirs to keep; those who use the things of the world, as if not engrossed in them. For this world in its present form is passing away."** I tended to get really excited about new purchases, especially if it was a pink tulle skirt or a new pair of boots. I needed practice to be less "engrossed," and my closet was providing it.

The day concluded with a fresh surrender:
"The money is Yours; the house is Yours; I am Yours.
My clothes are Yours; my stuff is Yours.
My limits and extravagances must be Your call. I don't trust myself to do it right.
Handsome is Yours; our girls and their destinies are Yours.
Our time on earth is Yours, written in Your book, days numbered and accounted for.
Help me live out those days in a way that brings You glory and makes You smile.

Cheers to You, Beloved Father. I love You, Jesus. Thank You, Good Spirit."

~elllero

As I adjusted to Woodbine, March invited springtime to revive the neighborhood, yet I felt a sadness that was a few weeks old. It was underneath, like a base coat of paint on an old wall. Activity and work kept it sub-sensory, but it was still there, and rose to my attention when I was quiet.

I happened upon the beautiful young woman who bought our former property, the 6.6. I asked her how everything was going, and she said musically, "Gooood," with her eyebrows raised. There was a sense of adventure glowing in her face and anticipation in her voice.

"We're excited, but our children are like 'What?!? What are they *doing*?' I had to explain that this is called **demolition**, and it's all going to be okay." I heard the word *demolition* and didn't hear much beyond that. Her enthusiastic voice became a bell in my ears as I began to reel inwardly.

Demolition of the house we'd built, where we'd become a family ... oh my. Deep breath. Only certain parts of the house, I reminded myself. But I felt the bucket of the backhoe dig right into my soul, into the place where memories and images rested undisturbed and solid and beautiful.

The walls of our bedroom, the place of safety and affection and stories and dreaming and fussing and forgiveness;
the place of being tangled up together all night long, of letting the temperature get into the 50s in our bedroom just so we could be naked and warm under the feather comforter;
the place of hiding Christmas gifts and shotguns and love letters;
the place where my Kroger-parking-lot-starving-artist-paintings hung for over a decade;
gone.

I felt that subtle sadness because every March the 6.6 was burgeoning with life and scent. The deer were happy, the birds were mating, the female foxes and skunks were pregnant, and the daffodils were almost done. The air was fragrant and everything sang *life*.

It was just different here on Woodbine.

I missed the celebration of life that happened there at every turn: sounds of coyotes and loads of stars and loud spring peepers and cautious, erratic squirrels. Flowers and free-wheeling hawks and neighbors taking walks again after winter hibernation. The thaw in the ponds, the slow swish of the koi. I was reminded of

27

the scent of jasmine, the sweetness of figs, and I felt it. It was an ache, a longing, a sweet remembering, a letting go of what I loved. One day during church, West Knox experienced a light morning shower. When I got outside after noon, I heard spring peepers whistling their song. I restrained my tears until I got in the car, grieving the natural beauty of my former life.

There were times when I realized I was still not fully given over to all that Woodbine was and all God was asking of me.

Here on Woodbine, my focus was different. It was on adjusting to the bass *boom-boom-boom* in the cars that drove down the street. It was seeing my neighbors' roller shades drawn down and their doors shut and curtains closed. It was listening for shots fired and sirens at night, and praying for my single female neighbors to be safe. It was enjoying the kids playing on the street, riding their bikes with no brakes, running away from the dogs that seemed so threatening. It was trying to not spend too much money on curtains or rods; it was figuring out how to make this house our own, yet hold it loosely. It was mapping out which way to turn on which street, the fastest way to the interstate, and how to get to the urban YMCA. It was seeing saggy pants with full briefs exposed, and doo-rags or bonnets, and darkly-tinted windows, and fences with watchful canines. It was cars going too fast down streets where children play. I just felt blue.

And yet … a gift. And yes, I know this is a bit weird.

One evening I got home late after teaching. I went into the kitchen, turned on the light, and saw a shadow move … and move again … and then there it was: a mouse. A mouse, here on Woodbine! Honestly (and I know this is hard for many people), I instantly felt at home. I wondered if the cat had brought it in to "play," because it was slower than the mice on the 6.6. It hugged the corners and hopped onto the gas stovetop and then went back behind the oven. I thought with horror about roasted mice. Its tail stayed visible for several seconds, and I thought, "If only Ninja Bear (our kitty) could see this," and then it was gone.

Then sirens began and were very close to the house. Wiley, our dog, went outside and sat down, listening, turning his head to the side as dogs do. Soon, he lifted his voice and, nose pointing to the sky, howled like a native wolf. I was overjoyed, lost in delight. He was singing, and it was as if I was transported to the wild again. I was surprised he received no answer. His classic howling form and his melody felt like home.

God knew I needed His special touch that night. It had been such a full week, so many thoughts, so little time to process, so much energy going out of me, such concern for others … too little prayer, too little time alone. As odd as it sounds, His kiss was in those critters.

28

Grant is such a present person and is so much more comfortable with Woodbine that he didn't really think about the 6.6 much. He also felt more purpose, a sense of contentment, and relief that we were not just living for *us* anymore. We were *together*, learning the sweetness of being *together* in an adventure as we took risk *together*, stepping out of the boat and walking on the water *together*. New bonds were forming between us through dependence and change. At last, a diverse environment! Finally, seeing homeless people daily, and brown faces, and hearing the refreshing lilt of a foreign language or two, and marveling at the black culture around us! Ah, being a minority in our own city! All this added up to a strong *yes* to Woodbine for him.

This was a favorite part of marriage for us, the temporary gift of being *home* to each other.

And I eventually got there, to that contented place. I just needed to grieve the changes in the expression of springtime. I grieved a bit every season that first year because I was (and am) so attached to *land*. Land has always marked time for me and I have appreciated its gifts. I am energized by its flourishing. I was taught by agrarian principles.

As I wrestled with giving up the beauties of my former life, I did not see the new beauties God had put in front of me. With giving up silence and quiet, I did not hear the sacred in the urban cacophony around me. With giving up control of my time, I did not understand the perspective of eternity. This was a tension, an inner dissonance, and as much as I wanted it to be resolved, it wasn't. As much as I wanted to be whole-hearted, I wasn't. *Yet*. I had to be honest with myself and say it. I lifted my face to my good Father and just stayed in the tension, hands open and eyes closed.

The Loud House

Long before I knew about the television show *The Loud House*, we had nicknamed the house two doors down with that same moniker. They held holiday parties till way past the city noise curfew; hit their kids, even in their front yard; smoked so much weed that we laughed about getting high on the cloud wave rolling down the street; astounded me with the adults getting crazy, all jumping in unison to a song that said, "Motha fucka" over and over, fists pumping in the air. There were almost always four to six kids within the front yard's chain-link fencing. It really angered me that one larger woman screamed at them with foul language like "Get your G*D ass in the house before I pull out the M*F* belt!" When I tried to show kindness to them and their children, they showed no interest in relationship.

Every year, Mother's Day, Memorial Day, and Labor Day were epic. Starting at 2 PM and going till 12:30 AM, their house blared and rocked. Music was everything. One person sat in a car on the street acting as a DJ, doors flung open, tunes blaring. The way the songs talked about women outraged me; the way the female singers referred to other women scalded me. I was on edge, my frustration deepening like a sinkhole, and I couldn't escape it. I sat, fumed, and hoped that my noise-cancelling headphones would work. They didn't quite cut it. I asked Miz Janet why no one on the street ever visibly did anything about it. She said she had called the police on them before. But Rev Rena said there was a neighborhood code, unspoken, that you *never* called the police to deal with a black situation. Ever. The climate in our nation between officers and the black community was so tense at that time that I didn't want to open that door. What if things spiraled?

During one party, when I walked outside, all the children were playing in the fenced-in yard, two adult males were sparring, and the rest of the adults were arm in arm, bouncing to "Motha fucka," singing as loudly as they could, smiles on their faces, loving life. They knew every syllable. The cloud of pot we drove into was enough to get us high just by passing through. For over seven hours, the boom bass nearly dented our newly paved street.

On Memorial Day, even my noise cancelling headphones plus the fan on the white noise setting couldn't drown out the bass's boom or the occasional screaming. At 11:30 PM I was fit to be tied, super frustrated, angry, and craving quiet. I had to work the following day.

I prayed, "God. Help me. This is so cross-cultural and I'm not comfortable *at all*." The thought came to mind that perhaps all I could do with this family was pray for them. I may not have dialogue with them, may not be able to engage their kids, may not be able to cook for them, may not be able to love them in ways I was used to — but I could pray, and pray mightily. Could I be content with that? Could I get beyond my own framework and understand that their experiences of life and race and class were completely different from mine, and so were their celebrations? Pause … yes.

Mr F

I was working on my fledgling garden by the fence and back alley. I kept hearing a strong adult voice saying, *"Fuck that! I got this!"* and then a basketball would swoosh through the goal. F this, F that. Over and over. And over. In my mind, I started calling the young man Mr F.

I found out his name was Derrick. He was a father, ex-Marine, and an incredibly respectable man.

In the middle of our urban backyard, there sat a rusted, claw-footed, cast-iron tub; it was here when we bought the house. By the time spring came around, the azalea that had been planted in it by the previous owners was brittle and dead, and the weeds in it were flourishing. I pulled the weeds and asked some neighborhood children to help me pull out the azalea (one of the children could be an engineer, an obvious problem-solver — if only he could go to college, be encouraged by some adults, and value engineering). We tugged the azalea to a small burn pile with much complaining and exclaiming and woe.

Handsome mowed and came up with three bags of grass scraps; into the tub they went. Within two weeks of rain, sun, and a bit of stirring, I had gorgeous brown dirt in exchange for that old grass. The tub had a new purpose, but needed to be moved to the edge of the garden boxes. I am not remotely strong enough to budge that big baby, so there it sat.

Handsome and I talked about it as Mr F kept playing, filling the air with expletives and basketball shots. We peeked through the fence and saw he was a mountain-sized man playing ball with his stepson, "D." Grant didn't feel 100% about asking for Mr F's help, but I thought it was a good idea, and Handsome ultimately opened the gate, missed two free throws, and asked.

With Derrick on one end and the three of us on the other end, we moved that tub with ease. It was comical.

I started showing the magic of the garden to D — strawberries, red-tipped lettuce, broccoli — while Handsome and Derrick got to know each other. Derrick had been overseas twice through his military service. All I could think of was, "I want him on my side. I want him on the wall for me." He was kind, respectful, mentally sharp, well-spoken, and patient. Derrick could have been one of David's wild Mighty Men (1 Chronicles 11), the 30 men who would risk everything for whatever battle David entered, or one of Achilles' great Myrmidons. Fierce, well-trained, battle-hard combatants. What a gift to have one of them living in the house behind the alley. He was Mr F on the court, wild and competitive, but he was a good father and listener at my picnic table. Mr F in the war zone; "Derrick" serving his neighbors. I think we all have those two sides present within us; I know I do. I can be a ferocious Mama bear, but then as gentle and kind as a feather on your skin.

Among our neighbors across the back alley were three spirited boys: Kadeem, Kintay, and Kahlil. Kadeem was tall, lanky, and white. For a year his Facebook page had "Fuck the Police" handwritten on a picture of a skull with a weed leaf on it. He hid fruity, cheap booze in his coat pocket. Sometimes he would sit on our porch and talk with us about his life, tears brimming, his spotty face reddening with emotion. He was so young ... so wounded.

Kintay and Kahlil were brown boisterous brothers, bundles of joy and athleticism. They would call Handsome out to throw ... anything, really.

Football, mostly, but once Grant hit a three-pointer on their backyard rim, they were challengers.

And that was how it happened … loving our neighbors. It wasn't complicated, but then again, it was: it wasn't simply us meeting them and loving them. Histories of harm, injustice, racism, mockery, dehumanization, and gentrification made being a neighbor far more complex than we understood. But then again, there were times all we had to do was share our cookies or swish a three-pointer.

Handsome and I found we needed time to talk and think through not only what was happening on the surface — throwing the football — but also at a deeper level: building trust between races, ages, classes, and cultures. Proving the individual is accountable in the present, but acknowledging the impact of the past tensions between races. Giving love with no strings, no demeaning, no twists, no hidden motivations. For these discussions, we'd often pour a glass of an adult beverage, put our feet in the middle of the couch, and lean back on the armrests opposite each other. Oh, the philosophical discussions we had! The problems we unearthed but rarely solved! The glory we saw in people, and the fear, and the potential! The questions we left unanswered. And that's what our life looks like to this day: deep talks. Few answers. Much love.

Chapter Three: The Children, Spring 2017

I LOVE TO WEAR AN APRON when I cook, though that may seem a bit antiquated. A protective, pretty apron is always the start of my cooking routine: choose which cloth pattern that suits my mood, secure the neck so there's plenty of give, wrap the apron around my waist with a bow tie. I love all the pockets strategically placed to tuck in frequently-used tools and implements, and the extra lower fabric that I use for drying my hands. My aprons testify to what I have botched or tidied. At the end of a cooking session, it is completely normal for me to have flour from top to bottom like light snow, streaks of sauce like striations in a rock ledge, and damp edges like wet shorelines. But the mixing and messiness and measuring pays off when my people, led by their noses, would come into the kitchen and exclaim, "Oh, this smells so good!"

One day I absent-mindedly prepared a salad for dinner as I thought about the dynamics of culture in Knoxville. The salad was colorful: green and white lettuce on the bottom, then bright groups of red and yellow peppers across the north end of the bowl, red and white radishes on the south, pepitas on the west side, cherry tomatoes and carrots covering the east, a crown of yellow grated cheddar in the center. It dawned on me that cities are like salads. One class is grouped *here*, one racial cluster thrives in another area *there*. Chinatowns *here*. Central Americans nested on one side. The poor settled in the resourced city center. The wealthy on this side. Industry, tech, mechanics, education, farming, government ... all finding their spaces within a city. Such dynamic ingredients to blend into one metropolis!

Majority-black East Knox was a small angle of Knoxville, only about 15 percent of the city's population, but just as I didn't want to give up an ingredient in my salad, black culture is a vital part of the mix. Without it, Knoxville would not be all it could be. And the Indians, the Italians, the Hispanics, the Africans ... my mind pictured us as red and yellow peppers, ruby-encircled white radishes, deep greens of healthy spinach, energized orange of carrots, pitchy purples of a crisped cabbage, all put in the same dish — or city — to be creatively mixed into something far greater than its own flavor.

~elles~

As the weather warmed, we began meeting neighbors. It was all about the cookies: 9-year-old Cinco (nicknamed Sync) from three doors down rode by on his bike, saw me happily munching on a plate of cookies on the porch swing, and pulled a hard stop. Once he ate two, his friends Beels and Reyana, both age 8, had to have them too. Ah, a doorway! Of course it involved sugar.

And then more kids came: there was Yaden, with his incredible grasp of concepts at 8 years old. Misi-ell, a strong tank of a boy, athletic and purposeful. Junior, so little, and his brother Erik. Our wide front porch and brown plastic chairs were living invitations for the kids to talk about their days at school.

MeLissa prayed out loud with me about the frequent gunfire and gang activity and it was like I was at a spiritual symphony. Her intensity would crescendo, and I knew all the demons were driven out and *never* coming back! *A-men*! Yes, there was beauty on Woodbine. I just had to learn to see it.

"We are not afraid!"

Sometimes bizarre things happened on Woodbine, like a particular Friday night in our first spring. Grant and I watched the emotionally devastating film "Manchester By the Sea" (one of his Top Five Movies of All Time that is really a list of about twenty movies), and got into bed around 11:45. Not long after, we began to hear gunfire in front of our house. I stopped counting after 15 shots, and they were still ringing out but progressing slightly past our front porch toward the center city. I called 911; they were getting several simultaneous calls from our neighbors. Within one minute, while I was still on the phone, police cars were on our street.

Grant had gotten out of bed and walked through the house. He came back to bed and we talked about it for a while: Grant said his heart was beating *hard*. He was as bothered and wide-eyed as I've seen him in our four months here.

He turned the lights back out, stretched into the sheets, and we held hands, as we do, to briefly pray. Then two words into Grant's prayer, our bedroom's roller shades inexplicably flipped up with a loud *whirrrrrrrr*! We jumped, sheets exploding, Grant immediately on his feet. I started to laugh, and without thinking yelled, *"We are not afraid! We are not afraid!"* I continued to laugh for a bit, affirmed to Grant that I was so glad to be on Woodbine, and then we began to settle down. It was like a scary movie intending to bring fright and freak, but instead, it brought out my inner lioness. I slept like a baby, picturing my fearless God laughing at the pranks of darkness.

Then I was awakened with a 5 AM wake-up call: two shots behind our house. We didn't know why, but 4-5 AM seemed to be a time when we frequently heard gunfire. I tried to roll back over, but instead got ready for church.

Just before the service, I met Nona at the church parking lot. She gave me a leather bracelet that held a metal square etched with the words, *"She slept with wolves without fear, for the wolves knew a lion was among them."*

She placed it on my wrist and said it was for me. It *was* me.

I was floored. I *wanted* to be that lion — Nona *thought* I was that lion — but I said in tears, *I am a cub trying to mimic Jesus, tripping and falling and running clumsily along.*

The image I was drawn to in my head was Aslan of Narnia, from C.S. Lewis' profound book series. I wanted Aslan (allegorically, Jesus) walking our streets, roaring and bounding, blowing life into every person He saw. As the book says, the creatures whispered in awe: "Aslan is on the move!" I truly believed that God was on the move on Woodbine. He was the lion; I was like little Lucy, walking beside Him with my hand in His mane, feeling His powerful Presence, fearless at the Bridge of Beruna — *because Aslan was with me.* I had no delusions: God was the power, the force, the lion, not I. And there were so many others praying on Woodbine, not just me; people who had lived there for years, prayed for *years*.

You are large; I am small. You are powerful; I am weak. You are limitless; I am limited. You are mighty and loving and fierce; I am at Your service. Just let me keep my hand in Your mane. Then truly I can sleep fearlessly with wolves, because You, my Lion, are with me.

Her gift gave me a new vocabulary: I found myself looking at all that was fearsome as if it was merely a wolf and not a lion. "Oh that's just a wolf. He/It looks scary, but there is One who is much greater than he/it."

I asked, ***"Father, how can I pray about Woodbine? How can I pray about the shooting that happens? I feel sad ... it's that underlying sadness accompanying the gunfire again, knowing that something was wrong this morning, that harm was being done, that near me there is harm and unrest and (I sense) violence and anger. What can I pray? What can I do?"***

And then my mind was filled with an image that became a prayer:

Every time a finger squeezes a trigger ...
every time ...
something that opposed God within that person would crumble.
A wall would come down,

a stronghold would shatter,
the darkness would break into shards
and God's light would come shining in.
Where there had been harm,
there would be hope and healing.

The broken young man in a gang,
the fatherless, the motherless,
the angry, the restless, the enraged,
the control freak, the drugged-up lunatic …
you name them, God knows them.

With every pull of the trigger, my prayer became that
God will move to restore, to humble, to break godlessness;
God will call these folks to worship Him.
Out of death, life will spring.
Out of defensiveness, openness will flourish.
Out of rage, peace will rule.
Out of brutality, servanthood will rise!
Out of fear, faith will abound!

And this was not just an assertive prayer; this was an aggressive prayer. I would not see what happened in the realm of principalities and powers, but I trusted they would be affected, because God hears the prayers of His children.

This was actually an answer to my prayers. I had asked to feel more of God, and I had wept with sorrow over Woodbine. I had asked to be empowered in prayer, and my passion grew through sadness and exposure to difficulties. Oh, our good, loving God! How dearly He loves His lost ones. I also saw that if I was to feel and carry (some of) God's sadness, I needed more of Him to be able to do it. I looked forward to this greater intimacy.

At 9 PM, my neighbor MeLissa got home and I ran across the street to her house. She was behind in rent and trying to figure that out, and had just gotten served divorce papers.

It turned out both of us had been weeping. Grieving for the lost, for the women walking the street, for the pain and brokenness, for the wounded. It was such a relief to hear her say it too. We prayed and listened to each other.

Emotionally exhausted, I laid down to rest. I went to sleep knowing God is a God who cares, who leans toward His lost children, who is mighty to save, who is powerful, who is the real Lion on Woodbine. And if I was awakened in the night by gunfire, I was one of many who were going to be praying, and the principalities and powers were going to have to obey the Lord. They hear His

36

roar and feel His claws and dare not defy the One who holds their destiny between His canines.

~ellee~

In praying for Woodbine, images really helped me. I pictured our long street lit up with a spraying, upward light, like sparklers or fireworks shooting toward the sky. The light started at a street level and had a brilliant whiteness to it, a blossoming holy fire 7-10 feet into the air. I pictured that white-bright light as God's goodness lighting up the street, calling all of the residents to a pure and holy life, a life of worship and community and shalom. I started humming my prayers and a little song formed:

Woodbine, Woodbine, find your place
Turn your eyes to God's good face
Let His power sin displace
Be filled with His truth and grace
Oh, be filled with truth and grace.

Woodbine, Woodbine, bright as a bride
Find your place at God's holy side
Light and love in Him reside
His goodness be multiplied
Oh, His goodness be multiplied.

This neighborhood began as a beautiful place to live, then slipped into decay, then destruction. I wanted to see that trend shift back to wholeness and wellness. How could I contribute to that? I decided that making a home of hospitality and creating a safe space, a place of beauty and creativity, was one of the most gloriously rebellious things I could do here. A holy courage rose up in me. Put me in a dark place: I'll bring light. Put me where there is no song: I'll sing. Put me where there is conflict: I'll speak peace. Put me where there is destruction: I'll become a builder.

It was a profound practice to pass every house on Woodbine, one hand on the steering wheel, the other pointing as I prayed out loud:
For God's holiness to be welcome *there*.
For God to heal all trauma *here*.
For God's peace to be on *that* home, *that* relationship, *that* family.
For God's saving grace to be known and practiced under *that* roof.
For God's good timing and salvation for *that* home.
For God's mercy to be on every person living in *that* house.
For the grounds and home to be cleansed of all evil influences and experiences through the blood of Christ, the Lamb of God who takes away the sin of the world (John 1).

37

For the beauty of the Lord to be experienced inside *those* walls.
For the children to grow up in peace with strong role models of good.
For drugs, prostitution, harm, or addiction to get out of *that* home.
For God to save, to rescue, to scoop up the people who live *there* and hold them
tightly to His holy chest and speak life into them.
For joy to erupt *there*!

Oh God, how kind You have been to us, how good!
Thank You for this place, this space called 2330 Woodbine Avenue!
Bless this house.
May Your light shine brightly here, God!
May this street be bright with Your glory!
May Your love roll down Woodbine like the winds that blow our trees
from west to east.
May Your peace extend from the start of Woodbine to the finish.
May You bring people to these vacancies.
May people on Woodbine share lives and stuff and food and time and
hope and sorrows of life.
May they gain skills needed for meaningful employment.
May they delight in steady, stable families and stay together in good
times and bad.
May our schools improve. May our teachers be encouraged.
May the poor teach us great lessons of trust and relationship.
May the wealthy open doors to networks and necessities and things.
May the community thrive, in Your Name and under Your protection.
Keep the Destroyer far from us. Bring that abundant life You talked
about.
I love You, God. Cheers to You. Amen.

～elle～

Handsome and I have found Woodbine to be an ever-changing place. Each year
seems to have a certain flavor, a specific focus. Like a ladder that must be
climbed one rung at a time, no year could be sped up or skipped over. This was a
purposeful learning curve, a path of learning to see, and of all things, our
foundation was laid by … children. Isn't that perfect, so like God, to choose
children to lead us?

Our life on Woodbine, while a gray struggle for me in some ways, was colored
brightly by three young ones: Reyana, Cinco, and Beels, our personal Woodbine
Trio.

38

Reyana

Reyana has a singing voice like a rising iridescent bubble and a giggle to match. Her laugh is a cure for the gray I sometimes feel. Whenever she starts bubbling over with laughter, I have no option but to crescendo from a smile to a belly laugh. I am like a balloon when she is around, unanchored by the weights I normally carry. She is quick to exclaim, 'Ouch!' at the slightest brush with danger. She usually catches herself when she gets whiny, giving herself the three-fingered 'W' (the dreaded 'whiner' symbol) and rephrasing her requests. She falls apart emotionally when she is tired and doesn't get her way. She's at that playful age where dolls, drawing, cooking, and cleaning were all fun as long as she's with me.

We talk a lot. Reys always wants explanations: "Why does the kitty sleep all day? Why is he so fat?" She ends sentences with prepositions (*Suzy, where you at?*) and all her text answers are one word ("Reys, how are you? *Good.* What are you doing? *Nothing.* How was school today? *Great.*") She speaks *urban*, which I'm still getting used to: "*Where Handsome? Where Ninja?*" She is comfortably thick; *never* one to take a long walk; able to answer every times-table question I fling at her unsuspecting mind; and one of my most consistent companions.

Her family is complicated, as I find the majority of EastKnox families are. There are more aunties than I can count; many boyfriends and girlfriends and ex-this-or-thats. I hear her describe numerous houses where she stays, especially Granny's or Auntie Tangie's or her dad's Granny's or Auntie Coco's. Reys tells me about family drama with excitement; she loves it. The crazier the better.

Reys and I were upstairs one afternoon. I was folding laundry, and she was looking at our United States of America map. (When we first moved to Woodbine, I was surprised that the kids didn't know how to picture the world, where major world cities were, and where we lived in comparison to other points within the US.)

As I folded, Reys said, "Oh! This is Florida. That is Texas." She pointed her brown finger at each of the states correctly.
"Where is Tennessee?" I asked.
"Right there," she said, pointing incorrectly. I clarified where Tennessee was, and then she continued.
"There's Vagina, and there's West Vagina," she said with authority. I lost my laundry, shrieking with laughter. "Ver-gin-yah," I said, giggling. She corrected herself and kept going.
"Up there is New Hamster," she pointed, "and over there to the left is Oregena and Montoya."
"New HamP-sher, Or-eh-gon, and Montana," I chuckled.
"Down here is Latoiniana, or something like that." "Lou-ee-zee-annah," I wheezed.

I could not contain myself. I almost had to curl up on the hardwood because I was laughing so hard. So was she. Don't let me give you the wrong impression: she's clever and perceptive and will probably own her own business someday. But now every time I travel through Virginia ....

~elless

Reys was very observant and for a child she expressed her heart very well. At dinner one summer evening Reys popped by and explained that a while back her daddy had left, and that another man was sometimes at her house, and she was glad that now her daddy was back.

She illustrated this with her hands. She folded her fingers into a heart shape and said her parents were once in love (hands together framing an entire heart), but then they fell out of love (she distanced her hands so the heart was "broken"). They had a big fight and he left (hands separated as far as she could reach).

Then came the other man, Damion. And fights. And name-calling and yelling. "You be triflin'."

Then her dad came back and they began to fall in love again ... her hands came closer together, but not quite touching. She took great care to show that her hands were almost together, like her parents, but not quite. I was so moved to see her explain how her parents were relating. Grant and I locked eyes ... another holy moment on Woodbine.

A few days later she came over at 10 am, following the scent of fresh cinnamon rolls. She and Beels had helped me make the dough the previous day, so of course they shared in the gift of cinnamon, sugar, butter, and bread in a cast iron skillet. Everyone got a skillet-load for their family.

She left at 3 PM after much play. As I cleaned the toilets, swept the floors, washed windows, and cleaned the kitchen, she played pretend. Sometimes part of her pretend was to help; she had never swished a toilet clean before and was simultaneously intrigued and repulsed.

Otherwise she pretended she was a moody kitty cat; a 17-year-old who could drive and fetch eggs, milk, bread, and cheese from the store; and a baby (human). Misi-ell came over too, and he was nicknamed RockStar and he became a strong bobcat, crawling everywhere and going through the dog door and meowing his words.

So this is the Kingdom:
hours of content play,
a basic lunch,

40

creative imaginations,
and delightful simplicity.
Staying dry during a thunderstorm.
A water gun fight.
Calling us Mama and Daddy.
The kids watching from safety as Grant sprayed four wasp's nests (and I screamed and ran).
Not a care in their worlds, even in their imaginary worlds.
It was such a gift. To all of us.

Fast-forward to October. My suspicions were true: Reyana picked up on everything. Her keen observations will serve her well as her understanding of life matures. The adults were mired in a destructive love triangle. Reyana explained the love temperature in her home using her hands: again she formed each hand into half of a heart shape, then gauged how close or far the couple was by moving her hands.

At this time, her parents were cooling off (hands wide) and Damion and her mom were heating up (hands in close). As she moved her hands, we could see her evaluating what was happening ... but to a 9-year-old mind, it was boiling down to what she liked and didn't like. She wanted her parents to be together, but Damion was part of her reality. She crinkled her nose; she raised her eyebrows. She was aware that she couldn't fix her parents' situation. She loved them both.

On the first day of fourth grade, she bounded up to the door, full of the excitement. I was surprised to see her hair in a slightly nappy bun — the first-day-of-school-hairdo is considered very important. Last year Reys had extensions down her back.

She loved her teacher, made some new friends, ate a tasty breakfast ... a perfect start. Listening to her made me want to be the room mother for her class. As a former public school teacher, I know the first day is very special; the tone of the classroom is set. Each student wants to know if he or she is valued in the eyes of the teacher. Each teacher wants his or her learning environment to be safe and productive. Everyone watches out for rough spots.

Reys played with some of my old dollhouse furniture while I prepared dinner with Collins, a young adult who lived with us at the time (you'll meet him in detail later). She later joined us in creating a salad dressing, adding lime, cilantro, yogurt, and mustard into a blender. She was a cheerful helper in the kitchen.

About an hour later, we sat down to dinner. Reys couldn't get her mom on the phone, so I divided my salad and gave her half. She had told us her mom was frying shrimp tonight — yum! — but it was already 8:00 on a school night. I asked Reys about her bedtime; she put herself to bed, usually around 9:30-something, she said. Sometimes she takes a bath, taking care not to let her hair get nappy.

We walked her home around 8:40. As we tucked her bike into the front room of the house, the smell of smoke was thick, so I exited quickly, bidding Reys a good sleep.

Grant and I fell quiet as we walked home, both of us reflective.

Cinco

In a mint green, four-bedroom voucher rental lived a blended family: white mom Ray-Mee, black dad Henry, Cinco (from Ray-Mee's previous relationship), and their two striking daughters. Both adults had other children elsewhere.

By appearance, Cinco was a fair-skinned black ten-year-old boy with full lips, caramel eyes, and not a single hair on his body. He has *alopecia*, a condition in which he has no brows, no lashes, no hair, period. When he realized he was different (and would always be), a caustic shaft sank deep into his psyche, bifurcating Cinco into two parts, two roles, two opposites: an energized bully or a devastated victim. He had neither quiet confidence nor gentle humility. His *modus operandi* in the world was bully or be bullied.

He had been called all the names, even though he was just in the third grade — Cueball, Homer, Full Moon, Humpty, and several I refuse to acknowledge because they are so crude. Cinco had to learn to armor up as a little child. He had a big personality bundled up in his lanky boy-body. He could trash talk with the best of 'em on any playing field, but was neither old enough nor skilled enough to deliver when he went ballin' with the street's more muscular teens. Since it had always been that way, he would quickly give in to a victim mentality. It didn't take much to upset him; he was expressive and felt deeply. He was quick to tears when he was disappointed and quick to spout off when someone came at him. He talked big and dreamed that the future Cinco was a powerful, dominating, wealthy persona with gold in his teeth.

Frequently he would come over and have dinner with us. He didn't like salad, which I often fixed, but he would eat meat and apples. We often had to cut him off at his third glass of orange juice.

He clearly enjoyed our affection and attention. He ranked himself relative to the other neighborhood children. "How long have you known me compared to Yaden and Reyana and Misi-ell and Beels? Who are you closest to?"

42

While he and Grant threw any ball available, they discussed table manners and talked about school and tending to teeth and how important it was that he be good to his sisters. He was so responsive to our love! Almost as important to Cinco, though, was gaining Wiley's confidence and affection.

Wiley, our rescued black dog, was afraid of children — all 75 furry pounds of him. I don't know what happened to him as a pup, but he was nervous and fearful around kids, pulling hard on his leash to *get away **now!*** Cinco set his mind on gaining Wiley's trust. He toned down his exuberant personality in order to get licks from tentative Wiley. Cinco would calmly put out his hand, say Wiley's name, and wait. The first time Wiley came to Cinco and licked his hand, Cinco's face lit up and his caramel eyes flashed brightly: "Look, Suzy, five licks!" That was the day he felt accepted into our family.

Although we did not know it as it was happening, 2017-2019 were our golden years on Woodbine with the children, led by Cinco. Our house became a gathering spot, a place of refuge, a haven of food and play, of outdoor games and indoor creativity. We began to truly know our neighbors because of the kids running in and out of our doors. It was the little things ... the small adventures ... the spontaneous, unexpected moments ... the daily crazy ... and always, Grant and I would look at each other with a smile because we did not know what we were doing.

～eelees

Boys swarmed around Grant our first May, ready to play any kind of outdoor sport possible. When they were worn out, they piled onto the porch. I asked, "What are you doing for your Mamas for Sunday? It's Mother's Day, you know."

Expressing love and gratitude on Mother's Day was crucial; in the 'hood, you *never* dishonor your mother, and you never let anyone else dishonor her either. I asked the boys at our house if they wanted to raid our roses (thank you, former owners) and take their mothers and grandmothers a bouquet. Affirmative!

With a mason jar in hand, one boy cut his immediately and went on his merry way. Not Cinco. He wanted *me* to cut the roses; he didn't like "those thorns, man! They hurt!" He would point to the rose, and I would snip, then he would arrange it in his jar. It was *very* serious business. He had to make sure that his jars were equal; one for his mom, one for his grandmother. He loaded up, even to the point of saying he wasn't sure he would be able to carry the jars all the way to his house (three doors down — *come on, you're fine*).

The following day I found a four-leaf clover. It was a tradition for me; I can usually spot them easily; I think it's all about pattern recognition. I plucked it

43

out of the strip of grass between the street and the sidewalk, happy with it, feeling gratitude to God for such a little thing.

As we strolled back toward our house, we saw Cinco playing with a soccer ball and yelled over to him. He ran to us, still handling the ball, and said he was emotional and sad. When Grant stole the soccer ball from him, his face broke into a massive smile, and a game of Keep Away began. It was amazing to me how a simple game of Keep Away, like a simple four-leaf clover, could light up the day.

"Cinco, go take this to your mom," I offered, giving him the clover. Immediately, with absolutely not one shred of hesitation, he yelled as he turned from my hand, "Mama, I got somethin' for you!" He bounced toward their porch, avoided his two little sisters, jumped over the toys strewn in the yard, wound around his grandmother on the steps, and stopped at his mom's chair. As we neared our house I could hear her exclaim, a smile in her voice.

~~~~

Father's Day is a much-celebrated holiday in my family. I asked Cinco, "So what do you do for Father's Day?" I tried to stay very general, since I wasn't sure what to say or not say. Henry is not Cinco's dad, but he is a present male father figure in Cinco's household.

"I haven't heard from my dad in a while," Cinco stated factually, "so he might be back in jail. I don't know. And I don't really do anything for Henry," he said, trailing off. I nodded, hoping he would go on. I have so much to learn about family systems that are not like mine.

"Henry has been lettin' me know about life, though. He been teachin' me."
"Really, Sync? That's great."
"Yeah, he's been showin' me YouTube videos of cops killin' black men. Just for no reason, too, just because they're black. There was this one …."

Cinco went on to explain with vivid gesticulations about a video where a police officer punched a black man in the face, then another where an officer shot a black man in the back multiple times, then another, and another …. Cinco was very serious, very cautious, and very alert to the reality of "white-washed justice." It was sobering to see Tigger-like Cinco so somber.

"Cinco, I'm so sorry this is the situation in our country. How does this make you feel? My compassion and righteous anger rise up when I see how the black community has suffered injustice."

"I feel sad and scared, Suzy, but I'm glad I know now how it is."

44

"For officers of the law, acquittal — do you know what that means? — and lack of consequences has been the historical pattern in the US. Sync, I see that this trend is shifting; Americans *need* this to shift. There must be honest accountability for all who hold power. Racism has no place in an officer."

"Yeah, Suzy," Cinco offered thoughtfully. "But it's scary, because the officers in the videos are definitely against black men. And I know I'm light, but I'm still black. Why are they like that? Why would anyone want to target another person because they're a color? I don't get it, but I know it happens. And I gotta be ready." He looked determined and afraid, grim as he walked home, scared to his scrawny child-soul.

I mulled. How can I enter into this as a white, Christian, law-abiding, female citizen? I caressed my Bible with my hand, pondering, flipping to the New Testament. The Biblical model of the body of Christ says when one part hurts, the entire body hurts: **"If one part suffers, every part suffers with it; if one part is honored, every part rejoices with it. Now you are the body of Christ, and each one of you is a part of it"** (1 Corinthians 12:26,27). When one part is wounded, the body doesn't shut down, but it does soothe and protect the ailing area.

I began to pray out loud:
"God, may Your people recognize that no matter what a Christian's class or color, when a Christian hurts, we all should feel each others' pain. We bear this burden (Galatians 6:2) through the strength of the Holy Spirit, knowing Jesus carries the heft of it (Matthew 11:30). When it feels too heavy to empathize with people who feel such deep pain, help us remember Paul's words in Galatians 6:9,10: Let us not become weary in doing good, for at the proper time we will reap a harvest if we do not give up. Therefore, as we have opportunity, let us do good to all people, especially to those who belong to the family of believers."

I looked at the news. At this time in history, America, instead of protecting the unprotected or including the excluded, was in the pattern of polarizing, blaming, and prohibiting. How did I view our nation? Are we "one nation, under God, indivisible, with liberty and justice for all," or are we "nationalistic cliques, many segregated tribes, under whatever authority we deem currently correct for our particular public, gladly divided into subgroups and separate societies, with liberty and justice for the dominant community in power"? I know what Jesus prayed in John 17:21-23:
"... that all of them may be one, Father, just as you are in me and I am in you. May they also be in us so that the world may believe that you have sent me. I have given them the glory that you gave me, that they may be one as

we are one— I in them and you in me—so that they may be brought to complete unity. Then the world will know that you sent me and have loved them even as you have loved me."

I phoned a white friend of mine, Rachel, who adopted a black daughter and teaches at a predominantly black magnet school. She was crystal clear:

"Unity in His Body is our Heavenly Father's way. It's a unity *for*, not a unity against, the person who is *other*. He commands His people again and again to welcome the stranger and foreigner, remembering their own times as sojourners. To humbly recall how it feels to not be able to read the signs, to not know a culture's mores, to not know where to turn or who to trust or how to enter the workforce … this remembering becomes empathy, softening our hearts and tenderizing our territorial tendencies. God knows our penchant for self-centeredness and survivalism, so He counters it with a challenge to be sacrificially kind.

"Consider Jesus, a refugee at almost two years old, fleeing the violence of Herod and caravanning to Egypt with His shocked, brave mother and determined father. Think of Him as an immigrant, settling back into Nazareth years later.

She swallowed. "If violence were happening to you and your family, wouldn't you do everything you could to get to a safer place? Of course you would; so would I, and with haste. So did Mary and Joseph."

"Rachel, as you experience life with your daughter, I know you want her to have safe spaces where she can simply *be herself, be a kid*. But I'm wondering: where can my black neighbors flee injustice? This is their home; whites imported their ancestors here hundreds of years ago and built the United States on their striped backs and calloused hands. Black folks adapted, they survived, yet subtler forms of racism continue to threaten their peace and wholeness. How does this make you feel as the white Mama of a black daughter, as well as your other white kids?"

Rachel sighed. "I know God hates injustice. And it's not just about the black race. What about the Hispanic immigrants who settle in Knoxville during the strawberry season and the vegetable harvests? What about the Burundians, the Congolese, and the Iranians who are settling into my school's community, hoping for a new life in a safe place? Do you know that according to research about the most dangerous place in the world to be a woman during the past decade, the Congo is consistently in the top ten? Of course I would welcome Congolese women into my neighborhood and home! Wouldn't you? Wouldn't you want them to feel peace, to know that they are not going to be raped as a weapon of war, not sold as a child bride, not victimized and limited because of their gender? That they can dream and hope and go to school, uninterrupted, and

46

not just survive, but *flourish*? Wouldn't you want that for your own daughter or sister or wife or mother?"

"Absolutely," I said earnestly.

"And what about the gentleman who was a qualified, educated doctor in the Congo but can only find a job here making pallets, because he doesn't yet know the language? Who are the doctors who will allow him to shadow them, who will pay for his language training and exams so he can re-enter his field at some level? Put yourself in his shoes. Imagine this happening to you, to your own son or daughter. They have so much to offer, so much to give, but they are trapped in systems they cannot fully engage. Someone has to mentor them, take interest, and help. So what can you do? Find the foreigner in your midst who needs your help. Sacrifice your leisure time, your energy, your money. Go love."

I sighed as I put down my phone. I believe relationships form us. How could I help form our beloved Cinco into a responsible, strong-minded, able-bodied black businessman in Knoxville? How could I love my precious neighbors? How could I have empathy for their oppression, disorientation, and exclusion? And didn't this also apply between classes, not just between races? These were my questions as I looked out my window at Woodbine Avenue.

~elle~

Cinco, restless on a Saturday, came over and challenged Grant to an arm-wrestling match. He bragged: "Of course I gotchoo! Yeah, I gonna own you! Punk!" Keep in mind that Sync was ten. And wiry. Grant was 48 and blue-collar-worker strong.

Grant knelt to our coffee table and put up his hand. Cinco pounced on it and took Grant's hand down, then yelled in triumph, dancing around the room with his arms raised, Rocky-style. Grant explained the rules, and Cinco bent to the table, offering his hand with his elbow in proper position. Grant took him down and held him there … for about one full minute. Sync was like a comic book character as he pulled and tugged and heaved and strained.

Reyana came over to make chocolate chip cookies. After washing her hands and putting on her favorite apron — the red tulle half-apron with the jingle bell — we got started. She could now run the KitchenAid mixer by herself, crack the eggs, pack the brown sugar, and hand-mix the flour. She had come a long way from whining to taste the batter! She protectively requested that she have a cookie for her family members and named them all: "Dre-man, LooLee, K'mia, TahTah, Auntie Tangie."

Cinco joined us as we loaded up the cookie sheets. After they licked their batter spoons whistle-clean, they began giggling through the house, playing hide-n-go-

47

seek with some tag thrown in. I finished making the batch of cookies; Reyana guarded the white paper plate loaded for her family: "Dre-man, LooLee, K'mia, TahTah, Auntie Tangie." She counted each cookie, making certain there was one for each person. While she and Cinco played, each time she ran through the kitchen, she would count, always attentive.

~~~~

Grant, Reyana, Cinco and I were in the kitchen. Reyana giggled and squealed, "My turn, my turn!" She and Grant were doing the Trust Fall. She was at ease falling back into his strong catch, and giggled through the whole thing. In fact, when she was back on her feet and steady, she would just laugh out loud, her eyes disappearing like the slimmest crescent moon.

Cinco, on the other hand, kept looking back over his shoulder, asking if Grant was ready, if Grant *could* do it, if Grant *would* do it — he was so nervous and scared! He never fully fell back, never fully let go. Not once. Each time he would buckle and put back his foot, lowering himself to the ground. "You weren't going to catch me!" he would accuse, and Grant would patiently say, "Yes, I will, but you've got to trust me and not try to save yourself."

Was I more like Cinco or Reyana when I faced the impossible, when God said *move* but it was easier to stay safe? I wrote later,

"Still my soul; move my feet. Trust God and do it. We Christians are children of light, and we walk by faith, not by sight. We say YES, LORD, even when we don't understand, because we can trust fall into His love. We trust in Your rescue, we listen to Your Spirit, and we take that step. Yes, Lord. May I trust fall into You."

~~~~

The Cinco Family

Mama Ray-Mee is a blend of red velvet hair + Snow White skin + trailer park in a tizzy. The wrapping paper of her childhood was poverty, but as I've gotten to unwrap who she is, I've discovered rich promise within her rowdy package.

No one taught her to dream of a stable, financially secure, productive life. She was taught how to stay within government-funded limits for home utilities, food, rent, and health care. That translated to this: stay home. Live small. Live with lots of irrational fears, especially of sicknesses. Don't waste your gas on adventure because you need it to get the kids to and from school. Keep your nails did, of course, and add lots of bling; you need to look polished and bad-ass in public. Always wear trendy, cool sunglasses. Have sex young, because what else are you going to do? *Everybody* gets pregnant at 16 or 17, and it's not surprising if you can't keep your kids, because *they* take lots of kids away. You can get 'em back, just straighten out your life. No drugs during testing. Keep your house clean when *they* come to inspect it. Talk nice in court, get your hair did, and play nice. But bitch it up by text or on social media — who the hell do *they* think they are? You gotta be tough. Live your own life on your own terms. Push back. Don't take any shit from anyone or you're weak. Feel completely at ease with making dark assumptions about people; suspicion and superstition will keep you alive.

Ray-Mee is the mom of four children; one lives under the care of another adult. Cinco is the eldest, governing his two younger half-sisters who are less than a year apart and twin-like. The girls are bright balloons in a limited world, full of light and bounce and smiles and mosquito bites. They delight in sidewalk chalk and wands for blowing bubbles and toy horses. Their affection for me is always sincere.

Ray-Mee also lives with Henry, the older black man with whom she has spent almost all of her adult life. Henry, the size of a large grizzly bear, is gentle and chronically shy, lumbering and watchful and kind. Ray-Mee has taken care of him through his times of depression. I've wondered so many things about his life. Did anyone mentor Henry? Did he have teachers who loved him well? Did anyone see his potential and applaud his good choices? Did anyone give him a chance? What were his experiences with racism and classism? I didn't know him well enough to ask such personal questions.

This family seemed to be stuck on an icy financial lake, slipping and sliding back toward all that was familiar and safe: a government-funded life.

When we met Cinco he was nine. Beels and her little brother, some of Henry's children, came to live with them for a time, but that did not work out — after drama, lying, defiance, and frustration on all sides, they were soon out of the house. I trembled for Beels' life; there was something terribly vulnerable about her. She was rail-thin, tall like Henry, and had a lazy eye. She kept losing her glasses and getting picked on at school, and she struggled academically. She seemed unaware of her crusty nose, of how to not shout back, of how to disengage a fight, of how to take care of her body. Already at age eight, she did not see adults as helpful and safe. Why? What adults had betrayed or used or ignored her? Even at her young age, I could tell a piece of her puzzle was missing, with harmful consequences.

While Beels was on Woodbine, she became one of "the Three," constantly moving in and out of our home as if it was her own. When she left to return to her mother's, I felt lonely for her. Our one-on-one time was always rich. She extended trust to me, and I never violated it. After being gone about a year, Beels came by, a taller version of herself, doe-eyed, irises straighter than I'd seen them in the past. She seemed okay … at a different elementary school, fifth grade, making A's, B's, and C's. When I asked if she was safe, her eyes fluttered briefly.

Damn.

One of the first things I noticed about Ray-Mee was that she would not look me in the eye. Ever. Never ever. She could be telling me about the boyfriend who was stalking a girl at the halfway house or the man who was high and yelling at his girlfriend on the street or how the kids did at school that day … it didn't matter, she would not meet my eyes. She focused on the frightening — what the latest shootings were, or who was robbed, or how the bikes were stolen again.

Nor did she smile. Ray-Mee's teeth were a mess, so she never smiled and kept her lips tight. Her four upper front teeth looked like black beans that someone had pincer-squished and shoved back into her gums. They were extremely deformed and discolored. All of her "smile teeth" were too small from decay, various shades of ivory to black, and had pits or dents. I think she hated her teeth, but what can a poor woman do?

Because of her teeth, because she didn't smile and didn't have that marketably open and hospitable face, she could not get a "frontside" job. She couldn't be a hostess, for example, who greeted everyone eye to eye, fresh-faced and smiling openly. "How may I help you today?" intoned in a happy greeting and grin. Not for Ray-Mee. She could have "backside" jobs where she watched the fryer basket or prepped the food or put together the sandwiches, wrapped them in paper, and put them on the chute. She ran the register a few times during the graveyard shift.

We connected first through Cinco, who wanted permission to come inside our home. For him to be out of her direct sight was a fearful thing for Ray-Mee; she could recount everything horrible that had ever happened to a child within a five-mile radius of wherever she stood. She was always outside on her little porch fighting off the mosquitos and watching her kids play, not with a relaxed joy, but with fierce vigilance.

Though suspicious, she decided I was okay. Cinco was allowed to come into the kitchen, cook with me and Reys, and watch every Vol football game we could get on our pitiful TV setup. He would yell so loudly at the coach, the players, and the refs that Ray-Mee could hear him from her porch.

Our relationship began to build, as trust does: in the small things over time. It took a year for her to really sit down and have a conversation with me about personal things. Who was she? What was her story? I had to be so patient, but after a year, I received her most precious gift: trust.

50

I hoped that just as Year One on Woodbine was about relationships with children, maybe Year Two could be about relationships with adults. While we had exchanges with three main families, we still weren't what I would call close to any of the adults here. It was not that I blamed them, or us. We were busy; we were working away from home; we were leading full lives and had limited capacities for relationships. We were honestly doing the best we could. Plus, there was much injury between classes and races represented on Woodbine; my best posture toward my neighbors was humble, patient curiosity. Why should they trust *me?*

That made a sweet text series from Ray-Mee my best Christmas present. Because Cinco and Beels had spent so much time at our house, we had asked her permission to give them small Christmas presents.

Ray-Mee: Thank you for everything! U r such a perfect role models for the kids you and Grant both. I really appreciate you guys!

Suzanne: Y'all have been a huge blessing to us as we have transitioned to Woodbine Avenue! We're grateful for your friendship!

Ray-Mee: Thank you. I'm glad you all are here i was going to move before you guys came!

Suzanne: [series of three yellow hearts] I'm so glad y'all stayed!

Spring included an addition to our family: a set of six chicks. It's amazing how animals open doors of friendship. I wrote:

Today was an ideal Spring day, illuminated by sunshine, Cinco, Beels, and six new chicks.

The chicklets are nestled in a box with their heat lamp, and I can already tell the black olive-egger is starting the pecking order. How human of her.

I see this pecking order in the neighborhood: Who is cool, who has to work to be cool, who is too young to care, who just wants to be loved and fed.

These children ... oh my. They've become important to me, to my soul's reconstruction. That they come to our porch or back yard is now such a beautiful, beautiful thing that I can get speechless and tearful. Let us not forget the power of love. Let us not forget how priceless children are. Let us not lose sight of them.

They are right here, noisy attention-seekers, wild and restless and poor listeners and always eating. They are rowdy and silly and they wound each other so quickly! They love a good game of Hide and Go Seek, Go Fish, or just want to make up songs as we do chores together (meaning, I'm working on home management and they're typically bystanders). God, help me see them and treasure them.

Ray-Mee is low on food. Earlier this week she asked if I knew anything about local food pantries, said she needed a job, and that the kids need warm-weather clothes. There is a part of me that wants to fix everything. I took her leftover sandwiches from a church event, and I know that helped, temporarily.

We could run to the grocery and stock their house. I could have a "No one on my block is going hungry, no way!" kind of attitude. But is that really the best way to love them? I have so many questions. What does her man do vocationally? What are her work skills? What help do they get from the state — what is not covered?

I asked this morning if they needed pancakes and syrup ... YES ... and added a ham, six eggs, half a loaf of bread, and lots of fruit. I've grown to love them. I don't want them to be hungry. I've opened up my heart, so opening up the refrigerator seems easy. But her "provision bucket" always seems barely shy of empty, while my bucket always seems full. Why is that?

Ray-Mee and I were able to sit down and talk about her life. I felt so buoyed by encouraging her and getting closer to her. I think her mother is younger than I, so maybe I have a mother/grandmother voice to her. I care about her more and more, and I believe she is gifted, able, and somewhat overwhelmed by her circumstances. She is two years older than our daughters and has five kids living with her (for now). Wow. Our girls aren't dating anyone, much less have 10-year-olds; they're working on building careers and figuring themselves out.

She says — earnestly —that she is doing her best. She thought she had graduated from high school but upon checking has one math class left. There's a local community college that could help. I think it's possible

52

for her to get some hefty scholarships from the state for college — we have lots to discover and research. We pulled out my laptop and surfed through certificates at local community-style colleges; we looked at a few degrees. The financial commitment is daunting, but the time commitment with five children seems insurmountable. I'm reminded that God enjoys moving mountains.

Father, would You intervene in Ray-Mee's circumstances and create pathways for her to succeed in every way in Your eyes? Would You show her what to pursue educationally and vocationally? Would You remind her You are with her? I want her to succeed, and I want her to be okay, and I want her kids to have what they need.

Is this what church really looks like? Is real church, real faith, simply opening up the refrigerator, letting squirrelly kids pick up baby chicks, singing made-up songs with Cinco as he helps me dig in plants, and talking to a neighbor about her future? Is church holding the little one who is scared of Wiley, giving out wipes for sticky fingers after sharing oranges, pulling up a fresh, real radish for the kids to see? Is this Your love? I think so. I can't help but join my life and heart to theirs — is this what You mean about loving your neighbor as yourself?

~elles~

"Yes," Ray-Mee said. "It's all in my name — the house, the voucher, the food stamps, everything." We talked about the difference between a job and a career. We both dreamed about what it would take for her to be a teacher. A beautiful, relaxed expression came across her face as she reminisced about playing school as a child. "I was always the teacher with my siblings and my dolls. It's in me. My Mama used to say it too."

She texted me pre-interview with a request for a bit of money. She explained the circumstances: The interview was originally scheduled for the next week but the personnel manager called to see if she could possibly interview the next day. Ray-Mee jumped at the chance to interview and then tried to figure out how to get there. The day before her van had broken down. Henry was going to pawn their chainsaw but the pawn shop did not open until after her interview, so she was stuck.

She was so embarrassed to ask me for money. And I was hesitant at first. I'd been through this same thing with others, and I ended up feeling weird. When we Christians lend, it's supposed to be with freedom, with an open hand — in other words, you may get it back, or you may not, but keep your heart open regardless. Could I do that? Would that be best for Ray-Mee?

53

Then I remembered what God had been whispering to me lately: "Live generously. You've received so much help along the way; live generously as others have lived with you." I thought about 1 Corinthians 4:7, "What do you have that you did not receive?" And it was done. I had a $20 bill and gave it to her. She was shy about it but grateful, still never looking at me in the eye.

She got the job! I was so excited for her. This would help get them through this tight time and encourage her till her education was figured out.

She sent me an epic text: "Thank you again your greatly appreciated. I love you Ms Lady. U are a great support and friend to have." My heart and eyes were full.

God, may she work out her education and come away from school with a career, be employable, be competent, be hard-working, and not get distracted by drama. May those who try to keep her down, who tell her she's "gettin' too big for her britches", be quiet. May she be strong enough to oppose them and get that career.

Oh God, give her vision for her life and family! Help her rise up! Help her break the cycles that keep her down. Bless Henry. Help him be supportive of her. Help him be an active, involved Daddy, and help him love Beels wisely. I know he addresses You as Jehovah; be his Jehovah Jireh, God the Provider.

~ullus~

Ray-Mee texted, asking me for $100 for gas. Ugh. They were going to Atlanta for a family reunion and needed gas money for their old Cadillac; their van was too broken-down to be trusted on a long trip.

She went to a local money lender and they were going to charge her $100 to borrow $100! That should be illegal! It infuriated me.

But neither Grant nor I felt we should lend them the $100. We felt we were contributing to them becoming dependent on us, like we were the Woodbine Bank and Loan.

It was such an awkward situation. We were growing in friendship with the whole family, and wanted to do the financial side in a very healthy way. What was *Toxic Charity* (a helpful book) in this situation? Would this qualify for *When Helping Hurts*? How did this fit into gentrification?

Our hope and desire was to lift up our neighbors, empower them, and encourage them to be self-sufficient, contributing citizens who loved and served others in this community and beyond. That was why I was okay with helping Ray-Mee with fixing her black-bean teeth: she could not get a better job with the wrecked teeth she had; no one would hire her for a well-paying position.

We were both uncomfortable with the gas money. We felt they should provide that for themselves or not travel.

"You cannot help the poor by destroying the rich.
You cannot strengthen the weak by weakening the strong.
You cannot bring about prosperity by discouraging thrift.
You cannot lift the wage earner up by pulling the wage payer down.

You cannot further the brotherhood of man by inciting class hatred.
You cannot build character and courage by taking away people's initiative and independence.
You cannot help people permanently by doing for them, what they could and should do for themselves."

Abraham Lincoln's wisdom helped us clarify: I told her no. It wasn't easy. The potential for misunderstanding was high. "I get paid Tuesday I just needed it til then. I've been trying to do my best. ... I could've left my debit card if you guys didn't trust me." But for us, it wasn't about trust. We didn't want to be manipulated or pressured; we wanted to care, and did. We did our best and had to rest.

So, Jesus, when You say to "give to whoever asks you, expecting nothing in return," how exactly does that work?

~elllee~

Just down the road there was a *(shhhh, don't tell anyone)* halfway house. I don't know what their crimes were, but the women there "laid low" and didn't want any trouble. They were always responsive when we walked past with Wiley. Big Mama sat on their porch as the Monarch Matriarch over that chrysalis house.

Just as I sent the kids home —Reyana, Beels, Misi-ell, and Cinco — a red Mustang with no muffler revved its way down Woodbine and parked in front of the halfway house. It seemed as if a tingle went down the spine of Woodbine. I watched from the porch, broom in hand, sweeping up the remains of play and fall leaves. What was it about the car and the man that made me stop sweeping and watch? Something was amiss with the driver, who was a large black man with a determined step and a loud, foul mouth. The children were told to get inside.

A yelling match ensued. The man yelled at the women on the porch, and they yelled back at him. The man from next door came out and did not hesitate to stand his ground near the women's porch. I clearly heard a man's voice say, "You keep your fuckin' hands off ...." I began to pray as the aggression intensified. Yells turned into screams as the man advanced up the porch steps, and then all I saw were arms flailing and fists flying.

Mustang Man went back to his flashy car, got a gun, and walked back toward the porch and male neighbor. "Do you want me to shoot you?" he yelled. And he drew the gun and fired.

I held my breath: no one fell.
Everyone scattered, screaming, running.
The porch cleared within seconds.

Wiley tried to run away from the pop of the gun, and I realized it would probably be best to go inside. I must admit to my own fascination; I watched from a window. Once he was armed, Mustang Man was alone but still angry. He railed around and someone yelled they'd called the police. He vroomed away and quickly after, two police cars arrived. The women filled the porch, talked to the officers, replayed the events, and the mood of fear lightened. I was concerned for the women who were trying so hard to stay on a good track.

Who was that man?
What or who did he want?
What was the history between him and the women on the porch?
Why was he so aggressive and why the abusive verbal exchange?

I stayed outside for almost an hour, watching and waiting and praying. I sat on the porch swing, pondering this place. Who tells my neighbors the gospel? Who brings the good news of freedom and beauty and reconciliation and strength and humility and Christ to Woodbine, to my neighbors? Who is willing to take the physical risk, to give up a stronger school system, to put in the time, to make new friendships? Who is willing to put aside their status, their notoriety, their niche of fame, their comfort, their brand of flash, to be with the former offenders and prostitutes?

And the scripture from Isaiah came flooding into my mind to answer my own questions: **"Here am I; Lord, send me"** (Isaiah 6:8). But what if they don't want me around? What if I mess up? What if they just want their own space? What if I don't feel safe to them? I laid out all my apprehensions and arguments for God to see. He knew them all anyway.

The Street Walkers

The first spring on Woodbine Avenue not only brought out daffodils and rejuvenated pansies, but it also brought out the prostitutes, walking day and night.

It was March, an easy afternoon to be outside, the kind of day that makes you lift your face to the sun and think, "Ah, spring is coming. This is a glimpse." I took Wiley on a quick two-block walk before I had to return to work for an evening event.

Two women got out of a car on the corner, but I couldn't really see them well because of a tree with low limbs. Evergreen shrubs crowded the base of the tree and jutted out, so as I turned the corner, I realized one of the women was behind me and one was in front of me. They'd gotten out of the car and gone to different corners.

The woman in front of me had her hand well down inside her colorful tights, frontside, and she seemed to be … arranging herself and her clothes? Putting something into place? Her dyed blond ponytail swung as she groped. She continued forward and Wiley and I fell into step behind her, while out-pacing her. She obviously thought I was her co-worker, who was behind me but still a short distance away. She started blowing off steam, sort of like I do at the end of the day. "Wooo!" Again a few times. When I didn't respond, she glanced back at me.

"Hey there," I initiated. Could we talk?
"Hi, pardon me, I was jus' adjustin' my self."
"No worries, I understand." Pause. "Has it been a good day?" Ugh, I don't know what to say.
"Yeah. Yeah, it's been good."

Then she turned and looked at me as she started to cross the street. She *saw* me. Me in my pencil skirt and boots, my swingy sweater, a fashionable package fresh from my workday. And I *saw* that she saw me, and an invisible wedge crashed into the concrete between us, and I lost her.

"It's been a real blessed day, ma'am. A real blessed day." Even her tone of voice changed into that of a dutiful Sunday school child trying to be sweet, rather than a wild one who'd just finished getting half-naked with a stranger.

And I thought, "Now, why did you just 'church it up' when you saw me?" The unseen wedge grew wider, laced with my frustration. I know people tend to homogenize and stay in their safe relational spaces, but the gospel instructs us to value people who are unlike ourselves, to resist the bait of division by cultural categories, and to close gaps, in the Name of the One who bridged our relational gap with the Father.

Her friend was also crossing the street, both women leaving me on the opposite side, but their crossing was interrupted by a low-rider, a brown four-door with a boom-boom-boom vibrating the rolled-down windows. A man with a medium-sized fro leaned out of the passenger side, made a cat-call sound, and said something crude.

Then he looked up and saw me.

Immediately he held up his hand, which was opened wide and palm facing me, and said, "'Scuze my language, 'scuze my language," and they boom-boomed off.

What did he see or sense that he so quickly held up his hand and made a request for pardon? I wondered, not having an answer but wanting to pursue one. In his split-second judgment, how did he know I condemned his behavior? What was the gap between us that did not invite connection?

Is this how police officers feel when they merge onto the interstate and everyone slams on their brakes, slowing to the appropriate speed limit, trying to be better than they have been, all of a sudden mindful of honoring the rules they've been breaking? Is this how people were with Jesus? Did some people start using religious language and "get their act together" for a conversation with Him? Or did others finally let go of trying so hard and just blurt out whatever was on the tip of their tongue?

I said to the woman who was nearest to me, the one who was the recipient of the crude comment, "I just wish they would treat you like a lady." My Mama-Bear was coming out, my care awkwardly and quickly trying to find words as the women were distancing from me. Me trying to bridge a physical gap that was far deeper, far more profound than the unseen, crashing wedge.

Without fully looking at me, she said, "They never do."
And then, with a feathery lilt, she quipped, "They don't know how."

Her comment settled on me like tar, fastening me to her cycle of sex and strangers and a cheap view of life and love. I felt instantly heavy.

Unless Handsome is sweating in the summer, when we sleep at night, we are naked and intertwined, legs all over each other, nested into each other's bodies. He is my heater in the winter; I am his soft comforter all year long. It may sound strange to bring this to the forefront, but in my understanding, we are souls and spirits within corporeal bodies. We are embodied, grounded by physical touch, interpreting life through our senses. Bodies are a gift from God.

Our sex life is mutual and happy. It's a rain-swollen bubbling brook, a passing storm, a high tide, billowed clouds passing speedily in a blue sky, a sumptuous feast after a long day of work in the dirt. He cares tenderly for me and attends to my aging, shifting body. His animation helps me know I am loved and wanted, and that secures me. He accepts my body, my flaws and faults acknowledged and included.

I think of how delicious our love life is when I see the street-walkers. They are not known; they are used and paid. Their physical intimacy is transactional, like paying for a meal. Who cares if she ever has an orgasm, or two, or four? Who sees her as more than a sexual release, a woman to dominate, a tool for tricks, a wage, a jackoff? Who sees the little girl? Who treasures her the way Handsome treasures me? Where were her 6'4" fierce father and spitfire 5'2" firecracker mother to care for her? Did they love and protect her the way my parents endeavored to protect me? What chance did the street-walkers have? What are their stories?

She may never know the pleasure of a man who loves taking his time … raking his bristle-beard across her belly … whispering things only lovers know … laughing out loud because she can't contain all the endorphins rafting through her artery-rivers.

Yet this is the picture of Christ and the church, of a man and woman who are one, of unity and grace and peace and pleasure and working out all of life together, of vows to never leave or forsake each other. A good marriage is a sign and wonder to the world, sex included.

The street walkers are another sign. They show the cheapened side of intimacy, the side where people are used and abused, not known or cherished. I see when they have a black eye. I hear when their pimps yell at them as they exit the car. I've heard people say that sex workers are just fine, thank you very much, stop judging. But don't try to tell me this is her joy, her highest ambition, that she's fine. No. She's tired. She's hurting. She's sick. She's trafficked. For some, they anticipate up to 30 sexual encounters in a single day. That body of hers? It's used like a tube of toothpaste, rolled up and brittle and empty at the end of its use. My informal research supports this; the life of a street walker is so short, so painful.

As they walked away, I earnestly wanted to talk more, to offer my house as a safe place, to let them know they are highly valued by my Father, but they walked away, and all I could say was, "Have a good day …" and choke on all the rest. "I love you, women, and you have so much value and worth. Stop this.

Is a pimp threatening you? I'll help you find a job. Tell me about your lives. How much education did you have? My dentist will help you with your teeth. Can I give you a hug, a plain and simple and innocent hug? You could be safe and leave this life today, right now, *right now!* Are you addicted? How can I help you?" I knew I was naive; I saw myself. My love, like oil; my lack of experience, like water: I didn't know how to mix them.

I had the privilege of going back to work that evening to learn from a remarkable, earth-shaking woman, Jane Overstreet of Development Associates International. What a seminar, what an example she was, what a strong work ethic, what solid principles! She set the bar not just high, but took it to a different plane altogether. What a contrast: she was flying all over the world training men and women to lead their nations and communities; my neighborhood walkers were hooking up and wiping away the semen. My heart broke.

It was late, very dark, when I reached my neighborhood. I turned onto North Olive, which then fed into Woodbine Avenue, and saw a woman walking on the sidewalk, purse over her shoulder, sporting jeans and a t-shirt and a ponytail. The white work truck in front of me jerkily swerved toward her and pulled to a halt. She got in.

The truck moved extremely slowly. I started thinking I needed to go around them, but the truck's blinker flashed and they turned onto Woodbine. Still inching along. I began to pass the truck when they pulled to a stop … right in front of our simple gravel parking place in our side yard. I looked over to begin communicating with the driver that I needed to be exactly where he was parked, but the woman got out, shut the door, and briskly walked back toward North Olive. That was when it hit me.

She must have been negotiating price or position and the hook-up didn't work out. She went back to wait for the next person. The truck moved on.

I parked quickly and moved as fast as I could to the sidewalk, but she was already gone.

Bottom line: I was totally unprepared to love these women. Their lives were staring me in the face and I didn't know how to love them. I had so much to learn.

I felt a vast gap, an "us" and "them" (which I detest), even as I longed to reach out and talk to them about their circumstances. If they had had my family … big, gracious love; the finest schools; networks of two generations for work and opportunity; medical and dental care; endless encouragement; who would they be today? Who would I be if I had been raised as they were? These women were a mystery to me. I felt lost and inadequate, sidetracked by my questions and aware of my assumptions. *God, help me.*

～ellee～

At the end of the summer, I was walking Wiley early one morning and saw someone enjoying a bicycle ride. There was a light-heartedness about the rider and the way she tilted the wheels into a slight back-and-forth swerve. I could tell the rider was having a grand time.

And then she rode closer and I saw her face, and to my surprise, it was one of the regular prostitutes who often walked North Olive. Her face was lit with a smile, bright as day, and her few teeth were shining! As she whizzed by I shouted, "Woohoo, looks like fun!" She responded, "It is, it is!" One side of her head was shaved, and the other had ear-to-chin-length hair, and that short crop was flapping in the breeze. Given the light in her eyes, the shine on her remaining teeth, and the delight that surrounded her, I felt buoyed. The little girl within her was alive and happily riding a bike.

Before all the tricks and johns and customers and kinky sex and fallen-out teeth and neglect and physical usage, there was a little girl. I saw her.

I burst into prayer:
"Father, You are Father to this woman. Call her to Yourself. Hold her like the daughter she is. Guard her today.
I love You, Lord.
Your other little girl."

Word of the Day: *Edentate*: toothless. An *edentate* smile.

～ellee～

I recognized a street walker striding with purpose, never stopping, walking north-south as I walked east-west. At the crossroads, we passed within 10 yards of each other. I was elated, even hopeful, because I had wondered what to say to her for months. How could I start a genuine conversation? How could I open the door to friendship with her? How could I show her that I care, that I *see* her, that she matters? Was this going to be my moment with her?

Just as I said hello, she noticed we were now walking in the same direction, that Wiley and I were just a few paces behind her. "Well fuck, I can't do this shit," she said, and turned and walked in the opposite direction.

Door of opportunity, slammed.

～ellee～

As our area gentrified over the years, the street walkers migrated off of Woodbine. Sometimes at night I wonder where they are, what they are doing, how men are treating them, if they've eaten, if they are sore, if they need medical treatment ... all the embodied things. I wonder about their inner lives. Can they be vulnerable with each other, or is life too ridiculously fraught to even think about soul care? Do they know Jesus in a way I don't, like beautiful Sonya in Dostoevsky's *Crime and Punishment*?

Occasionally I make the two-mile walk to our local farmer's market in the heart of downtown. There is one sketchy area where I pray that my angels glow extra brightly, a place I perceive intuitively that harm swirls and evil seeks. It's a spirit of consuming, of predation. I walk through there because I want that place to change, so I pray and bring all of the Kingdom light and love and holy power I can emanate. It's there that I've felt my senses go alert as a rental car slows down, a man rolls down his passenger side window, and he pats the clean seat. I shake my head and verbalize a firm "No," and they quickly move on, either afraid to get caught or so hungry for sex that they can't slow their hunt.

So I prayed for the street walkers, the predators, and the johns. I let my heart be grieved and moved, and my tears flowed for them. I prayed like Jeremiah and felt like Job. These were embodied men and women made in the glittering image of God Almighty, crusted with transactional, genital grime. They were made for better.

A Normal Day

We took Cinco and Reyana to brunch-lunch at a Market Square restaurant called Café Four. In the car we stated our expectations: be nice to each other. Napkins in laps. No eating with fingers except for the bacon. No phones. Engage in conversation. I must admit that I love these conversations and the resulting behaviors.

Reyana was very serious about getting that napkin in her lap. Like an old mother, she tsk'd Cinco into getting his napkin settled. I loved watching them and how she non-verbally instructed him to get that napkin moving! She gave him The Look.

We have a silly family tradition in our house of imitating statues, so after our filling brunch the three females posed for pictures of three suffragettes in Market Square. Then the two kids played in the water fountains, giggling and running through the water until they were soaked head to toe.

I loved holding Reyana's nine-year-old hand as we dripped our way back to the car. I was aware of other people's glances, but I felt as though we were family, and I didn't think people (in general) really marveled or hated or reacted to mixed-race relationships with the rancor they did in the past. At least in Knoxville, mixed-race families are more and more common.

Back on the street, a thunderstorm raged into Knoxville, slamming our chairs across the porch into the swing, propping it up at a steep angle. The doll house fell on its face and the furniture spewed out and tumbled across the soggy quilt. After the front passed, Grant played basketball with seven other guys, Shirts & Skins. Cars dodged the boys as they played to 21. I went in to get some water for everyone and when I opened up the freezer door, it hit me: strawberry cake! My sweet Mama had brought me a strawberry cake with cream cheese icing for Mother's Day. Because of doing the Whole 30, I had stashed it in the freezer. Perfect day to share! The street funneled onto our porch. Paper plates covered in deliciousness passed from person to person until everyone had their fill.

From Reyana's point of view:
All these days when I've been out to eat with y'all and stuff, it been awesome. Running through the fountain was awesome! Every time I ran through the fountain it like it goes in my face! I felt that I was going to fly. I felt like I was going up to heaven when I jumped.

Taking pictures with Cinco and Marlie was exciting and next Sunday I hope that Collins [our house guest] *will come with us. Today has been a good day on Woodbine. Now I want some SlimJims.*

A Normal Night

When I got home around 5:30, Reyana came biking over on her pink bike with the tassels. She was the only one on the street who had kept the same bike for a year and a half; all the others had been stolen, replaced, stolen, and replaced. Reys wisely took hers inside each evening.

Reyana and I, outfitted in our favorite aprons, finished slicing peaches about the time Cinco came over and Grant drove in. I had a large bowl of green grapes out for dinner, but they became a toy rather than food: the war was on. Who could throw the grape up in the air and catch it with their mouth, no hands?

Grant won hands down, Cinco earned a loud mostly-victorious second, and Reyana came in a giggling third. I fed "the girls" — the hens — their first snack of Cheerios floating in their water trough.

Reys joined us for dinner because she said the adults told her they weren't eating at home tonight … which meant no food for Reyana. At dinner Reyana chewed with her mouth open, the kids barely sat down in their chairs, no one used their napkin, and Cinco thumped Reys on the head when he went to get another spoon. Reys got in an angry funk, and just as we were about to send them home, their tension broke with the anticipation of a basketball game with Grant. But not before Reys had some time to do my hair (pronounced "her").

She brushed my wavy brown hair out down to my shoulders, then combed it ("of course you have to use a comb!" which I would never do), then divided it to do braids from the scalp. She scrapped that because "it would take forever" (I have thick hair). She styled, swirled, braided, and decorated ... until I had three large braids, 2 barrettes, and much less (combed) hair.

The kids played a game of HORSE with Grant, Wiley and I were on the porch as the temperature dropped from 93 to a doable 83, the katydids were singing, neighbors were out walking their dogs, and the sky was deepening toward dark. Cars were slowing down when they saw the game on the street, and drivers waved and yelled "Reyaaaaaana" as they passed. Cinco was out of his mind about the coming UT football game and was effervescent; he and Grant would be sitting on the 45-yard line together.

This was a good night. No gunfire, no drugs, no half-alive characters walking the street. Just our beloved kids ... and one pesky mosquito.

Chapter Four: Walking, Summer 2017

BEING HUMAN ON WOODBINE AVENUE means we welcome weakness and strength, the unseemly and the generous, the holy and the profane. There is room for all of it. This is divine hospitality, an expansive welcoming of all that is in others and ourselves. We don't despise their failures or our own; failure is one of our best teachers. We don't shame others for their fractures and faultlines; we've got ours too. We laugh with and at each other; we point out the joy in daily life and give thanks.

Rather than mask up, harden off, or steel ourselves, we welcome weakness and vulnerability. We see it, look it in the eye, and say, "Hello there. Come into the light. Let me dust you off and see you more closely. Come, sit next to me." No running. No hiding.

This takes guts.

It's challenging to not be disgusted with myself when I fail.
It's challenging not to judge. To be brave and meek, strong and soft, at the same time.
It's challenging to rest in my own (very imperfect) presence sometimes. But this is what I do when I am healthy: I see myself and others, whether in glory or filth or simply plain, and open the door.

There is tremendous value in *living with*, in being *in* the mess, not just near it. I began to realize how knowing what happens in our neighborhood was dependent on being physically present. As each day bound itself to its yesterday, it became more clear that I had my two feet solidly planted in radically different worlds. Through daily interactions at work and at home, I saw the value of proximity wherever I was.

Be with me, I whispered to God.
Be with me, sobbed the lady with cancer in my office.
Be with me, fumed the woman in the middle of a divorce as we sat outside the courtroom.
Be with me, danced little Reyana in my kitchen.
Be with me, jabbed sporty Cinco underneath the goal.

Be with me, breathed the broken-hearted mom as her child was taken away.

Two worlds, one way: *Be with me.*

Thankfully, I knew someone who had far deeper insight into my two worlds than I: Jesus. What a mystery He is: an infinite, invisible God embodied into mortal, limited flesh. He had two homes; one, eternal; the other, temporal. What did He experience in the highest heavens? The birth of galaxies when He flicked His wrist? The creation of souls with His every loving breath? The dance of protons and electrons, axons and synapses, hydrogen and helium bending and bursting to universal laws He spoke into being? The melodious, mysterious worship of angels?

Yet He came here … here as a man with pores and poop (no disrespect meant). He proved His true love for the fallen and fractured as well as the rigidly religious and the morally misguided and the sinful self-destructive. Jesus' heart and head blended into wisdom, guiding Him into relationships, putting all things to right again. Lame legs, blind eyes, guilty consciences — He ably aligned them all to His own concept of wellness. He challenged the cruelly critical, the broken bitter, the indefatigably insolent with His grace and truth. Some responded with joy and dancing; others tried to kill Him, and did.

And Jesus scattered His glorious life and truth wherever He went: with the wealthy, with the poor. With the privileged, with the oppressed. With the illiterate and the learned. With the cynical and the saint and the sinner.

Now, I had a chance to follow in His footsteps. I would not even consider walking this path without the Holy Spirit; it was too treacherous a way, too tricky a terrain, and I was too naive. Here I was in my vocational life, one foot in the world of white wealth, honor, networks, privilege, good intentions, safe relationships, intellect, defensiveness, and fear. All this was familiar to me.

Woodbine, on the other hand, was rich with variance. On my block were whites and browns and blacks, shades of personalities as varied as the shades of skin. The experiences represented by my little block were magnificently motley, mixed by race, class, and every sort of economic status.

I marveled at this: we were a microcosm of what it was to be different, "other" from each other, *and* in proximity. Without proximity I would not — could not — experience the understanding gained only through relationship. Scholarship could augment what I was experiencing but not replace it. Being a reader, I leaned on books to bridge my knowledge gap. This was important, because I could unwittingly cause harm without first knowing history, without gaining awareness about the conflict and significance of the history of black and white, the interplay of government policy, and the current challenges faced by the black community.

If we weren't on Woodbine, we wouldn't see what was happening at a deeper level. Someone could tell me about Woodbine, but it's different than actually *living* on Woodbine. It's similar to the difference between explaining with words what a lemon is like in appearance, taste, and texture vs. actually seeing, tasting, and handling a lemon. Words could acquaint me with the lemon; I could imagine the lemon; I could relate the lemon to other objects or fruits to get an idea of its being. But it is different from actually holding a lemon, feeling the roughness of its skin, the weight of it in my hand; or tasting a lemon, allowing it to wake up my mouth with its bold, sour, citrus flavor and delight my nose with its singular scent.

We wanted the full flavor of Woodbine — the zest, sweetness, and tang. How to taste all of our street? Three-four days a week, I began walking our roads.

Stuck on the Porch

I was on my morning walk moving back toward home, bouncing and happy, when above my music I heard a yell in a Southern drawl. "Hey! Hey, help me! Can you help me?"

I looked across the street and there was a large woman in a chair motioning for me to come to her. "I called 911 over an hour ago! They still aren't here. I don't know what the problem is." She groaned in pain. "I think I broke my foot last night."

Her foot was indeed swollen, her ankle rounded out so you could no longer see the bone. I asked her some questions — do you have any ice I could put on your foot? May I elevate your leg? What is your name? 911 Ambulance Dispatch said they had had several life-threatening emergencies they had to tend to first, but they promised they would come.

She moaned and tears poured down when I elevated her foot onto her purse. She was staying in a church's community house while she attended the funerals of her parents; she lost them both within four days of each other. She had locked the door behind her when she hobbled out to the porch, so there was no way to get ice from inside. She yelled to a black young man across the street, asking him for some ice, but he said his mama didn't do ice. A true Southerner.

I ran home. I gathered a baggie of ice, a cold water bottle, a bowl of peaches, some of my homemade whipped cream, one of my books, and drove back. She was still there.

I sat with her, listening. She was so sad about her parents, but appreciated their tender story: After her father died, her mother died of a broken heart. "I think she just didn't want to do life without him."

This woman was feeling uncertainty, sorrow, and pain — a heavy load to bear. As she explained her story to me, tears rolled from her eyes, down her cheeks, and onto her chest, and made a wet, spreading spot on her shirt. I prayed for her and encouraged her as best I could, then drove home to get ready for the day. I checked her porch when I drove past on my way to work; she was gone.

I became reflective, thinking about the story of the Good Samaritan, Jesus' instructive parable about a man who was robbed, beaten, and left for dead (Luke 10:25-37). Two religious men walked past the wounded man; Jesus did not go into detail about why they walked past. Perhaps they were in a hurry; perhaps they were afraid or did not want to become "unclean" by touching him. A Samaritan man stopped to help him. This was very significant because Jews and Samaritans were at enmity like Palestinians and Israelis, the Rwandan Hutu vs Tutsis, or the Unionists and Nationalists of The Troubles in Northern Ireland. The wounded man was Jewish; the despised Samaritan could have walked on by too, because of racism and ethnic animosity. But he paused.

In his care, the Good Samaritan was sacrificial, other-focused, and financially generous. He was not afraid to step into the mess, the blood, and the harm shown to a stranger.

The point of the parable was to answer the question, "Who is my neighbor?" Another way to ask that question is, "God, who are You asking me to love and serve? Who is crossing my path today — do I have the resources to help? Am I willing to be inconvenienced, to pay a bit, to change my schedule, to care, to listen, to network for his or her good?"

What else could I have done for her? I chose to go to work rather than go to the hospital with her. Did she know how to advocate for her own care in a hospital setting? Did she know the questions to ask, would not having a solid current address hurt her level of care? Where was she going to stay tonight? I didn't know. I felt that sense of, "Next time, follow through more closely, go further."

I settled into a routine: morning walks down to the park. These were lovely days — the heat was coming, but there was morning-fresh crispness lingering in the shaded portions of our broken sidewalks. Weeds were thriving. Robins were hopping about and mockingbirds were scolding anything within their territory.

One morning as I neared the park, I had a sudden sense, like an inner holy Amber Alert, to listen. *Watch, be fully aware.* And then I saw her.

She was in a salmon-pink shirt, surrounded by multiple plastic grocery bags that were almost translucent because they were so full, pressed to stretching. She was simply sitting, gazing out at nothing. When I passed within 15 yards of her I said hello with a shy wave, then kept walking. When I looked back at her, she was slumped over at the waist ... and she stayed that way for a while.

I couldn't take it. Again, the Good Samaritan story, my training, and my job in loving women pulled my heart to her with magnetic force. I knelt by her, being as gentle as I could, acknowledging she might be scared of me. I asked her if she was alright. She said *Yes*, but her answer was slow and foggy, like she was completely, utterly, irreparably exhausted.

"Are you homeless right now?"
"Sort of ... it's a long story." Her full lips were gorgeous. High cheekbones. A classic African beauty.
"I'm sure. I'm sorry." I paused, trying to think of what to say.
"Listen, do you need anything right now? Are you okay?"
"Yes, I'm alright." She spoke slowly.
"Do you have a place to stay tonight?"
"I'm not sure."
"Do you have a phone? Can I give you my number? I do not want you to stay out here tonight. It's not safe for a woman alone. You are welcome at my house."
"I don't have a phone right now...." She trailed off. Her exhaustion made me want to just take her into my arms or tuck her into one of my beds at home, all of which were full of visitors at this time.

"The Lord is with me, I don't feel afraid," she said slowly, thoughtfully.
"I'm so glad. I do believe He is with you." We paused, just sitting together for a while.
"Okay, please: remember my address." I told her my street number, told her our evening schedule, and left her with a caring hug.

I realized later how my mother would have been upset with me for telling her our schedule. But Grant has never thought of theft as a deterrent for being on Woodbine. I was grateful for that as I told him about the salmon-pink exhausted lamb and that I'd told her when we would not be home. He wasn't worried about it. We put our blow-up mattress on standby. On the way back home I looked for her, but she never showed.

For a while, on my morning walks, God asked me to not listen to music, but to listen to Him. I still took my phone but was no longer plugged in. I simply tried to listen and be present to whatever God had for me on Woodbine.

I heard four shots at 5:18 PM, May 28, 2017, on a Sunday near the direction of the park. A minute and a half later, I saw a huge man in a comically small car speeding down Woodbine. Within two minutes of the shots, we heard the song of the ice cream truck. Two minutes after that, we heard sirens. This place was full of contradictions.

We tuned to the police scanner, and sure enough, it was a 10-81 (shooting) and the police were starting a crime log. "There is blood in the front of a house [a few blocks down, Bertrand] and one block over [Fifth Avenue]. The keys are in the front door."

The crime was reported by our local news stations. Apparently a man was taken to UT hospital with life-threatening injuries; he later died. And we heard those four shots that got him just as he was turning his keys in his door ....

Months later Grant and I were looking at a house about two blocks west of us, pursuing it as a possible rental purchase. While I was outside, I watched a drug deal happen. Two women. One bag of white stuff. Hand to hand, quick and wordless. Another woman waiting in a car. Speedy drive-away. Serious and emaciated faces, blond hair, dyed and stringy.

That house had never held its renters for some reason, but now it had obviously become a drug den. Many cars were there when I saw the deal, and when I walked Wiley, there were always cars at the curb. I never smelled weed there, but my inner caution sensor was always on alert.

A few days later Handsome called me before I left the house. He left late that morning (6:30 AM), just in time to see a SWAT team, armored vehicle, police officers, four undercover cars, and two marked police cars closing a raid on the drug house. Officers were on the porch, suited up and strong. Arrests had been made and the house was being searched.

I walked past after work and to my surprise, all the lights were on, shades were up, and I could see into the house. I had never, ever seen into that house before; it was usually laced up like a tight pair of Jordans.

No one was present. There were about five cars there; were the drivers in jail?

Then in the wee hours of the morning, Grant and I awakened to an automatic weapon firing. I lost count of the bullets quickly. Whoever the shooter was pursuing only had a handgun; that was sobering. The sounds of POP ... POP ... POP-POP were quite different from the extended RATATATTATTATTATTAT.

I hated automatic weapons on our streets. I hated drugs more than ever before. I hated seeing skinny men and women strung out and doing courier work so they could have something to shoot up. I hated seeing their stress; they were meant to be free. They were created to be light, to laugh, to be well-treated, and to have meaningful work, but they had become shadows, a scandalous, patched-up version of who God created them to be. My heart ached.

~elles

Dream: Jewels

In my dream I was walking down Woodbine toward the park, full of marvel and wonder. Certain houses were bejeweled — green emeralds were leaves, cherries were garnets, water fountains were topaz laced with peridot. Flower leaves were jade, flashing with lustrous pearl centers and tourmaline petals. Windows were diamonds, and I could see brilliant colors like spotlights beaming through them, refracting in the sunshine. People exuded colors, and I could sense the glory of God in them.

Then I would walk by another house: grey. No sparkle. A shimmerless existence thirsty for color and joy.

Some houses and properties were dark, as if a storm had rolled in and I could not even see to the door. It was as if the land and house were crying out for relief, for life, and for joy, but was temporarily shrouded in fear and evil, like something was growling or thunderous or crouching there. I felt defensive. Wiley did not want to walk by these houses; it was as if he could see something I couldn't. I was reminded of Balaam's donkey (Numbers 22:21-33) and let him lead me across the street.

Then I would pass another home ablaze with beauty, and reach down to touch fiery, opalescent flowers beside aquamarine walkways. Amethyst porch pillars and ruby rails refracted cherry light onto the yards where children played, radiant with citrine purity. Tourmaline branches glistened as they sported dazzling fruit. So much light shifting into glorious colors! I realized I didn't have my sunglasses.

I intuitively knew through the Spirit that the difference in the homes was the presence of God. He was the light flowing through every jewel, the source of all that was beautiful and good, the spark of joy and the fulfiller of hope. He was calling to the other houses: *Through beauty, I'm knocking. Open your door and I will gladly come in and eat with you. You too can see light scatter My beautiful Presence through each room. Will you let Me in?*

The Challenge of Coming Home

The first summer the kids were out of school, coming home looked like this:
1. I pull in the gravel parking area beside the house.
2. I put the car in park and hear, "SuzySuzySuzy!"

3. I see smiling black faces running happily toward my car as I open my door.
4. I get inundated with questions like, "Can you hang out?" "Where have you been all day?" "What are you gonna do now?" and then hear the drama of the day as I gather my things.
5. I walk toward the front porch, taking in two-three voices at a time, questions and thoughts and comments flying around like dragonflies over water.
6. I unlock the door and Wiley the dog is bouncing up and down, but still scared of all the kids at the same time.
7. Sometimes the kids ask if they can come in and Wiley barks vehemently, getting the scraps of my attention as we all merge into the hallway toward the kitchen.
8. Lots of listening and conversation. Lots of orange juice.

May I speak as an introvert for a moment? This was a challenge. Yes, it was beautiful, but for me, it was also a challenge.

The nature of my job was to *be with*. It was a Gospel-centered approach to work: be with people. Listen. Love them well, serve them, call and text them, eat with them, and visit them. Go to their homes and to the hospitals; be with them quietly in my office or quickly walking on a boulevard; pray with them, plan for them, pursue them. Grieve with the grieving, counsel the confused, go to wherever the hurting were: city courtrooms, abortion clinics, private homes. I was with people much of my day, swimming in their seas, but knew I had a quiet shore nearby at the end of the day. I did well as long as my introvert needs were satisfied; I would classify myself an extroverted introvert.

In my pre-Woodbine life, I went home to silence, to an extremely peaceful setting. The creek running in front of our porch was blissful; the frogs' singing and bellowing made me happy. After a day and/or evening full of people, I could retreat and get quiet and re-fuel. Now the *children* were running in front of our porch and they also definitely bellowed, but it was a completely different scenario. With them, there was need. With them, there was hope for time together. There was emotion and conversation and (dare I say it?) saturation.

One day I got home from Sunday church followed by a deep meeting with a couple. I loved getting my hugs — three children this time — and hearing the drama of the moment. One kid had loaded up a nerf gun with tacks and shot his sister in the leg and another neighborhood kid in the hand. He was in T-R-O-U-B-L-E. I tried not to laugh.

I listened for a little while, then let them know I was going inside, and if Grant was napping, I was planning on snuggling in with him. Sunday naps are a favorite part of Sunday for us. It was hard for them to have me close that front door because they wanted to come in; but this time it was not hard for me to close the door. There were just times Grant and I needed to be alone with each other. The kids pledged they'd stay on the porch swing till we came out, even if it was hours.

He was indeed trying to nap, but the kids were so loud that it was not possible. Have I mentioned that our doors and windows in this old house are not well sealed, and we hear everything easily?

As Grant and I enjoyed some together time, we could hear, "Suzyyyyy! Graaaaaant! Are you coming out yet?" and "Hey, stop that! Gimme that!" and "I can swing higher than you!" and "Get off me!" and "Watch me do this on the swing!" We looked at each other and Grant said, "I hope that swing holds!" and we laughed and held each other just a little bit longer.

No one got hurt, and the kids all ended up playing at our house for hours, culminating in an impromptu hamburger and hot dog grill night. Corn, salad, potatoes from our garden ... we had eight young guests. Several times as we prepared food and space, Grant looked at me with sparkling eyes, and I could tell he was alive and happy to organically and spontaneously serve the kids. He checked on me a few times: "You okay, Babe?" And once, right in the middle of working in the kitchen, I felt God's Spirit remind me that it was for moments like these that we were on Woodbine.

The girls drew pictures, wrote stories, and gathered flowers and weeds to make pretty bouquets in red Solo cups. The boys played basketball and competed. A few of them stepped in Wiley's poop, so the hose came out to rinse shoes, then people got wet, and there was lots of squealing. Cinco argued with everyone. He has the instinct of leadership but not the skills, *yet*. Young Misi-ell held his ground, verbally firing back every time Cinco contradicted how tall Misi-ell was. Reyana held her own ground too, all four feet of her little feisty self. Beels just wanted to be loved. Kintay shook his head at all the arguing, loved to be on the move, and was a positive, polite foil for the others. He didn't get drawn into drama. His brother Kahlil was creative, interesting, and loved the garden, especially the strawberries. The Big Brothers were interested in more mayo. Simple things. *Be with* things. That evening I sleepily murmured,

Thank You, God, for the feast of being with these children. You fed our souls as we fed their bodies. I know You say with You is abundant life ... even for introverts and children. Amen.

There are two boys with impeccable manners that I called The Big Brothers. That's because of their girth: in 'hood terms, they were thick. Very thick.

As The Big Brothers and their friend DJ were playing basketball at our goal, cool air blew through, the dark skies lost their load, and it began to downpour. I was delighted to see the boys stay and continue heaving the glistening ball to the goal. There's something completely delightful about kids playing in the rain. It's free and pure and fun and out of the box. It's like a rascally smile, a playful invitation, a grin with energy and a feisty plan behind it.

Eventually the boys knocked, asking for water. I invited them in and they quickly filled the kitchen. I opened the refrigerator and the idea light bulb went off.

Two days previous, my dad had given me a baggie filled with the first-fruits of his blueberry bushes. How else can one celebrate the first round of blueberries than with homemade whipped cream? I added heavy cream, a bit of powdered sugar, and some homemade vanilla extract into a cold bowl and churned until the delicious, fluffy whipped cream begged to be decorated with blueberries.

I had six little cups filled with this heavenly goodness and offered them to the boys, telling them the story of my dad's blueberries. DJ smiled! This was a rare thing around me. "I've never tasted blueberries with flavor before. Usually they're just ...." He searched for a word but ended up crinkling his nose. That said enough.

I asked if they wanted another cup full and all of them exclaimed, "Yes!" with their eyebrows up. My Mama-heart was so happy.

God Almighty, thick with power, bless these boys. May they find their thickness and well-being in You. Cheers to You, Lord God.

One day I was walking in our back yard, lost in thought, until an uncharacteristic scent interrupted me. I followed it to our HVAC unit, where I found tucked into a private corner, a neat pile of human poop ... with a dollar bill right beside it. Wow. At least they left a tip.

The Tornado

During the first summer, life on Woodbine constantly surprised me. For example, one day, on my way to work around 7:50 AM, I passed a woman in handcuffs with a police officer at her left and right. She looked bewildered. I didn't know her or her story.

That same day after work I met two young entrepreneurial women to give them our painted kitchen table. It seated four, and we needed more space than that for the kids and guests they bring, so we donated it to their start-up. We loaded the chairs easily but they were going to have to make two trips, so we put the table down outside by the curb. I told them I'd stay on the porch so the table didn't walk away by itself. I went back in for my book and came back to the porch. The girls were still there, in their car, but the look on their faces had changed from happy elation to horror.

When I went inside, apparently a man pulled up in a rage. He was wearing the ubiquitous white wife-beater shirt and pants, but his belt … was wrapped around his knuckles.

A boy of about middle school stature had been bunting a soccer ball along the curbside, quietly playing by himself. I thought he was just hoping for some of the kids to come out and play with him. The furious man was a father figure; he was like a tornado, yelling, flailing his arms, and, sadly, wrapping his belt around his fist and whipping the boy. The boy melted into tears and sorrow and wailed. By the time I got out of my house door, the grown-up had stopped beating the boy with his belt but was still beating him up with his words.

It was awful. Everyone on the street had stopped; The Tornado was just losing it, sucking up all the air on Woodbine.

He forced the boy to get into the car, which the boy did not want to do, and screeched away. Grant pulled up as we were all exhaling, trying to make sense of this trauma, when the man pulled up again, this time by himself, still spattering and sputtering and flailing. I think he had moved from a Category 5 to a Category 2.

I reflected about this situation. If I had seen The Tornado pull up and start beating the boy, I imagine my Mama Bear (which I consider a sacred part of female DNA) would have kicked in and I would have run over to defend the boy. I imagine it would've ended up in a bad assault. For some reason this did not happen.

What of the boy? I don't know.
What of the Tornado-man? I don't know.

I prayed in equal measure for both of them, pondering what had shaped The Tornado into such a storm. Was he beaten as a kid too? Was there mental illness involved?

And the boy … oh God, for that boy, that blue-shirted, soccer ball boy who was losing the color of simple joy as his tears dissolved into the driving rain and clouds of The Tornado.

God have mercy on them both.

It may have been easier for *me* to open doors and make initial contact here on the street, but it was Grant Standing who was loved. I was eating it up ... and maybe a little jealous.

It was the boys. They flocked to him. He was steady, good-hearted, straight-forward, and an athlete. He was a father figure, available after work, and he treated these kids like they were real people with real feelings. He looked at them in the eye, listened, and was responsive. He was intellectual but reachable. He didn't treat the kids like they were an inconvenience or a mistake.

They were responding to his consistent masculine voice so well. Often the footballs were flying or the basketballs were bouncing, and he was just simply being with them in a uniquely masculine way.

For example, one day Zack-Attack got jumped. He stuttered relentlessly as he told us about it, but seemed alright physically. He said a bunch of guys got out of a silver car and tried to beat him up. We were able to comfort him — his stuttering slowed — and walked him safely home. I wondered if this had anything to do with the new gang symbol we saw on a dumpster in front of a Woodbine house that was being flipped.

Why did Zack-Attack run to our house? Grant. Zack-Attack needed a man.

After work, Grant played miniature football with the boys (Cinco, Kintay, Kahlil, and Kadeem). He bought a football and a basketball and upon presentation to the boys, a sense of awe rippled through conversation: "Wow, Mr Grant, how much did these cost?" That awe lasted about ten seconds and then everyone wanted to P-L-A-Y.

My favorite part of the epic matches on our mini-field (literally about 30 feet by twelve feet) was the quarterback's preamble. "49! 62! Go left! Set! Hike!" became far more colorful through Grant's creativity: "06:42! [the time] Babe in the garden! Boys from the alley! Hike!" Soon the boys were doing it: "37! 91! 7! [Our zip code] Miz Suzanne in a white shirt! Wiley running crazy! My hair's getting wet ... HIKE!"

Woodbine felt like home that day. Boys giggling and trash-talking and running through the waterhose ... me picking squash and putting roses and sunflowers in mason jars ... Grant pouring out his firm love and direction. I felt like such a rich woman, replete with love and grace, thankful for Woodbine.

My parents invited the family to vacation together, a dreamy bucket-list cool-weather trip. It was hard to leave the wild wilderness of Alaska with its 50-degree temperatures, tempestuous weather, muskegs, glaciers, orcas, brown bear, salmon, white thunder, magnificent mountains, spectacular vistas, rich food, the sense of exploration and intrigue …

… and come back to work and Woodbine. 90-plus degrees and humid, brown burnt grass, wilted flowers, weeds in my garden, overgrown zucchini and loads of dog poop-land mines in the yard. 170-something notable emails at work. A new spider had set up house in the bathroom. Sigh. But yes, it was home.

The hardest part about returning, though, was getting the news that Kintay and Kahlil had moved while I was gone. Grant came home one day before me and the boys had come to say goodbye. I never got to hug them and send them forward with kisses and prayers.

There was no explanation. I wonder, was it the bills, the rent? Did one of the parents lose a job? Did they find a better deal somewhere else? Will they stay at the same school? I'll never know.

I had read about transience as a part of life in the 'hood. We identified a cycle: people got adequate housing, stayed as long as possible, circumstances changed or difficulties culminated, and they had to uproot quickly to the next place, rarely getting ahead or saving money. Always a crisis. It was very difficult to have enough money to put down a security deposit, cleaning deposit, and two months rent up front. Housing for the marginalized is incredibly stressful, and that stress transfers to the kids.

The kids' lives seemed so vulnerable. In spite of sometimes feeling overwhelmed by the kids on our block, I cared deeply for them. School had started back, and they were in some of the worst-ranked schools in our city.

Unfortunately, we soon identified another cycle with a damning domino effect.

As I left the house I heard my neighbor yell, "Are your tires okay?" I wasn't sure what she meant until I looked at all the cars parked along the street. All but two had flats. "Someone slashed or punctured all our tires." Oh no!

Did someone think that was funny, or mean, or vengeance for some wrong?

Grant and I parked in our side yard off the street, and our tires were fine. But up and down our block and well into the next one, cars that parked on the street had at least one flat.

The domino effect of a flat tire:
▷ A neighbor comes out to go to work and realizes he/she has a flat.
▷ They call work; how will their boss react? Inflexible? Understanding? Yell at them? Be patient?

- They might not be able to get to work, or at best are late that day.
- They can't get the tire replaced within a day, or a week, or even a month depending on their income. This can be an unexpected expense, a real setback.
- Without transportation, they lose their jobs.
- If they lose their jobs, they lose their housing.
- They lose their housing. Will someone take them in, will they couch surf, will they be homeless? Some renters around here do not have the cleaning deposit plus the two months rent to start plus the utility activation fees necessary to move on short notice.

Even now, if you were to drive up and down the streets in my 'hood, you would see cars parked with flat tires — sometimes for months. Transportation is crucial.

~ellee~

The Three (Cinco, Beels, and Reys) rubbed the sleep out of their eyes, realized it was Saturday, and bumbled over for Smart Start cereal and blueberries. Once fed, their usual energetic and silly selves kicked in and they delighted us with their antics for four hours.

We baked cookies and cleaned that up, then vacuumed and played pickup sticks and cleaned that up. Then they ate a simple lunch and cleaned that up. But the best part, even over the slow-mo videos of them blowing air through their bouncing lips, was the dancing.

Please note: you must dance in our kitchen. This is a requirement. It doesn't matter that it is a tight space, or that the moves will cause things to crash or people will flail about and knock each other in the head. That's a given, and if the dancing is good, will be laughed off. And who would want to dance in the family room, where there's space?

Also note: no one knows the proper lyrics to any of the songs. They make them up or mumble along, then pipe up when they are secure about what they are singing.

Also note: for the kids, if there is a cuss word in a song, it's off the play list. Even Bruno and Beyoncé. And yes, among Woodbine's third and fourth graders, the "b" word is still considered a bad word: "All the kids know *that*." *My Dick,* anything disrespectful to women, and anything with "fuck" in the song is not allowed in our house, although we hear it on the street all the time. The kids all know that those are inappropriate words, but by age twelve, most of them use profanity so they will be considered street-hardy.

Last note: the dog vacated the area for fear of his very life. Someone trying to whip and nay-nay might accidentally topple over and scare him even more than

78

someone who was popping, locking, biz marking, wopping, preppin', or smurfin'.

And, of course, I was learning constantly from the children. Atticus, Cinco's cousin, had speech patterns similar to Freddy:

Be ri theh.	Be right there.
Lil bih mo.	Little bit more.
I fiktuh moo.	I'm fixin' to move.

Cinco was saying, "No cap!" with authority over and over. He paused, looked at me, and saw my blank face: "You don't know what that means, do you?" Bingo. He started loading up the skillet with bacon, carefully laying out each piece. This was his first time ever cooking bacon — no cap.

There have been more than a few times Cinco and Reyana have to clue me in on street slang. They always laugh, implying I'm old or I'm out of touch. True dat. But they patiently try to explain the meanings behind the expression, which can be comical.

Cinco said there's a good way and a bad way to use *no cap*. He only uses it in the good way, thank you very much. As he turned the bacon he paused: "It means I ain't playin.'" From then on, he ended almost every single sentence with no cap.

Suzanne: You need to turn that piece of bacon, Cinco.
Cinco: I got this, no cap. Aww, look how good it looks now, no cap. I'm hungry, no cap!

He also let me know that no one plays Ole Town Road anymore — *nobody*. No cap. Cue eye roll.

I also received a massive compliment when someone told me I was *drippin'* — so *hot* that the *ice* (gold, jewelry, etc.) on me was *dripping* off. I saw a lot of t-shirts on women after Mother's Day that said *Drippin'*. No cap.

~elles

Over the past year we made friends with Gizmo the Tiny Dog. He weighed in at 4 pounds soaking wet, but his heart was large and his bark, rapid. Once I learned his name, every time we passed his fence he leaned out to us for a loving neck scratch.

As Grant, Wiley and I were returning to our house, we switched to Gizmo's side of the street so the dogs could greet each other. In front of Gizmo's house was an intimidating car: the windows were tinted black and the boom-boom-boom bass was shaking the car and the house windows. I've learned to not avoid, to be less afraid, that someone's just jamming to their favorite song. But sometimes I feel fear knocking.

As the dogs sniffed hello, a young man with braids rolled down his window, and out of the blue queried, "I wonder what they're sayin' to each other, ya know what I'm sayin'?" His smile stretched across his face in a childlike wonder. "I know!" we both responded in unison. After a bit more chatting, we strolled on.

Handsome loved that interaction! "He didn't have to say anything. He could've totally ignored us and let us walk away, but he engaged us. He was so friendly and thoughtful and it was easy to jump right into conversation with him." We had no idea what his name was and haven't seen him since.

At home, Handsome poured me a home-made Cosmo after grabbing a beer for himself. As he peeled the yellow rind from a lemon, he mused, "Given all that white folks have put black folks through historically, I am amazed at how kind our African American neighbors are. Given the mass incarceration and the subtle systemic racism that is still operating in our country, I value every single positive interaction between races."

I chimed in: "Here we are: we are white people with white voices and white connections and white influence and loads of white privilege. If white privilege were an alcoholic drink," I said, lifting my Cosmo, "I've been tipsy all my life, so much so, it feels normal." I paused. "And our black neighbors are not running away! Maybe some are suspicious, a bit, but why wouldn't they be?"

He continued: "As a white male, I want to shift *power over* people to *power to*, *power with*. I want to do this, at work and at home." He sighed. "God, help me do this."

We went out to the front porch swing at dusk, still contemplating life and racism, when I heard a car engine revving toward us. The driver punched the accelerator hard, the car kicked into gear, and there it went, a sports car trying to take flight on our straight runway stretch of Woodbine. Not the first to try. But in the flashes of streetlight I noticed something: there was a black young man holding onto the roof, sprawled out across the rear window and trunk in baggy jeans, grinning at 50+ miles per hour. They didn't hesitate at the stop sign.

Ah, Woodbine.

Both the driver and the roof-rider reminded me of my brother. When he was 16 and 17, he would load up his Jeep with friends (and me, the little sister) and go to a flat where the lake had receded and the mud was thick and starting to crack. He would sling us through the mud as he did donuts, over and over until we were barely able to hold on. Of course, we were standing up, holding onto the

80

roll bar, screaming with a mix of fear and delight, asking for more. We both drove too fast down those county lanes, taking the wide curves at 70 mph, having the time of our lives, blond hair whipped by the wind, sunburned faces smiling as we sang our favorite songs at the top of our lungs.

Ah, youth.

~elees

Our porch was crowded with bright young black and white master's degree students in their 20s. We had gathered for a meal and conversation; everyone there was motivated to understand, to grow, and to build our city into a better place, but backgrounds were quite varied. No one knew where the discussion would go.

Grant stirred things up, which is his forté. Pointing, he asked, "Have you white people ever heard American history from a minority perspective?"
All of the white kids shook their heads.
"Could one of you who are black lead us into that? What were you taught at school versus what were you taught at home?"

"Completely different," Tyshawn stated authoritatively. "At home, I was taught more about slavery, the purpose behind it — and it was economics. Black people were used and abused to make white people rich. No offense," he directly said to his listening white friends.

"Of all the books I've read about this topic," I agreed, "my favorite was the memoir of a white, privileged, insulated woman who began to understand systemic and cultural racism when she took a course in history … US history taught from a non-white perspective." I grabbed Debbie Irving's book, *Waking Up White*, as they kept talking.

One very quiet black guy spoke tenderly. The way he chose his words carefully made us see his circumspection: he was a thoughtful person, contemplative.

"It was about power. Power over others, *use* of them. The disregarding of their humanness. White Americans were, in that era, quick to dehumanize anyone who was not like them. Consider the Native Americans, the Trail of Tears, the breaking of signed agreements — even here in East Tennessee. Consider traders stealing black people from their homes, transporting them across the ocean, one-third commonly perishing during the journey, being stripped, separated from your family, not knowing the language or culture, being treated like the lowest of beasts, crying out to your God in faith for His rescue, learning about the Underground Railroad through quilts and songs, hearing the stories of Harriet Tubman and Frederick Douglass, President Lincoln, the war, emancipation, freedom … that was one era.

"But black freedom was taken back in underhanded ways. You may have heard it said that racism never dies, it just takes different forms. Think about the Jim Crow laws, lynchings, government benefit exclusions, the Civil Rights movement, the hopelessness of being considered a criminal just because you were born black, the law creating harsher penalties toward black people … that was another era."

The porch was silent except for this young man's voice. His hands had flown to his chest when he said, "born black," and rested there. No one moved.

"In my black point of view, the criminals were the traders, the people who worked the slave-selling block, the plantation masters. The legislators, the manipulators, the owners who were blind to black humanity. The lynchers, the politicians. the Christian folk who said nothing or remained 'moderate' because of social pressure. The dehumanizers."
A tear rolled past his glasses. We stayed in respectful silence for a time.

"How is that fair or righteous in God's eyes? It can't be," commented a black girl.
"Oh I don't think He's happy about slavery at all," said a white guy. "I just can't figure out why He didn't stop it with a clear command. A really clear *Thou shalt not*. Actually, I guess He did with *Love your neighbors as yourselves*, but we disregarded that! And the masters used to quote the Bible all the time to keep their slaves in line. That's downright wicked. And manipulative. Exploitative. Why didn't He destroy them?"

Another white girl agreed: "What about our own East Tennessee with Hispanic workers during strawberry season? Brown-skinned short men ride in the back of pickup trucks to pick the fields. When I was in my teens I saw them and honestly did not know the scale of what was happening. It wasn't until I got older and immigration issues were in the news that I learned of how little they were paid, how they were used and not appreciated, how most were still grateful because it was safer and better than what they could earn in Central America. I felt they deserved better, that Americans should have the integrity to pay them fully for their work. Because they were probably in East Tennessee illegally, they were taken advantage of by legal business owners. It's all just wrong."

"My problem is, I have no idea how to step into that debate or the policies around immigration; but I'm angry. What do I do with this?" asked one young man.

"Has anyone ever been in a conversation with a black person and just bluntly apologized for the white race — our white race — about slavery?" asked a white girl.

"I have — yes," I said. "Three times. And I got different reactions each time. Once, the women just brushed it off: 'This is a different day and time. There was personal accountability.' Another man who grew up in the Jim Crow era said that he had moved on, that we should *all* move on. But the third person — oh my. Her eyes filled with tears and she broke down. I had said, 'I'm so sorry. It was wrong, all of it, horribly wrong.' 'No white person has ever said that to me,' she said. She just wept. I wanted to hug her, to touch her somehow, but didn't feel like that would be accepted. The last thing I wanted to do in that context was disrespect her body or her space. It just proved to me that the existence of one person's experience with racism does not negate another's experience. Different experiences of racism don't invalidate the experience of racism. A spectrum of experiences and responses exist. And there's grace for all."

One young man looked up from his phone, his face illumined by soft blue light. "On biblehub.com the Greek word *doulos* meant *slave*, and it was used over 125 times in the New Testament. Historically, if someone was a doulos, they belonged to someone else with no rights to self-ownership. The New Testament Scriptures say I am both a slave and a son, voluntarily subject to Jesus as my Master and yet *also* His friend and brother. And Jesus said that if you wanted to be a leader, **'The greatest among you will be your doulos.'** A slave! That reverses all of our images of success and prosperity."

I asked, "What do you think about Paul's letter to his friend Philemon? To me, Paul seemed to be telling Onesimus, 'Go back to Philemon' in order to begin a reorientation process between them as Christian brothers. Jesus changed the very nature of their relationship. I think Paul was saying, 'Don't look at him as a slave, look at him as a brother.' Isn't that a powerful story for that day and time? How then could slavery have flourished so in the South? How could Christian people ever justify slavery if they read this letter?"

Tyshawn agreed. "To me the bottom line is in verses 15 and 16 … let me read it: **'Perhaps the reason he was separated from you for a little while was that you might have him back forever—no longer as a slave, but better than a slave, as a dear brother. He is very dear to me but even dearer to you, both as a fellow man and as a brother in the Lord.'"**

"Southern masters did not look at their slaves as brothers," scoffed one young woman. "How did Christian people go from this letter to lynching?"

We were sobered at her blunt question, devastated that in the name of the Christian faith, black people were manipulated into being "submissive," then brutalized. There was a level of angry electricity, along with sorrow and confusion.

"Sin," said Handsome, putting his drink down too hard on the table. "Greed. Arrogance and pride. It was only a matter of time before pride led to dehumanization. Cultures throughout history have fallen into this trap: 'I want to own you, I want to have *power over* you, so that I may succeed. I will take care of my family and property at your expense. I will expand my business through your labor and not pay you fairly. I will disregard your needs, feelings, and agency because I place my own life above yours.'"

"Think through the Scriptures," I commented. "You've got Pharaoh. He enslaved the Hebrew race to promote himself, his class, his people, and his vision, regardless of what happened to the Hebrews. Then you've got Haman in the book of Esther. He is probably the prototype for racism. He was offended by the Jew named Mordecai, and he transferred his hatred for Mordecai onto the entire Jewish race. It wasn't good enough to kill Mordecai; he wanted to kill every Jew. He worked within government systems to establish a cause for completely wiping out the Jewish race. Then in the book of Acts, you've got Jewish Christians working through what it looked and felt like to welcome *any* human into faith, no favoritism allowed through works or heritage. All of these Biblical situations feel weighty."

One young man just shook his head, mumbling, "Why are we like this? What is our problem?"

"You, in your 20s, are hoping to change the course of racism in your generation. We can't change the past, so how do we relate to it as modern people who don't want to be racists? How do we acknowledge a heritage that harmed black people and benefitted whites, and firmly reject it as our future reality?"

"Those are key questions. From what I understand, in your studies you are going to explore that question for an entire year. Come back and give us your answers," Grant requested.

One student began to scribe the group's favorite questions:
What do the Scriptures say about race and class?
With race in mind, how are we going to hire and fire? What are we looking for in a future work environment?
What businesses do we support? What are we going to do about racially exclusive business cliques?
How can we acknowledge another person's racial or ethnic pain?
How can we share power with others?
How can we create safe spaces for friends who have had traumatic experiences due to race, gender, class, ethnicity — all the things?

Chapter Five: Going Deeper, Fall/Winter 2017

A PROFESSOR FRIEND, Mary Terry, recommended that I diversify what I read. How many minority authors, minority cinematographers, minority vocalists, minority podcasters, minority performers did I follow? Excellent suggestion. I began by reading *I'm Still Here* by black author Austin Channing Brown, a modern societal commentator who is a fierce voice against white supremacy, which she also identifies as white privilege.

Austin Channing Brown came to the University of Tennessee to speak with students and faculty. There was just enough room for people in the community to fill in the seats at the back; we squeezed in.

She was fantastic. Her comments about majority-white institutions and spaces of whiteness were quite sobering. Addressing black students and faculty, she thoughtfully advised them to adjust their expectations. I took these notes:

"The institution cannot love you. The rhetoric is friendly, so it can be confusing. Your job is to survive. You won't change the institution. Get what you need and get out. You let friends you choose, in. Most institutions were not created with blacks in mind; thus we end up with an unequal education. There are significant micro-aggressions: how do we heal? How do we heal when we are disappointed with a person [like a professor] who is not better at race? Get your joy from relationships, not American institutions. Build your own table where it's safe for you. Most institutions love themselves. Work to remember where you actually find intimacy. We must love ourselves intentionally in a world that does not love us well. Don't internalize shame for having the hope that things would be better or different. Survive by being in spaces where we are loved. Be intentional about finding healing spaces."

She reiterated her famous statement, "White people can be exhausting." The audience knowingly chuckled along with her, even though the moment was serious. I've heard many of my black neighbors agree, even as I asked them about their experience of being black in Knoxville … but kindly, they gave me the grace of opening up, and I'm certain they entrusted their stories to me because we had a real relationship. My mind wandered to their faces and stories when ACB said, "Can you *just believe me* and leave a person of color alone? Don't re-traumatize people of color when they tell their stories of racism. *Believe them.*" Yes ma'am.

Someone in the crowd said, "If you're a bridge [between black and white communities], you get walked on both ways." This was profound to me, a startlingly concise truth I was experiencing. This is what I was feeling when I told our story, especially in the political landscape of East Tennessee and in the dissonance between my job and home settings. At times it seemed as if no one was ever completely at peace with who we were becoming or what we were doing. We were judged or misunderstood; some friends were disengaging or distancing.

One of my black acquaintances later remarked, "Do we have to be integrated *everywhere*? Can't I just have some safe spaces with black brothers and sisters, with no white people? Can church or neighborhood be some of those spaces? Can't I just be with those who get me, who have lived my same history, who know my language? Being in white majority culture so much is exhausting. I just want to relax and be black."

I've thought about his remark often. On one hand, I think those safe spaces are necessary, absolutely. On the other hand, I think the Kingdom of God looks integrated. "Every tribe ...." So how does a modern Christian proceed? I think our first identity is as believers, brothers and sisters with the Kingdom in common. Ideally, being Christian creates the safe spaces for the other facets of who we are, but in reality, Christians have not proven safe, especially to many black people who live in my 'hood. So here we are, white people working gently to love and listen to our black neighbors, trying to convey the love of Christ with every glass of water, every conversation.

Knoxville Tour with Kenin Boise, Wisdom from Christena Cleveland

I went on a a tour of the urban city center with a local black historian and activist, Kenin Boise. His background was rich: Christian Community Development, urban planning, and work at Knoxville's Emerald Youth Foundation. He quoted Christena Cleveland's article, *How to Actually Fight for Racial Reconciliation:* "We begin our journeys of reconciliation by doing the same—by leaving the comfort and familiarity of our racially isolated worlds, engaging across racial lines, identifying with people of other races and making their burdens our own. ...[The word] reconciliation is much more profound and beautiful. In the Greek, reconciliation is katallassō which literally means 'to change, or exchange; to effect a change.' The word katallassō is often used by the apostle Paul to describe the restoration that can occur after two groups have been at odds (e.g., Romans 5:1-11)."

86

Kenin took us by shuttered Rule High School, once a hub for the black community. My mom taught there when I was in high school and college. For her master's degree she created a class for high-school-aged parents so they could simultaneously learn parenting skills and stay in school. She wrote grants for the funding, was awarded the grant money, began the class, and it lasted over two decades.

I smile when I think of how she used to pull up to "Roo High" in her black Mercedes all done up in privilege. Within a few weeks into the semester, she usually won her teen students — 50% black, 50% white, on average. There was life at Roo High, then … but no more. It was sobering and discouraging to see the glinting razor wire and the boarded-up windows. Kenin asked, "How did watching that bustling hub go silent affect the community?" He paused. "Adversely: it indicated giving up, of moving on and away, of a lack of investment. A negative voice, a hollow echo." We turned back to our tour van, sobered and thoughtful.

"KCDC (Knoxville Community Development Corporation) is a very powerful organization," Kenin said, eyebrows raised. Yes, indeed. Knoxville's East Side was deeply impacted by *eminent domain* during urban renewal. After hearing Kenin, we checked on details during dinner: to build the Civic Coliseum in 1961, 72 residences, 9 businesses, and 2 churches were razed. This grieved us. It was difficult to clothe my feelings with words. It felt like an ache that spanned hills and valleys, homes and driveways and mailboxes. It was brown-skinned boys on bikes and girls in pigtails playing dolls under the trees; it was the rhythm of spring daffodils and fall oaks, neighbors on porches … gone.

Living on Woodbine opened my eyes to both racial reconciliation and racial justice. Two levels emerged: change through personal relationships (quieter, relational) and change through structural policies (civic-oriented, administrative). Justice must thrive on both levels. We looked up the textbook definition of *eminent domain:* "… is the power of a state … or national government to take private property for public use. The most common uses of property taken by eminent domain have been for roads, government buildings and public utilities. Many railroads were given the right of eminent domain to obtain land or easements in order to build and connect rail networks. In the mid-20th century, a new application of eminent domain was pioneered, in which the government could take the property and transfer it to a private third party for redevelopment. This was initially done only to a property that has been deemed "blighted" or a "development impediment", on the principle that such properties had a negative impact upon surrounding property owners, but was later expanded to allow the taking of any private property when the new third-party owner could develop the property in such a way as to bring in increased tax revenues to the government" (Wikipedia).

When we all stood in the parking area of the police station, it was heartbreaking to think of all the people who had originally made these spaces their homes. How devastating to be helpless. The black East Side community is still very sensitive to government moves, understandably. In spite of the good intentions of many, urban renewal did harm. In the black community, I heard many speak of "urban renewal" as "Negro removal."

I asked specifically about the rapidly decaying, defunct Knoxville College property, a beautiful college campus that drew black people from all over the South for an excellent education. Kenin got somber. Knoxville College to him was very personal. I had hopes that part of the reparations money from the *African American Equity Resolution* could be used to revitalize it; he was unsure. It was as if he was afraid to hope for it. He referenced how crucial Knoxville College was to forming community, networks, and a sense of city safety.

We looked up more information about Knoxville's *African American Equity Resolution*: "The African American Equity Restoration Task Force will study, review, and identify strategic solutions to improve areas of disparity and disenfranchisement in the black community, work with existing agencies in the community, and develop policy, programs and recommendations that will establish opportunities for generational wealth building in the black community." None of us were on the task force, so we decided to keep each other informed as we saw things develop.

Kenin spoke about American history from a black perspective and one woman on the tour, disgusted, exclaimed that her "white-washed history books" were infuriating and deceptive. I agreed. I had never heard history recounted from a black perspective until I moved to Woodbine. Rev Rena, Mr. Bob Booker, my neighbors, and now Kenin taught me about Knoxville history from their vantage, and it was eye-opening. What bothered me? Lack: the lack of opportunity, equality under the law, mentoring, power networks, transparency, and banking opportunities. The limits placed on black-embodied people. How white people were always cast as good but clearly were self-serving and thought little of gaining at the expense of black people. The blindness and malaise of the Body of Christ to God's heart for a multiethnic church. The complete silence on racism in my young years.

At dinner we also looked up the Christian Cleveland article: *"Reconciliation work is costly because it is the work of the Cross. We kid ourselves if we think we can enjoy restored relationships without paying the price for them.… Reconcilers have the honor of following in Jesus' footsteps, but we also must recognize that reconciliation will lead to our own deaths. …Racial reconciliation isn't a goal; it's a way of life. The way of the reconciler requires constant self-sacrifice and self-giving. It leads to places and experiences that will stun you in both terrifying and beautiful ways. Reconciliation costs everything but, like the Cross, it also offers everything."*

My great hope is that our part of Woodbine can become an oasis of shalom for all races and classes; that we will know our neighbors' names and stories; that we will love well; and that we will impact future history for good, in Jesus' Name. To God's glory and our neighbors' good.

Eight for Dinner

After work I was planning on meeting three young women from Parkridge at our house to get to know them, their vision for their entrepreneurial endeavors, and their community-minded lifestyle. I stopped by Abbey Fields Urban Garden to pick up some fresh veggies for a light tomato vegetable soup to compliment my fresh sourdough wheat bread.

The three expanded to eight, from age 14 to their mid-20s. What amazing young women! Brown Joyful: her smile lit up the back porch deep into that night. Dark Simiya, erudite and articulate, passionate about life, leaning in. Brown Nicia, guarded and wise. Their white house-parents, Carolyn and Hannah, eager to engage, very attentive and thoughtful about the girls' responses, wise beyond their years. Sisters and friends, listening and supportive.

"Can we talk about race?" Handsome asked, and the porch blew wide open.

We discussed "black on black" pressure to 'stay ghetto', to not be influenced by living with white house-parents. "Aw, you jus' bein' white now," the girls' friends would jive. It was an accusation.

Handsome's sarcasm, quiet humor, and questions drew them out. They talked about school situations — a freshman and senior in high school getting together. They talked about dating: "Black boys just want grown-up stuff," they said. Grant said *all* boys want grown-up stuff. They laughed about how they used to dress like "Hoochi-coochi Mamas". They had high hopes for their volleyball team.

As we learned more about how they all lived together, Handsome probed, "How do you all make decisions?" They truly had a community mindset; the Romans 12 body analogy was real to them. Rather than compare or envy, they were glad that another person had a gift to bring to the family. They had gotten used to being together, to living as a large family, and loved it, fitting together as pieces in a puzzle make a complete and lovely picture.

But at first, when they all moved in together, the girls were suspicious and uncomfortable. They hid their clothes and their money; they couldn't sleep because it was too quiet. But as they saw how their houseparents lived and loved, they opened up.

And, as always, we learned new words: flex = so funny. Slap = cool. *Handsome is so flex.*

We had so much to learn from these girls and their housemamas. When they left, we spoke with awe in our voices about their wisdom, experience, and circumspect thoughtfulness. We wanted more time with them.

Family feel: Brunch

Sometimes you've just got to have breakfast for lunch … eggs, bacon, and homemade sourdough toast with butter and honey.

Just as I was finishing prep-cooking a package of bacon (11:15 AM), the kitchen filled with kids. The energy level in the house soared as they smelled bacon. Bacon makes everything better, whether you're in the 'hood or in the city or in the country, no?

Instantly there was a family atmosphere. "Can I have some of that?" they asked, pointing to the bacon. "Of course you may," and I distributed one piece per child as I got the toast buttered. Grant started cracking the blue, brown, and pale eggs from our hens, and the kids asked for fried eggs, not ooo-gross-scrambled eggs. Reyana asked for "bald eggs." We were stumped. Turns out that a "bald egg" is a boiled egg. "You know, the ones that are hard like a ball. Balled eggs." They got me giggling as they salted their eggs, crunched their toast ("Chew with your mouth closed, please"), and told stories.

It was a family feeling. They waltzed right in, asked for their share, and enjoyed every bite. No pretense, no sense of exclusion; just a come-on-in-and-eat-with-us-of-course-I-will-why-not?

Beels refused to let anyone eat until we said the blessing. She recited "God is great, God is good" and everyone joined in to finish the simple prayer. That was a golden moment, heaven shimmering there in our dining room, lighting up the faces of the children and bringing a deep satisfaction to my smiling soul.

Perhaps these precious ones, these three, are why we are here. Bacon, eggs, toast, love, laughter, and a safe place around the table. What beauty God has brought in unexpectedly as we have trusted Him.

P.S. Handsome gave me another reason to love him … again. We had a rainy day recently and he was late getting home. Why? Traffic? Work? No. He had given a man on the street his raincoat, then stopped by a local store to see if they had another one he could purchase. He found one on sale and wore it home in the downpour. You've got to love a man who gives his jacket to a stranger.

Poverty and Teeth

I listened to a TedX Talk by Shawn Duncan. He asked the question, *Why do the buckets of some people remain full and others remain empty, after years of charity?* He drew a distinction between crisis poverty and chronic poverty: Ray-Mee seemed to live in chronic poverty with frequent crises.

Shawn Duncan proposed a strategy: If the poverty is chronic, it is likely development-based. So, he asked, how do we disrupt the systems that keep this poverty in place?

For Ray-Mee, it seems that education will enable her to rise out of their poverty, if she will keep the job. It also seems that the job must lead to a career, which would include benefits and vision for her life and skill set. Who will take the risk, see the gold inside her, and patiently develop her?

Shawn also posed these sets of questions based on how we evaluate the good work we do in our community:
1. Are you the hero in your community? Are you a rescuer? Are you just affirming their material, vocal, and power poverty?
2. Poverty is a lack of voice, power, access. Who has been left out of the conversation?
3. Is the bucket still empty, requiring you to still fill it? Look at systems, not just symptoms. "Give a man a fish and he'll be fed for a day; teach him to fish and he'll be fed for a lifetime." Sounds good, but maybe already know how to fish. Do they have access to the pond? Are there fees to fish? Can he get a fair market rate? Is the community flooded with free fish? Are we rushing to fix symptoms rather than disrupting systems? Is the charity part of the system that needs to be disrupted?
4. To disrupt chronic systems, we need skilled professionals, not just volunteers. How can you leverage your job skill set to effect change?

I thought much about #3, thinking that the system of Ray-Mee asking me for money needed to be interrupted. She needed to be able to generate her own money. How could I support her? Pick up her kids from school? Take them a dinner once a week so she can study? Buy her basic school materials or books?

~elle~

Ray-Mee sat on my porch, nervously looking everywhere but into my eyes.

"I need some help, and I hate to ask, but I'm gonna. You know my teeth. Ugh, they're horrible. I can't do anything with them, but I heard about a place that my state insurance will work with, NoCo Dental. I went on their website — they're national, you know — and I can get dentures if they pull these front teeth, and I only have to pay $35-$50 a month. I *think* I can do that. But I need a co-signer because the total bill is over $5,000. I'm here to ask you if you'll sign with me. I know it's a lot, but I'm gonna make it happen. I gotta do something about these teeth."

After praying, talking with Grant about it, debating every scenario in my mind, and going on the website for myself, I agreed. I thought it would be her best chance to boost her confidence, start smiling, and get a frontside, better-paying job.

Ray-Mee and I went into NoCo Dental and went through the paperwork. I was instantly on guard: I had a bad feeling. The woman emphasized monthly payments, not a total cost. She did not talk about the length of time needed to pay off this loan. She did say financing was at 29.9%, which was, in my opinion, exorbitant, *outrageous*! I asked about a plan for interest-free payment and a pay-off date. Ray-Mee had no idea what I was asking about. The woman then told us we could have 18 months same-as-cash to pay off the $5,000, but if we missed one payment, we would have to pay all of the interest for the total $5,000. *Robbery*.

I was frustrated. I felt they were taking advantage of the poor. The bait: pay only a minimum/month for an immediate set of new teeth. The catch: you'd be in their debt for over a decade and paying far more than $5,000! I did the math; Ray-Mee did not know how.

And when I talked with Ray-Mee about it, I discovered:
- Ray-Mee had no clue about interest — what it is, how it works, how different places charge different interest rates depending on credit scores and other factors
- She was thrilled to get new teeth in three weeks, even though they would be pulling ten (!!) teeth at once
- She knew my credit would get her the loan, and was thankful, but had no vision for building her own credit score
- No one had ever taught her financial basics
- Her sights were on the short-term and the immediate, not the long-term. I think some institutions that advertise and charge such rates count on that and take advantage of the poor person's lack of knowledge, familiarity, and experience with such systems
- She did not understand how to calculate how much she needed to pay each month if we wanted to pay off the $5,000 in 18 months

After seeing how she was about to be taken advantage of, I was quite determined to help her pay off the $5K in 18 months. I showed her how to figure out how much money we needed to send them each month: 18 into 5,000 = about $278 per month. That was out of her reach, so we made a deal: monthly, I would pay some, she would pay some, and I'd see if any of my people would contribute, just to encourage her. They did, here and there, enough to alleviate Ray-Mee's gut-wrenching feeling of pressure.

We set up a payment system online as we sat on my swing. Our password was "Suzanne&Ray,"and that felt so good! *In it together.* We scheduled a payment so there would be consistency and reasonable expectations.

There were many months Ray-Mee could contribute only $50-$100. Her fast food job paid very little; if the kids got sick, if something changed with their food voucher, if the van broke down — they were always on the edge of financial oblivion. Their rent, $800/month, a fairly normal amount for around here, was paid with a Section 8 housing voucher. At least their rental home was secure even if their food, utilities, and other smaller necessities were not (this was pre-gentrification tsunami, which I will discuss later). Other people kicked in where Ray-Mee could not, and in 18 months, we paid off her dentures! They look absolutely perfect. They fit well and NoCo Dental has graciously taken care of any requests she has made.

Now, for that frontside job….

~elle~

The Basketball Goal

All Handsome wanted for Christmas (2017) was a basketball goal. He imagined playing with the kids and Cinco on the street, getting closer, bonding over competitive hoops. Enter Cinco's trash talk:
"I'm gonna school you, ol' man!"
"I got you, Grant, and I'm gonna whip you. Guaranteed."
"You can't play! You too old!"

Handsome won their daily HORSE games 96% of the time. At first.

The basketball goal was a kid magnet. For two years, community formed under the goal: athletic brothers Rocky, Deshawn, Chris and little sister Marshay; Cinco; and neighbors Walter, Tarion, and Josiah were there almost daily.

The goal brought life onto our street: competition, bravado, and energy. As the boys became more accustomed to the routine of afternoon ball clashes and rivalries, they settled into some bad habits, such as cussing like I'd never heard, belittling, and near-fights. Grant was very patient; I was aghast at how they treated each other. "That's street ballin', Babe," he would say. We missed quiet Sunday afternoons, but we loved the boys more, so I'd load up the porch with cold water, fruit, and on occasion, cookies for post-game snacks.

Cinco, Beels, Deshawn, Marshay and I were on the front porch inhaling small clementine oranges, enjoying the scent of orange as it sprayed into the air. Athletic, competitive Rocky was on his fourth, peeling it quickly, when Cinco, on his second, turned his head in a reflective manner and said, "Ya know, I haven't gotten into trouble at school this year."

Was that an earthquake I felt? Or just the porch swing?

This was a profound observation. Last year Cinco came home with tales of fights, suspensions, and conflicts with students and teachers. I had not even thought about the change until Cinco brought it up.

Instantly my mind went to Handsome. Had my sweet husband — so patient with Cinco, so good with this boy — had his love and attention made a difference? Had all of those basketball games, all of the throwing the football, all of the talks on the porch, all of Cinco's tears, all of Grant's prayers, had they made that difference in Cinco's life?

"Yeah, I haven't either," Deshawn said.
"Boys, what's made the difference? Why do you think you're doing so much better this year?"

Cinco spoke up first. "My mom says I'm maturing." He stated it as a fact, without hubris or bravado. A smile broke out on my face, seeing him so matter-of-fact about himself. He looked up. If he had had eyebrows, they would have been high. "Yeah, I think I'm just maturing."

Deshawn piped up between bites and picked up on the phrase. "Yeah, I'm maturing too. You know, I used to be bad in fifth grade, causin' problems and fightin'. But not this year. Seventh grade is different."

Years ago I taught seventh grade, which is usually the year most people try to forget as quickly as possible, or at least push down into their subconsciouses. Is there a more awkward time in life? Kids want to be friends but have poor relational skills. They end up in fights with fists and words and phone battles and bullying. They want to be sweethearts ("goin' out, talkin', hangin' out, 'together'") but only know what they see in media, and they aren't emotionally or physically ready for that. Their gangly limbs, their oily faces, their braces, the changes in mood and hormones and physical features bungling and bumbling toward adulthood.

Some of the kids tried on a new friend group for a few days to see how they fit, then shed them like an old pair of socks to try on a new one. "Should I be more loud and rambunctious? Should I be flirtatious? Should I be studious and disciplined in class or should I be a slacker so I don't get the teacher's praise and get embarrassed?"

Handsome Standing helped.

He would never say so. I love his humility. He was "just being with the kids, it's no big deal. Just shootin' hoops." But all of those connections, the subtle instruction, those approving glances, his strong example, his care and detail and rebukes, they added up to a whole lot of relational beauty. They formed character. They re-formed character.

Grant was like a window. The love of God and the graces of his own dad shone through him like light through glass onto those kids. Grant was unaware it was even happening; that was his humble nature. If these boys mature into a Grant-man, I will just sit down on our porch and weep. They could not do better.

~·eelee·

To live in Knoxville, Tennessee, is to be orange-minded. Rare is the person who is not a Vol in this territory. Ten-year-old Cinco's blood ran orange. He knew all the players and their stats.

Grant arranged a surprise with Ray-Mee. A confluence of events led to this magical day. Beels' birthday; my parents (the ticket owners) were out of town and we inherited their four tickets; and the time of the game, 6:00 PM, fit into the family's schedule.

The kids had never been to a men's Vols basketball game. Ray-Mee did not tell the kids our plan to take them to the game, but let them know they had to be ready at 4:15 PM for a surprise. All day long they fished: "What should we wear? Where are we goin'? What're we gonna be doin'? Is there food there? When we gonna be home?"

At last the time came. They came across the street, burst into the house with happy energy, and saw both Grant and I in orange shirts and guessed it: "We're goin' to the game! We're goin' to the game!" they yelled as they bounced around the kitchen. "Suzy, is this your second game ever?" I felt my privilege: I had been to games since I was younger than Cinco.

We piled into the car. We planned to get there early so we could walk around Thompson-Boling Arena, grab four hotdogs, buy both of them a "happy birthday Beels" Vols t-shirt, and get to our seats before the introductions. Fortunately for the kids, there were tables of fun freebies: posters, stickers, shakers. They both grabbed shakers and promptly lost them. Then they misplaced their posters. Beels didn't want to lose her sticker so she put it right on her face!

It was delightful to walk them to our seats. At first they thought they would be in the nosebleed section, way up high, but we guided them to section 122 opposite the Vols bench, then all the way down, down, down to row 6. *Row 6!* It felt like we were almost on the floor. Cinco was in heaven. Beels lit up when she saw cheerleaders and dancers. "That's the way it's gonna be for us: Cinco's gonna play football and I'm gonna cheer."

We told them we had very high expectations of them: we expected them to get along, to be good to each other, to stay very close to us while we were in the crowds. They did wonderfully. Cinco even gave Beels some of his nachos: miraculous.

I heard Cinco use the phrase, "He broke his ankles." That translated to a player faking one direction and leaving his guard in the dust. The first time I heard that at our goal on Woodbine, I quickly moved toward the first aid kit when Cinco, laughing, said, "*No*, Suzanne, not *that* kind of broke ankles!"

The Vols men played well, broke lots of ankles, and won. During the game, the JumboTron showed Josh Dobbs, a former UT quarterback who also has alopecia. Cinco and Grant left to see if they could go meet him in person, but they did not see him.

Cinco and Beels sported their matching $17 Grant Williams #2 jerseys and held our hands as we wound our way back to the car.

The cool winter air refreshed us all as we recapped the evening. We dropped them off while Ray-Mee waited on the steps for them, eager to hear about their surprise. I think she was every bit as excited as they were. I had texted her pictures throughout the evening.

Grant and I smiled and talked into the night about the evening. Did we buy them too much? No, they saw the expensive shirts and hoodies; they knew their t-shirts were $17. Did they eat enough? Yes, but not too much. Did they show respect? Enthusiasm? Delight? Yes. Were they good to each other? Yes.

So we thanked God for the opportunity to take the kids to the game and felt the joy and slept like we'd run a marathon.

Miz Janet: the Fence

George, the man who renovated our house on Woodbine, took it back to the bones and recreated it. It was a blighted property, literally falling down on itself, until George intervened. The house had been chopped up into smaller apartments: stairs went nowhere, there were kitchenettes and bathrooms crammed into odd spaces, and doors led to the outside ... on the second floor.

In the process of rebuilding, he also tore down the relationship with Miz Janet. In response, George built a privacy fence, a non-gated six-foot wall of wood so he would not have to see or interact with her. After hearing the *why* behind the fence, Grant and I decided to tear it down. That fence represented the exact opposite of why we were here.

We teamed up with Adam, a strong brown man with a huge love for Jesus and young people who were looking for work. He brought over a team of four young adults and within fifteen minutes, they had broken down and removed that barrier. I saved one section so I could scribe "Woodbine" on it in calligraphy and put it on the porch.

A day later Miz Janet came out to say hello after I returned from work. She was wearing her bathrobe and pajamas (very modest) and her hair was wrapped up high. (Note: Some people in my neighborhood wear pajamas at any time; this is something I've had to get used to.) She warmly hugged me over her short chain-link fence, said she loved me and Grant, and gave me a gift, a decorated pine Christmas swag. I was happily overwhelmed, so surprised.

"You know, I didn't really have a neighbor over here before. When I saw people taking down the fence yesterday, I thought, 'these people are real neighbors.' Sure is nice to see … to not have that fence there. Now we can see each other, be *real neighbors*." Her voice was warm and emphatic.

Miz Janet's gift is placed on our front door each Christmas season, a prized possession.

The following summer, Miz Janet and I began walking together almost every morning at 7AM. It hit me between the eyes: she initiated us walking together, simply as neighbors who wanted to enjoy each other. I answered with a hearty *yes*. My impression of her was she was a woman of strong faith, a survivor, able to navigate both white and black cultures, and loved her extensive family. She was quick to laugh, thoughtful in speech, and knew every black person we passed.

For some reason, she was not sleeping well; we both agreed that exercise might be helpful to reestablish a good sleeping pattern. For a mile and a half each morning, Miz Janet and I would catch up and then pray over Woodbine Avenue, our families, anything we saw, whatever came to mind. We blessed each other. We prayed for our children. We dreamed about the Kingdom come on Woodbine. When she prayed, she quoted a lot of Scripture … it just flowed out of her mouth like water, mixing with praises and concerns.

I remember staring at the barbed wire curled on top of the concrete wall and the way the sun glinted on the razored edges. It was like there were mirrors and diamonds hidden among the bright pink flowers of the bougainvillea. I was in a residential section of Addis Ababa, Ethiopia, and the guard had just let me into a person's home. All the streets for miles — and this was not the nicest section of town — had guards with AK-somethings at the ready, a stern warning.

I remember staring at the green walls of living arborvitae in West Knoxville, deep olive stretching upward and separating home from home. Drawn property lines in hues of emerald with unspoken cautions of "This is mine, don't cross," and "We want our privacy" and "Don't intrude; this is my yard."

Why are we like this? Why all the fences? Why don't we want to be welcoming, relational neighbors? Even as an introvert I can still be kind and ask personal questions of those who live around me. If I don't know my neighbor, how can I love my neighbor?

Miz Janet was the one I texted when Grant was out of town and I couldn't zip the zipper all the way up on my red plaid pencil dress. I strained and stretched, but to no avail; the zipper was in the no-man's-land of my mid-back. On my way to a wedding, I stopped at her front door and she zipped me up, patted me on the arm, and told me to have a good time. On my way home, I stopped at her front door and she unzipped me, asking how the wedding was. Now *that's* knowing your neighbor! She's the first one I call if the electricity goes out and the first one I ask to spend the night with us if it hasn't come back on by 9:30 PM. When the bullets used to fly near or between our yards, we'd text to check on each other.

The best reason I can think of to have a fence is to have something to lean on as you talk with a neighbor.

～∼ellee∽

Winter settled in like snowflakes, cold and cloudy, and the neighborhood went into hibernation. The streetlights came on by 5:30, and chilled darkness emphasized Knoxville's bright red winter sunsets. Our quiet nights extended, so we read voraciously and tallied our new books:

A Place at the Table, Chris Seay (done during Lent)
Being White, Paula Harris and Doug Schaupp
Beyond Charity, John M. Perkins
Children of Fire, Thomas C Holt (Grant read this one, but I did not take the time)
Christianity and Wokeness, Owen Strachan
Divided by Faith, Emerson and Smith
Every Good Endeavor, Timothy Keller

98

Dignity: Seeking Respect in Back Row America, Chris Arnade
Dare to Lead, Brené Brown
Between the World and Me, Ta Na'hesi Coates
Everybody Always, Bob Goff
Generous Justice, Timothy Keller
Half the Sky, Nicholas D Kristof and Sheryl WuDunn
I'm Still Here, Austin Channing Brown
Interrupted, Jen Hatmaker
Jesus and the Disinherited, Howard Thurman
Just Mercy, Bryan Stevenson
Les Miserables, the section on the priest's life, Victor Hugo
Let Your Life Speak, Parker Palmer
No One Ever Asked, Ganshert
On That Day Everybody Ate, Margaret Trost
Our Little Secret, Stanford Johnson
Restavec: From Haitian Slave Child to Middle-Class American, Jean-Robert Cadet
Same Kind of Different as Me, Ron Hall and Denver Moore
Strangers at My Door, Jonathan Wilson-Hartgrove
Tattoos on the Heart, Gregory Boyle
The Art of Neighboring, Jay Pathak and Dave Runyon
The Beautiful Community, Irwin L Ince, Jr
The Color of Compromise, Jemar Tisby
The Gift of Being Yourself, David G Benner
The Gospel Comes with a House Key, Rosaria Butterfield
The Hate U Give, Angie Thomas
The Insanity of God, Nik Ripken
The Lost Letters of Pergamum, Bruce W Longnecker
The Power of Proximity, Michelle Ferrigno Warren
The Space Between Us, Thrity Umrigar
This Beautiful Truth, Sarah Clarkson
Tightrope, Nicholas D Kristof and Sheryl WuDunn
Waking Up White, Debbie Irving
White Awake, Kadeem Hill

Our conversations were rich with issues of race and class:
What does positive gentrification look like? We were beginning to see negative gentrification in our 'hood on the city-side of Woodbine.
What are practical ways to be a bridge between classes when classes have so many hidden behavioral rules?
We don't know how to speak 'urban'; sometimes others here know how to speak 'suburban.'
How do we earn our neighbors' trust so it's not just, "Hey, how ya doin'?" but it's sharing life? it's not just surface, it's stirring the waters?

How do we engage in helping our neighbors who need structural housing improvements, without seeming like a bank or like we have all the answers and resources?

How do we work on job disparities in Knoxville? Is the local high school a good place to start?

How do we communicate to *all* of Knoxville that each side of Knox has gifts to give the other — that we do better together?

What do we do about the fear — the stereotype that East Knox is scary, full of drugs and crime?

How do we engage the stereotypes characterizing our poor white neighbors?

～ellees

Just before the Super Bowl, we took Cinco and Wiley on a two-mile walk. Cinco started in with all the usual complaints: he got tired of dribbling his basketball … his hands got cold … he was thirsty … and in his silliness, he began calling Grant "big ole sleepy head silly head Grant."

How he showed affection and security was so endearing. He kept intentionally running into Handsome on the sidewalk, thigmotropic as he walked, a vine constantly reaching out to touch Handsome, hoping to curl a tendril arm around him.

"If something happened to my Mama … or Henry … could I live here? Would you and Grant take care of me?"

"Of course, Cinco. You would be welcome here."

"Silly little goofy head ole Cinco Woodbine boy" settled right in to watching the first half of the Super Bowl with us, cheering on the Eagles, checking in with his mom, and being a kid. We have a normal-size couch, but Cinco was snuggled up next to Grant, always in physical contact with him, a rowdy cub wanting to play with Papa Bear. It was healthy and sweet to see.

Another afternoon, Cinco and Beels and I went to the Fellini Kroger and they played tag, begged for sugary cereal, and skittered off to get their free cookie from the bakery section. They were so light, so silly, so happy. Other patrons smiled patiently at me when Beels kept steering on the wrong side of the aisle; there are many unspoken rules in a grocery store, and she did not yet know them.

Back on Woodbine, Cinco wanted to have a talk over a bowl of cereal. He was ready to open up about foster care; Beels chimed in too. Then both began to count the people in their lives they had lost through death. Cinco — age 10 — had already lost six people. Beels — four. Given their personal experiences of trauma, the fact that they were as healthy as they were was astounding to me.

100

In our second round of winter on Woodbine, Handsome and I spent a few days in Florida visiting my parents. The word I used for their community was *pristine*: lush, green grass; brilliant flowers (in February!); order, loveliness; no trash, no debris; sunshine and blue skies and 75-80 degrees. The food was sumptuous and fresh. Our schedule was relaxed. We spent some time on their boat, shelled, drank fine wine, and feasted on fish. It was a remarkable oasis in the midst of our cold, cloudy Tennessee winter season.

When we arrived home, Knoxville was gray, dim, and dismal. The man (still) living under the bridge greeted us with a wave as we entered Parkridge. As we pulled onto Woodbine, everyone's windows were closed tight and doors shut. No leaves, no flowers, no children running around, no bikes, no signs of joy. It was downright depressing.

Reflectively, I decided Woodbine was like a flower bulb:
papery on the outside,
hard to the touch,
no outward signs of life,
devoid of color.
In fact, it looked like something to throw away.

But I knew the truth: Woodbine was full of life and beauty. I just couldn't see it. It was coming. There were parts and pieces and cells and tissues waiting to burst into life, but they were hidden ... *for now.*

By faith I said aloud, "Beauty is coming!" I started pointing at houses like my finger was a magic wand: "Color is coming! Life is coming! Winter will give way to spring! Better yet — life is within *now*, brewing, creating, stirring, ready to push upward." Handsome just smiled his patient smile and said, "That's my Babe."

I must see with eyes of faith. I must not give in to the gray and dim and dismal as the final word. Soon there will be greens and reds and pinks and yellows. Soon there will be tender stems and baby leaves and pink petals on cherry trees and the brilliant yellows of daffodils. People will be out and about again, the boom boom boom of the cars filling the air.

Soon.

That spring, finally, Woodbine felt like our settled home. What happened? Why then?
It was a combination of loving our neighbor Cinco,

being so content to come home after a wonderful Easter celebration to nap with Handsome,
and later having kids knock on the door to tell us about their day.
And the news from my daughter that she saw a cute field mouse in the kitchen stealing Wiley's dog food.
And Ninja decapitated a baby bunny.
And eating leftovers around the kitchen island without utensils or plates, licking our fingers and going in for seconds and thirds, all manners suspended.
And the smell of cookies in the house.
It all added up … it all fit into "home."

This feeling felt hard-won. A gift, but also a choice. It was still evolving and growing, but at least it was there, burgeoning with promise, like the yeast expanding my sourdough bread, like the flowers pushing up from my bulbs.

Chapter Six: Tensions, Spring 2018

Dream: Going Low Like Jesus

I AWAKENED AS THE DAWN SPREAD vanilla light onto my thin curtains. I didn't want to: my dream was so intriguing that I didn't want to leave it.

I was with a small group of Christian friends, faithful people who saw the world as it is and felt the pull of Jesus into the harder places, the hurting places, the uncomfortable places, the lower places.

We were unified: the mission of a Christian is always to seek the lowest place, like water. What, in this world, was the lowest place? Let's go there. We looked as if we were in a mine: we kept tracing down a shaft, going lower, then leveling out, then walking deeper again, then plateauing.

I began at the top, in the light, normally dressed, simply plain me. Then I and my friends would go a layer lower, pause at the plateau, and then descend deeper. Eight to ten friends would stay at the previous level, but new people would come to me and rally to the next lowest layer. I was never alone; when a friend would stay at a certain level, new friends would come, always seeking to be like water: to go low. At each level there were people and activity, but it got gnarlier and rougher as we descended.

I was constantly going lower. Lowering myself, my pride, my materialism, my sense of importance, lowering everything about me, yet within, becoming more and more full, more and more radiant. The lower I went into the darkness, the more the Holy Spirit cast His complete, pristine, magnificent, pure light within me. The darker the setting, the brighter the Spirit's luminosity within my companions. The deeper we went, the brighter we became, lit up from the inside. When I got to the lowest level I could go — and there, a sense of finality, of knowing, of completion and fullness — it was lit up by the effusive brightness of the Holy Spirit beaming within His people. Others continued lower, but it was my time to stop. There was a contentment and usefulness at the level where I was, a settled feeling. I blessed others as they went lower and warmly prayed over them, and they were gone.

~~~~~

Questions with Handsome

While on staycation, Handsome and I went to our family's cabin for a day away. It was so good: a lazy morning, talking for hours and cooking brunch, a long walk in the woods, a bath in the lake with a grease-cutting soap to get all of the poison ivy off of us and the dog, topped off with a bit of swimming. We ran off the end of the dock holding hands.

It had been a long time since I had been submerged in water; I felt like I had been submerged in Woodbine and work. Two good things, but also good to get away. We invited The Dinner Peeps to eat with us on the cabin porch.

On the spectrum of an ascetic life (left hand) to an extravagant, self-serving life (right hand), Grant naturally tends toward asceticism. He does not need much to live; he does not want a lot of things; he wants rest, meaningful time with me and other chosen people, and time to be on Woodbine. Although he is a very focused workman, he is not a workaholic. I love these things about him.

He is a philosopher, not a complainer, and he goes about things in a thinking way. I appreciate this about our marriage, but it became one of my favorite parts once I learned how to talk to and listen to my Handsome. He wants to clarify big picture concepts like *Kingdom of God* and *shalom* and *community* and *living as a good neighbor*: "How do you define that?" is a very common question when we begin these discussions. He tests the boundaries of every concept, then becomes practical. I am pragmatic; thus we discuss and solve problems in different ways.

He asks questions of himself, me, the cosmos, and God, such as:
•Is the Kingdom of God in heaven or now or both? (We all thought both.)

•What does the Kingdom of God look like for our lives *now*? What do we do with the prosperity and good gifts God offered the Israelites in the Old Testament, and the sacrificial, more ascetic life of Jesus in the New Testament?

•Does that mean it's okay to live in wealth, safely in an enclave with friends and family? Does that mean that we share, that we stop spending so much money on ourselves and invest it in other lives and our community? How would our lives change if we were more community-minded and less individualistic? What if those enclaves are homogeneous?

•If the Old Testament idea of *shalom* is wholeness, wellness, a sense of well-being personally and communally, how does it apply to us and Woodbine?

•What part does community play in shalom, practically? How does a community lead itself toward shalom?

•Why do materially, professionally successful Christians tend toward leaving city areas of hardship, rather than moving into them? Why weren't we taught this idea in church: "God has blessed me with a strong income and stable family, so I want to go to a rougher part of town and lift it up, sharing the good gifts God has given me"? It seems as if most of us Peeps were taught the exact opposite, in Jesus' Name. How can this be?

•Do we have to tack on "for us" every time we're talking to others about being with the poor, or being a good neighbor, or living out shalom on Woodbine Avenue? Why do people keep saying, "That's great *for you*" but they are not (by their own admission) willing to give up their school system or local benefits — are we supposed to just be quiet and not challenge them? Goodness knows we're still challenging ourselves — the don't think we're better than anyone else. *"Iron sharpens iron; so one person sharpens another,"* Proverbs 27:17.

We met some friends for dinner, reiterating our pondering. "Now we're getting personal," Bryant said, leaning in. "I like this practical talk. Yeah, I think it's great that y'all moved to Woodbine, but I don't want to live there. It's not a practical location for me to get to work. It's not safe for my family. I agree that the comment, 'moving to Woodbine is great … for you,' must be annoying, but I gotta say, the challenge of hearing your stories feels real. Just by personally knowing a friend who is choosing to live in a harder situation makes me uncomfortable, sometimes even confrontational and defensive for my own chosen lifestyle. No one, including me, wants to hear that they're wrong or feel *less than*; no one wants to be judged."

"Yeah, I don't either, Bryant," initiated Handsome. "So back to the getting personal part: why would you *not* raise a family here? Why not live in East Knox?"

Our table rattled off their top four challenges easily, in less than 30 seconds:
1. Poor school ratings across the board. They wanted their kids to get the best education possible. Parents felt their kids could be better prepared for business in a private or West Knox school (not that those schools were perfect, but they did get better scores).
2. Danger: shootings, robbery.
3. Drug availability.
4. How tricky it can be for white kids to navigate non-white cultures in a school and neighborhood setting. They were all worried about bullying.

"We're protective, what can we say? Aren't we supposed to be? Doesn't God want us to protect our children?" asked Bryant's wife.

"I feel like I'd be disobeying God's will for me as a parent if I brought my children to live here," added my friend Shelton.

"Aren't we all reading these same Scriptures?" Handsome asked. "What do the Scriptures say for us to do?" At that, we were off: we had as many answers as there were people around the table. It's not that we disagreed about the basics of obeying God, honoring Him with our lives and money, raising our families in love, grace and truth — we didn't agree about how to live that out.

"So I guess we have to walk in the Spirit, not quench the Spirit, pray in the Spirit … and do what we think He's telling us to do," I summarized. "We'll do what we think is right and bless each of you as you pursue your own convictions. We need to live Romans 14: be convinced in your own mind and don't judge each other."

Bryant agreed: "No judgment here, but lots of prayer, and let's keep up these conversations. This has been a legit challenge. I can say with honesty that there are things I don't want to give up … I don't even think it would be wise for me to give them up. How do rich folks not feel used? How do poor folks not feel embarrassed? And that bucket illustration — dang, that has me thinking. My bucket does always seem full. And then there's the foundational question: What difference does the love of Jesus make in all of this? It's a lot to consider."

Around the table, we were reflective: What about our neighbors who live *without* much of the time? What is our role with them? How do we love them, and how do we receive their love? What richness will we learn from them? And what of our friends who have so much money that they don't even know what to do with it, other than give a bit here and there, save up for retirement and do what they want? How can we help the two worlds meet? How can we foster real relationship? How can our rich friends use their networks and resources to help our poor friends?

Conversations with Handsome stir up beautiful things … and a lot more questions.

Josh Dobbs' Kindness

Seeing Josh Dobbs at the UT game gave us an idea. Lately Cinco had been dealing a lot with being bullied, even at our own basketball goal. Older boys, sigh. Boys with attitude, boys out to *prove*, boys ready to dominate and demean. Boys who wrinkled their broad noses when they said "pussy" or didn't think twice about bringing a younger kid to tears. Boys who threw the ball down the street and said, "Nah, I ain't gettin' it, *you* get it."

Hmmm: could we …? We called our nephew, Franklin, who was friends with lots of the University of Tennessee athletes. We asked Franklin if he knew Josh Dobbs, former UT quarterback and an NFL player. Josh also had alopecia, and I'd heard he had a kind heart.

Affirmative, they were acquaintances. I felt a tingle of excitement.

I asked Franklin if he could text Josh to see if he was in Knoxville for Easter: Affirmative, Josh was here for a few events. Oh my goodness, could this happen?

I texted, *Could Josh and I possibly set up a meeting with Cinco?* AFFIRMATIVE, he could come by to see him! I literally jumped around the house.

Josh was able to come to our house Saturday after he headlined at a women's empowerment event downtown. He looked like he had just stepped out of a haberdashery shop: all class. He paused for a moment to change into athletic shoes, then strode with Grant and me to Cinco's front door. The look on Cinco's face was priceless … his jaw dropped as his eyes lifted up! His UT jersey waved on his slight boy-build, compared to strong, muscular Josh Dobbs.

Josh extended a hand to Cinco, who shook it wordlessly. Grant had been working with him on how to shake hands like a man.

Within minutes Cinco said, "You look like I do." "Yeah, you're just lighter than I am," Josh said good-naturedly. They proceeded to play HORSE at our basketball goal. Cinco's mom and I sat and watched all three of the guys play. It was just a fun game, no pretense, no weirdness. One of the signs that Cinco was comfortable was he took off his hat. He almost always wore a hat, first because he was embarrassed that he was completely bald, but also to protect himself from the sun.

Josh guarded Cinco; I have pictures of Cinco trying to make a goal over Josh's man-sized frame. It was comical, but you've got to appreciate Cinco's lion-hearted attempts.

Those two transitioned into playing football. Cinco made several great catches, and every one of Josh's throws were perfect spirals, always hitting his mark. Then Josh pulled in closer and the two just talked. At one point Cinco's mom caught her breath and said, "He's letting him feel his head. Look." Josh had bent down low, and Cinco's hand was on his head. Bald boys. "Yep, just like mine," we heard Cinco say.

How beautiful it is to see a big man stoop low to love a small boy.

We tried not to be intrusive, but I confess I heard Josh ask Cinco, "Are your eyes sensitive to light?" Josh was bringing up the hard things … the awkward and unsettling parts of alopecia. Precious man, kind man to support and encourage one so small.

Ultimately, the visit concluded with hugs and pictures, and Josh drove away. Cinco was starry-eyed but not ridiculous, which pleased Grant, who does not like celebrity culture.

Hours later, Cinco's mom texted us that a friend of theirs had called the news station and Cinco would be interviewed at 3PM tomorrow about this visit.

Handsome and I were stricken. In our minds, this was a private, tender meeting not for public consumption. We had not told anyone except our family that Josh was coming, and we did not want any attention to take away from Cinco's time with Josh. To us, this had been a gift to Cinco without fanfare or money exchanged or paparazzi; it was to build up his confidence and comfort his soul. These were deeply personal things.

Cinco's mom totally understood our point of view, and we agreed that I should contact Josh to see what he thought. I loved being on the same page with her and I was so thankful that she was not territorial about the experience. She was only 28 and was temporarily caring for six children. She was rarely even off her porch, much less over in my yard and able to talk for a while. What a gift the day was for our friendship.

I communicated with Josh, apologizing for the turn of events. I was determined to honor Josh's feelings: If he did not want this to be public, I would call the tv station, explain everything, and call it off. Thankfully, Josh really considered it to be no big deal; he was even excited for Cinco.

Later Sync dropped in to watch the Final Four game. Out of the blue, he said, "Thank you. Thank you for today, for having Josh Dobbs come over." He didn't even crack a big smile; he just said it factually, like it was a precious thing to be treasured. "It was great."

Grant was also reflective after Cinco left. "Did we do a good thing? Did this perpetuate celebrity culture — idolizing people, creating a burst or 'wow' moment that really didn't have continuing relationship with it?" We processed verbally for a while, thinking about Josh's thrice-repeated promise that if Cinco needed him for anything that he could call.

It turned out that Josh kept that promise. Year after year, Josh continues to invite Cinco to training camps and athletic events. Josh is a solid man. I am so thankful Cinco could count him as a friend.

Local 8 News interviewed Cinco and his proud Mama about Josh Dobbs' visit. Cinco spoke bluntly about his visit with Josh. "We have the same *condition,*" he said emphatically. They cut to a clip of manly, powerful Josh Dobbs working out. Cut back to Cinco in his rocking chair: "When he hugged me, he called me … his brother." Ten-year-old Cinco looked reflective, even numinous.

~elles

When I was a child, I thought gardening was the worst waste of a Saturday that could ever be invented. I hated pulling weeds and being out in the heat. As an adult, I've negotiated the demands of a garden and have made room for all the joys of it: fresh cherry tomatoes. Cucumbers still warm from the sun slathered in homemade basil pesto. Pulling up potatoes and carrots, brushing off the dirt and welcoming them into the sun. Trimming asparagus, cutting fresh flowers for the house. Garlic, leeks, onions, herbs — I love it all. Cutting fresh thyme for a roast, adding mint and dill to an asparagus-wild rice salad, making my own salsa — yes!

Gardening with the kids amplified my enjoyment. They were so full of questions, opinions, and feelings about gardening.

- Why does this dirt stink?
- Why is mushroom compost so heavy?
- How do I mix the peat and the compost and the dirt together when it's all so … so … sticky?
- Why is that seed so little? I don't believe a whole plant can come from this thing. No way.
- Strawberries! Yay! I like strawberries! When can I eat 'em? Next week?
- Where do I put all these seeds? Can I eat these seeds?
- How can you eat the spinach if it's growing in dirt? It's dirty! That's gross!
- I don't like peas. They're gross. Why are you planting peas? (Cue disgusted face.)
- Are there any more potatoes to pull up?

I had packages of radish seeds (their seeds are small), peas (large), and carrot seeds (tiny). I made little furrows with the side of my hand, karate-chop style, for the radishes, but Reyana considered those to be loose guidelines, not law. Reyana was a sprinkler, not a planter; not only that, she sprinkled from afar, say, shoulder height, rather than right down on the furrows. It was clear that we were going to have radishes appear over about 1/3 of the raised bed garden box.

Beels grabbed the pea seeds and followed instruction well. Two by two; four planting spots down one row, near the supports; done.

Cinco … Cinco! Oh my. He enthusiastically grabbed the carrot seed package and in true Cinco style, ripped it open, just as I gasped, "Wait!" About half the package went everywhere in the box. His nose crinkled up, and he exclaimed, "Oh my gosh, they're so small!" Images of flying carrots flashed before my eyes as he turned the package upside down and there they went, hundreds of tiny seeds blobbed up together in one spot.

"Oops, I'm sorry," he said.
"It's okay," I said. "It's done. There is a better way ... next year."

We spread the seeds with our fingertips; no rows for our carrots that year, just area. (I harvested Cinco's carrots for three cool-weather seasons!)

The kids helped me give the seeds a drink of water, spread a protective cloth mesh over them, and then they had to go home.

I am sad to say that after the kids left, I straightened our rows of spinach seedlings. That was so silly. A structured garden does bring me a sense of satisfaction, like there is order in the world, but part of what I'm learning on Woodbine is that my sense of order and beauty is not the point. God's Kingdom, His beauty, His work, is the point. And thank goodness, He works with crooked things and out-of-order people. Case study right here.

<center>~~~~~</center>

I pulled into our driveway while listening to chapter 10 of *Hillbilly Elegy* by Yale lawyer and self-proclaimed Kentucky-Ohio hillbilly JD Vance. It was fascinating to compare the migration and situation of black Americans with the Appalachian migration of (his term) hillbillies. There were many similarities.

My mind was swirling with academic, social, and cultural paradigms when Beels collided with my door yelling, "SuzySuzySuzy!" Welcome to Woodbine ... shift gears.

Cinco, Beels, and Reyana opened the front door and demanded to see the new chicks. They needed a manners reboot! Once they asked properly, I brought the Chick Bin downstairs and out to the back porch.

We gave the "W" to Reyana numerous times. Reminder: *The W* was the dreaded middle three fingers held up at eye level and it identified *whining*. I was crystal clear about whining: not. in. my. house. If someone got that whiny tone, they got the W. Then they had the chance to restate their request or frustration with a normal tone. We had practiced this frequently, making it a game, and it was highly effective.

Grant pulled in about ten minutes after I did, and he and Cinco went out to shoot hoops after showing the chicks some gentle love. The kids were still a bit spooked by their quick movements and loud panic chirps, so we were taking the acquaintance slowly.

110

I heard more voices yelling for the ball as the girls and I settled into washing hands, slicing vegetables, creating a salad, and warming up a feast of event leftovers: pineapple and chicken; skewers of fruit; and cheesy twice-baked potatoes.

An entire pan of the chicken plus another of the potatoes went to Ray-Mee's family. It was God's provision for them in a tight time. We ended up feeding five children, but the thrilling part was who sat down to dinner. As we listened to Reyana say grace, I sat there agape:
Beels held hands with Cinco (they fought so bitterly when she first moved in with his family and had come so far);
Cinco held hands with DK (DK was the name-calling, cuss-mouth, dominating bully);
DK held hands with Reyana (this 14-year-old boy kindly and patiently holding hands with a 9-year-old girl, of all things);
Reyana held hands with Kumani (14-year-old sweet kid, excellent manners, great baller, DK's best friend);
Kumani held hands with Grant (who was the one who asked everyone to stay and eat with us in typical Grant style: "Babe, here we come, ya got enough for all of us?")
Grant held hands with me (squeezing love to me during the prayer);
and I held hands with Beels.

Tossed about in conflict and competition, this troop of kids had been in my prayers, and to my delight, our little circle of happy eaters ate in peace and fellowship. *This time.* No bad names, no animosity, no cussing. Good manners all around with a few training tips.

God! You are remarkable. You answered my prayers with such ease, with such speed. Thank You! I celebrate You! Cheers to You, Lord God Almighty!

They all loved dessert: fresh strawberries trucked in from South Carolina in a bucket, warm off the truck, passed around with homemade whipped cream, heavy on the powdered sugar and vanilla. Instantly, they loved swiping a strawberry through the creamy goodness and taking it straight to the mouth; no one had ever done that before.

It was as if God was showing me, "Not only can I easily bring enemies together, but I'll give you whipped cream too: friendship, dialogue, even prayer around a common meal." Wow.

As I journaled that evening,
I find myself greedy. I ask for more: real, strong friendship between the boys; for Cinco to get out of a victim/bully mentality and learn to lead;

for all of the boys to learn what it means to serve and love, even on the court; for encouragement to ring out at the goal, not foul words; for laughter, not tears; for Your Kingdom to come and Your will to be done. Cheers to You, Father God. Amen.

One of the children came over with her nephew, One-and-a-half-year-old BamBam. He was a bundle of energy and delighted in showing off his new skill: jumping. He was a solid little one, so he shook our house with each jump, and looked up to hear us say, "BOOM!" after each landing.

One of the other kids looked over at him and said, "He's a bad boy." I was stunned. He was not bad; he was little. Why did the older boy say that?

BamBam hits. Hitting has been modeled for him, so of course he hit others. I began to say, "Easy" in a very gentle voice, showing him how to be more mindfully kind with his actions. He was so gentle when he stroked the kitty's fur. But with people, when he wanted their attention, he hit.

And they hit back. I watched this and the irony hit me. He would hit them; they would hit back as they were telling him not to hit.

I spoke to the older kids: "Do you realize that when he hits, you tell him not to hit as you are hitting him? That makes no sense. Model for him *how to be* rather than hitting him."

One of the kids piped up, "But that's what you do. You pop 'em." And he totally, utterly ignored my advice. Never mind that he was 10 and I have raised two daughters; never mind that I had 124 students to discipline and nurture every year I was a public school teacher. Sigh.

BamBam's interactions with the older kids were unpleasant, so I took matters into my own hands — literally. I scooped him up, went into the kitchen, and told him all about dinner. I pointed out peaches and potatoes, salt and pepper, each of the vegetables — he soaked it in like a thirsty flower waiting to bloom after the next rain. We cooked. He tried to talk and repeat what I said. He watched me form words and you could see his mental wheels turning. He pointed, and I responded.

Ultimately, life was all about the peaches. They were so much like little balls, and he wanted them all. So I took the basket of peaches and put it on the floor beside another empty basket. He spent twenty minutes handling the peaches, putting them all in one basket and then transferring them to the other basket. Back and forth, he loaded and unloaded. He was dextrous and strong and had focus. He behaved so well.

112

At one point, "we" cleaned up and went in to check on the older kids, who were playing PickUp Sticks. He went over and picked up a red stick. A girl screamed at him — screamed! — and yanked the stick back out of his hand. BamBam stood there unsteadily, looking so confused. I was upset and defensive: "Don't yell at him, he doesn't know! He doesn't know the rules — he's only a year and a half old. Be patient!" She looked sheepish and said she was sorry. But clearly she did not want him near.

After about an hour his mama came by to take him home; she couldn't've been more than 20. Her voluptuous self spilled out from her clothing, her stretch marks visible from having BamBam. As I handed her his peaches, I complimented her son's behavior and told her what fun we'd had, and how good his developing fine motor skills were. She didn't really even look at me. They walked back down the street.

I shut the door and cried.

My grandmother, who smoked and enjoyed a lively flapper swing dance in the Roaring '20s, earned her Masters degree in Child and Family Studies. A woman ahead of her day, she earned her degree before she married and had five children (one passed just at birth). In her day, she was radical. Fascinating. Independent.

She was fully invested in raising her family to be savvy, kind, resourceful, and honorable. "To whom much has been given, much will be required" was their family slogan. They were community-minded, working class, good people. My sweet Mama followed in her footsteps, earning her Masters in the same field. For her Master's project, she wanted to interrupt the cycle of child pregnancy, poverty, and lack of opportunity by opening a childcare program at a local urban high school — Rule High, the school on the tour — so the students who had children could learn parenting skills. About half of her 14-to-18-year-old students were white, the other half, black. She loved them all.

Periodically in my adult years a beaming black woman would approach my mom and give her a huge hug and exclaim, "You saved my life! You taught me so much! Now just look at my baby!" And she'd pull out pictures of her children in their high school cap and gown or military graduation. My Mama would glow when that happened and give God the glory.

I had every advantage of having generations of matriarchal educators — strong-minded, competent, enterprising women who valued family and knew all the current knowledge of their eras pertaining to the development and care of children. They were excellent, educated, conscientious parents.

So what brought me to tears?

It broke my heart to see BamBam treated like he was an inconvenience.
Yelled at with no explanation appropriate for his age.
Handled without understanding of his developmental needs at a year and a half.
Not delighted in or treasured.
And he was so precious!

Rather than being hit
and hearing "No!" constantly without explanation and training
and being treated like an inconvenience,
if BamBam was raised by my sweet Mama,
poured into by my innovative, practical, networked tribe,
loved and lauded and encouraged and directed toward good,
who would he become?
Is it even a good question?

If he was taught he could reach any height —
as high as Obama, a black man like him, the former leader of the free world —
who would he become?

And then I'm confronted by my own faulty thinking: Who says he won't become a great man, a leader, smart in school, capable and interesting? Who says his adversities won't make him deep and good? Who says his Mama does not know how to train or love him well, or that he needs the same type of training my family gave me or that he needs to travel the same path as President Obama? Who says our "advantages" would serve him well? I needed to not put his situation in a box, but honestly, it was hard. From general internet research, as well as stories from my neighbors, I found that the statistics were clearly against BamBam and his mom.

I prayed honestly:
God, forgive me for thinking I know better, that my path is the best path, that everyone needs to grow up like I did. My childhood wasn't perfect, but it was good. It was loving. So help me love well — BamBam, his young Mama, all the neighborhood kids. I lift BamBam up to You tonight and ask You to protect him, enrich him, and help him believe in You as he grows up. Put his feet on a good path. Bless his young Mama. Send her encouragement. Thank You.

I prayed for the neighborhood kids, priceless to me; neighbors who had moved in, then moved on to other destinations. With care I lifted them to my Father, whispering their names with love in my heart, feeling the weight of praying for their lives lift like colorful Chinese lanterns floating up to heaven. Red for Reys, her vibrant joy igniting the sky; orange for Cinco, for his love of the Vol nation and his energetic dynamism reverberating into the clouds.

I wondered, vaguely, what my color would be ... ah yes. Gold. Gold like my hair when I was young; gold after the purifying fire of many tests; gold, like the crown that awaited me. Gold, as I reflected Jesus' light in the new city of the Lamb. My dreams that night sparkled.

Chapter Seven: New Perspectives, Summer 2018

WHAT DID JESUS MEAN by *the deceitfulness of wealth*? I re-read the parable of the soils (Matthew 13) one more time. This was frequently on my mind. Reflectively, I wrote what I'd pondered lately:

Lessons from the Poor:
1. *Wealth is in friendship.*
2. *Loyalty and laughter are currency (we want to be rich in those).*
3. *Dependence on each other creates community; it's not a bad thing. One body, many parts.*
4. *The power of prayer, song and community are almost indestructible.*
5. *Food is part of community; "thickness" is a good sign.*

What is the deceitfulness of wealth?
1. *Being bloated: fat with self-absorption, pridefully in a class or race, overfed on self, over-entertained, over-concerned with money and status*
2. *Being blind: blind to our own privileges and power, blind to other points of view, blind to other cultures' vantages and beauties*
3. *Being naive: thinking everyone will have a similar level of ease in navigating the white culture, the marketplace, and the systems of our nation; thinking everyone is like I am*
4. *Being deceived: by the lust of the flesh, the lust of the eyes, and the pride of life ... expressed through money.*

I also heard a quote that solidified generosity, wealth, and money: "If you have more than you need, build a longer table, not a higher fence." I felt my whole being say, *Yes!* If God chose to allow me to have money, it was not just for me. I was to let that river flow liberally into others' lives; I had everything I needed and more.

Suzanne, let it flow like water, lower and lower, nourishing and bringing life. Yes, Lord.

Mosquitoes are my nemesis, so I was quite upset with the bites at the base of my neck, just at my hairline. I must have gotten attacked by mosquitos when I was gardening with the kids.

Only …

It turned out it wasn't the mosquitoes. It was even weirder. And worse. It was lice. Or, as Reyana pronounced it, *lifes*.

I found an adult louse in my hair as I walked Wiley after work and freaked out right there on the sidewalk. I killed it with my fingernail after being sure of what it was (thanks, Google Images). Ugh.

How did this happen? And how do the animals and people of the world deal with this? Could they have come from the chickens? From the hotel where we stayed for a wedding recently? None of the kids were scratchy this week, and black kids rarely get lice because of the oils in their hair.

I had washed my hair most days this past week, even though it tends to be dry and I usually wash it only once or twice a week. But I read that was a perfect environment for lice: dry, clean hair.

My long-suffering husband earned his stripes by combing my thick, brown hair for *two hours* with a lice comb. Zillions of lice, most small, and nits (eggs) were on my head. It was a colonized planet. We were simultaneously fascinated and disgusted. Handsome was so meticulous that he did not stop until even the nits were consistently gone. We sanitized everything.

My hairstyle became a consistent coconut top knot: I smothered my hair in coconut oil to kill any critters we missed and piled it on top of my head in a messy, oily bun. Perpetually-just-out-of-the-swimming-pool look.

Cinco will never, ever have this problem. Lucky him.

～ellee～

Thunderbolt & Freddy

When we first moved to Woodbine, I saw a lot of people walk by as I sat on my porch swing in the early mornings. There are different styles of walking, you know: Strolling. Stop/start with the dog walking. Walk-and-talk with a friend walking. Exercise walking. Jus' wakin' up walking. High or drunk and stumbling walking. Swishy and eyeing the cars for a customer walking.

One woman I had not yet met would walk briskly by, thin as a young tree, barely disturbing the air she was so lean. She always carried bags; her walk was focused and deliberate. Eventually I was able to ask her about herself: she was a classic example of the working poor, barely making ends meet but always showing up to her cleaning job. Faithful. Inadequately paid. She strode to the bus stop and caught her lines to get to work, then walked home in the dark. I began to pray for her safety. There was something about her that activated my curiosity.

~~~~

During our second summer, storm systems buffeted Knoxville streets. With clouds ominously darkening, we put up the basketballs. Between downpours I was going to dash to meet Grant at one of our favorite local restaurants. Before I left I wanted to make sure Reyana got home safely, so from the porch I watched her bike toward home. Screaming caught my attention. It was anger-screaming, not terror-screaming, so I maneuvered around the porch posts to find out what was happening. Reyana was slowing down to watch, as were the three ballplayers.

A storm in the form of a drunk woman was hammering down on the lawn of Ray-Mee's and Henry's home. Foul-mouthed thunder rang throughout the street. I made my way over.

Quiet, tall, lumbering Henry calmly told her to stay off their property. Henry, so large and gentle, a solid wall, restrained; the woman, so frail yet so rageful, accusatory and aggressive.

From where I stood she did not smell like alcohol, but her mannerisms indicated she was smashed or on something. This was not the first time I'd seen her like this. She shrieked accusingly at Ray-Mee and Henry; there were a variety of offenses, even that they were going to kill her, that they had threatened her. Ray-Mee and Henry were on their porch, Ray-Mee in her black sunglasses looking coldly calm and offended, while the kids listened to the woman's harangue. Her language was a downburst of atrocities. "You can't be white around here!" she screamed, and her voice sounded worn like old smoked leather.

"Should I call the police?" one of the Big Brothers asked. "Give it a minute, then maybe, yes," I recommended. Her body language was becoming more contentious.

I approached her. "I'm sorry you're having a bad day," I said gently, trying to take her elbow and steer her toward her house.

"I've had a bad fuckin' LIFE!" she yelled, not at me in particular, but toward Ray-Mee's house. She angrily yanked away her arm. Using my body space and a gentle hand on her back, I turned her gingerly toward her front porch, hoping I could get her indoors.

118

"Freddy's not around much, it's *his* dog, and *he's with Ray-Mee*," she screamed, pointing her bony arms and looking like she was ready to rip Ray-Mee limb from limb. She was accusing Ray-Mee of having an affair with her man, Freddy. There was absolutely no way that was true. Period. Freddy's dog was loose, running about and scaring the young children in Ray-Mee's yard. The gravel-voiced thunder-thrower got the dog and put him in her smoke-scented house — and I thought it was over. I proceeded to meet Grant.

I reflected on this incident as I drove. She was a sheep without a shepherd, lost and grasping and hurt and snarling and furious. I wanted to love on her but knew God would have to make a way. I had no idea what to do.

The police did have to come out later that evening because she started throwing thunder again — it was categorized as a "noise complaint."

~elle~

We had a temporary addition to our neighborhood party named Atticus, an eighth-grader from Macon up visiting his cousin Cinco. He was so *street* in his speaking that I had to really concentrate to understand him. He rarely said his S sound, though he did pronounce his Zs. He often dropped the final syllable of a word. If I followed his context, I could often stay in conversation with him.

Atticus and the boys played basketball every day, several times a day. If it was cool enough, I'd stay on the porch and tidy up or read just to be near; porch time always gave me more insight into my neighborhood. For example, Freddy and our screaming neighbor, now nicknamed Thunderbolt, walked past the house as I read. It was so interesting: Freddy asked me if I was afraid to die.

Hello.

"No, actually I really look forward to being in heaven with Jesus." I smiled big, and he believed me.

Freddy quoted Scripture, saying, "Fe-ah (fear) does not have to do with love. If I fe-ah, I'ma not trustin' Gawd. The Bible say no eye has seen, no ear has heard, all that the Lord has planned. So why should I be afraid of dyin'?"

Thunderbolt chimed in. "I just don't think we can choose when we die. That's up to Him. He gives us troubles and takes 'em away when He's ready." (I disagreed with her theology a bit there; I think we can create all kinds of troubles on our own.)

Freddy put his hand on her shoulder, obviously enamored of God and glad to share this conversation. Thunderbolt just shrugged him off, gave him a look, and they kept walking.

119

Most remarkable to see them and to engage that conversation after their tempestuous week.

Atticus asked if he could "hep roun' the hou" and we began a project to put up supports for a grapevine. I asked Atticus about school, his grades, his hopes, his family, and ambitions. "Ah'm not afrai' ta die," he said with a smile. "I got the Lor'."

As he talked, it seemed that prison ran in the male lineage of his family; sadly, within two years, Cinco told me that Atticus was behind bars. Two years after that, he had two children with two different teenaged mothers. I've never seen him again. I lament what happens to these street boys. Who is there for them? Who is loving them, training them, showing them how to be men? Who could intervene in Atticus' life? I have no answers.

~ellee~

The first year and a half away from the 6.6 revealed much about my soul. At times I felt that I was the rich young ruler walking away from Jesus, yet at other times I was also like loving, focused Mary Magdalene running toward Him. I was fully *agathokakological*: a tumble of both good and bad rumbling within.

Grant was more comfortable with people who were poor, yet his job involved creating beauty on the properties of the wealthy — they have the disposable income necessary for landscaping. He had a foot — actually, a muddy boot — firmly in both worlds, but he identified more closely with the poor. I, on the other hand, was more comfortable with the educated, curious, and motivated of any societal class. I disliked snobbery or elitism. I delighted in finding enthusiasm (especially artistic or intellectual) in unexpected places. Grant was more comfortable *being with* the poor; I was more comfortable if I was doing something to empower them. This ensured that we were never truly comfortable at the same time, unless we were fully resting well in God's purpose for us: to love our neighbor.

Woodbine had exposed my heart, and it was true:
I liked the comforts of following me and disliked the cost of following Jesus.
I liked the way I had been raised, but wrestled with the way that raises others.
I was in denial about my inner diva and forgetting my inner warrior.
I was more self-serving than sacrificial.
I was self-centered rather than God-centered.

I was holding onto my self and my material satisfactions and my history and my standards. The crappy quality of the curtain rod that was thin and bowing in the middle, for example; the shredded curtains, the rollers with the holes … they all bugged me. We could do better. We could afford it. I could make this pretty. God

120

loves beauty and brings life and order. Wouldn't fixing these things reflect Him? Well, no, not necessarily. Not if I disregarded my neighbor's situations. Not if they were choosing between heating their home and feeding their kids, while I was picking out window shades.

I needed to rethink: What are the standards of heaven?

Generous and loving sacrifice now, "Well done, good and faithful servant" crowning me later.
Abundant living now, although I may not fit someone's standards of prosperity.
Serve your neighbor as you would Jesus.
Love your neighbor as yourself. Love as Jesus loved.
Love your enemy. Pray for and bless those who curse you.
Consider others better than yourself.
Let go of distractions.
Do not let your possessions possess you.
Wealth carries with it a deceitfulness. Be aware; beware.
Share. God loves a cheerful giver.
If you suffer as a Christian, rejoice!
Abundance is not in possessions or material wealth or physical perfections.
A person's worth is not determined by their possessions, their home, or their job.

I kept coming back to Jesus: He gave up heaven for this earth, for me. He kept going low: downwardly mobile. He gave, and gave, and gave, pouring out His life. What was ping-ponging in my head and heart was not about guilt: it was about how to follow Jesus' model and conviction of my sin. For me, it was being willing to learn rather than lead; to be like a child rather than a commander. It was about honestly feeling and acknowledging my own resistance to the One I confessed to love most deeply. It was about receiving from Him all that I needed, about letting the water of His abundance flow through me to others. As I was enriched, I was to enrich others. **A generous person will prosper; whoever refreshes others will be refreshed,** Proverbs 11:25.

It was as if I was holding an invitation from Jesus:

You are cordially invited
to shift your loyalty
from self-preservation and self-centered living
to trust, vulnerability, and unexpected joy
as I, your first love,
move according to what I deem best.
I am asking you to go low, like water.
You may suffer misunderstandings, griefs, and heartaches.
RSVP today.

Picture me reading the invitation and leaning back on the kitchen counter, stunned and unsure if I *really* wanted to be sacrificial like Him. Could I trust like that? Could I live like Jesus? Could I go low like water?

Disability: Two Definitions

One mama of three adopted disabled children wisely illustrated a profound truth to her non-adopted children:
"You know when you break a plate and it splits into four or five pieces … can you glue that plate back together?"
"Yes," her children solemnly replied.
"You know when you break a plate and it shatters into two hundred pieces, can you glue that plate back together?"
"No, Mama," with big eyes. "Is that what has happened to our new sister?"
"Yes. What you're seeing is the difference between being broken and being shattered."

Oh my.

Sometimes that is what we see on the streets around Parkridge. That is why we need a taste of heaven here: grace for being different. No one staring. You just pitch in and help your neighbor, it's no big thing. We celebrate small steps that mark big advances. We redirect mistakes. We receive and give lavish love … or sometimes we are completely disregarded … but God sees what every heart can sustain.

I learned that although someone looks typical, they may not be. While their outer bodies might look average, their inner contents were not. Through trauma or genetics, their needs were different and unique.

~~~

It was fascinating to me how often I saw disability in my community. When the disabled were right in front of my eyes each day, I started thinking about how to contribute to their health. I rarely saw anyone who was disabled in West Knox. In fact, quite the opposite: I saw people who were strong, working out, running or walking for their health, toting weights as they strode past, brisk and purposeful.

My friend Shelton asked a magical question at lunch: "What's been on your mind lately, Suzanne?"

"Take a mental drive with me down Magnolia Avenue, the big arterial roadway two streets over from us. You know the one. Here you have more dollar stores. You see more quick-cash places — 'Cash your check here for a fee' — which I have concluded are mostly scandalous places from the pit of hell that prey on the poor.

122

"One example: Ray-Mee went to get a loan to drive to Atlanta to visit family: gas money, fast food on the road, and some money to give the family for feeding them. Not even a cushion in case something went wrong. She figured $100 would cover her family of five. She went to the place, asked about their rate, and they told her it would be a $100 fee for $100, due the following Tuesday. So for a $100 loan on Thursday, she would have to pay $200 back just days later. God is very clear in His Word about usury: He hates it. I do too. It is *criminal*."

Shelton leaned forward in her seat as I spoke. "Wait, that's *legal*? That's just wrong."

"Back to Magnolia Avenue. You'll also notice more ethnic hair and nail salons with sexy posters on the windows, car repair places with piles of run-down vehicles in their lots, and run-down storefronts. Weeds grow in the sidewalks, which are often broken and uneven. People walk more, and loiter about. You'll notice bars across the windows and doors of some places, especially liquor stores, gas stations, and convenience stops. Parking lots are more trashy.

"But one of the most dramatic, affecting sights you'll see are all of the people in wheelchairs, usually with no legs. They're on the side of the road, often waiting for transportation or someone to talk to, or just hanging out. Sometimes they have a dog. Their stumps speak so loudly to me.

"One day I was on the front porch and a grizzly-bearded gentleman went booming by on his jacked-up wheelchair. He had no legs, but he had tunes. His boom box speakers were on the back side of the motorized chair, and he was nodding his head in time with the music. Toolin' down the middle of the street he went. I waved, smiling and incredulous, but he was too into the music to notice me.

"Once I heard a person blithely comment about how people in the 'hood make bad food choices. The sassy part of me wanted to respond with, 'Let's see … was it the effect red-lining had on his family and community when he grew up, with no access to healthy grocery stores? Was it when the interstate was intentionally put through the black part of town, destroying the black business district? That was happening in the 70's in the name of 'urban renewal'. Was it that grocery stores make their profit on non-food items, and with limited jobs and opportunities, our black community did not spend their money on non-food items? Was it the GI Bill that benefited white families through generational wealth building, but black veterans were not given access, thus restricting their possibilities of creating thriving, business-building communities? Or maybe he's a vet who experienced major trauma in a war? I admit my hackles went up.

123

"We currently live in a food desert. The nearest places within walking distance (or reasonable wheelchair distance) for food are the Dollar Tree, Dollar General, and gas stations. A non-driver can get an entire bag of hyper-flavored Hot Cheetos for 99 cents, but the local stores do not carry fresh fruit. A non-driver could buy fruit in a can for $1.99, with an expiration date of two-three years. He or she is likely on a fixed income; he may not have access to other transportation; and he may not like apples *or* Cheetos, but he can only purchase what's nearby."

Shelton laughed cynically, saying, "Of course every kid will choose the salt and sugar. I love it too."

"People who walk in this area of Magnolia also talk to themselves a lot, and loudly. It's definitely a mental, real conversation that's going on in some person's head, gesticulations included. Some of those dialogues are intense. Sometimes they even fight the air."

"I've seen that," noted Shelton. "Sometimes it seems like a debate. Sometimes I wonder what's going on in their heads. They are literally talking out loud to thin air."

"By the liquor store, there are always at least four to fifteen men and a few women sitting, standing, talking, and smoking, looking around and looking rough. It's a gathering spot. There's no condemnation there. You don't have to clean up to sit on the liquor store wall; you just come as you are and join in. You don't have to prove anything, just come talk. Actually, doesn't that sound like what church is supposed to be?"

"Absolutely. In fact, I think of church in so many metaphors: hospitals, bars, a dinner table. It's about being together honestly. About loving Jesus and each other in His light. Can we keep it that simple?"

We paid our tabs and committed to pray for our neighborhoods, each with their own issues.

~elles~

Tall Henry (not Ray-Mee's Henry) is one of the men on the liquor store wall. Almost everyone in Parkridge knows and loves him. He wears his official identification tag on a lanyard every day, all day.

When he needs money, he comes by, "just askin', no pressure. Ya got any jobs f'me to do? I don't wanna beg, *NO*, that ain't me. I wanna work. I'll do yard work, wash your car, even pick up the dog poop. I'ma good drag man: if Grant cuts any trees or bushes, I'll drag the limbs to the street. $15 an hour, generally speakin'."

You'll also see him walking dogs, playing chess with older gentlemen on their front porches, and mowing people's grass.

Tall Henry is a man of dignity and honor. He does what he promises, shows up on time, and keeps his wits about him. I don't know why he's homeless. When it gets bitterly cold in the winter or storms are predicted for the night, Henry stays at a woman's house for $10 a night. Otherwise, it's open skies. All that for a 76-year-old fellow.

To my knowledge, there's one homeless hangout where Henry will not sleep: the Standard Knitting Mill (SKM). A mile from our house is the spooky shell of the SKM, a massive building with blown-out windows on multiple stories. The homeless live there off and on, depending on current police priorities, and bathe in a nearby stream that has warning signs: "This water did not pass safe chemical testing standards. Do not drink." Grasses, flowering weeds, wild jasmine, and rabbits populate the broken concrete parking lot. It is littered with broken glass, and trash that's blown there by swirling wind.

Grant and I go near there with Wiley so he can run around adjacent to the baseball field and play off-leash for about fifteen minutes each day. For a week we noticed a man in a wheelchair, his right lower leg in a cast, pushing himself from the local park (with unlocked bathrooms) to the SKM or the corner store. This was July, and temperatures were routinely in the 90s with high humidity. "Poor guy," I thought, and began to wave every time we saw him. One evening Grant and I stopped to speak with him.

He surprised us with his cheerful attitude. "I'm Jason. I know I look a mess," he said, swiping at his hair, which was … yes, a mess. "I'm homeless. *Homeless, but not hopeless,*" he said, smiling like it was his slogan. So friendly, so congenial and mannerly! We began to look forward to seeing Jason. We asked about his upcoming surgery, his cast (it began falling apart due to exposure and his picking) and his water intake.

Soon we met Tobey, an older, long-bearded man who went about on a bike. He was Jason's self-designated caretaker and also homeless. Whenever he rode by, he would wave and tell us how many days it was until his birthday. He seemed less emotionally stable to me, and Grant decided that we should always go to the SKM together from now on.

Living in the SKM was simple. It was surrounded by a chain-link fence that was hardly tight. A human body could easily squeeze under or between certain parts of the gates. Between the spray-painted smiley faces, "titties" and penis images, and word grafitti, there were lots of boarded-up doors and windows. One of the doors was open, and the homeless just walked right in. To Jason's benefit, there was a delivery ramp, so he could wheel right up.

About three days passed with no sight of the guys, other homeless people, or pop-up tent squatters. Where were they? Was Jason okay? Was Tobey?

Grant and I decided to see if we could get a tray of cupcakes to enthusiastic Tobey for his birthday. The SKM seemed very quiet, but then we thought we saw someone. We parked off the street, walked down the railroad tracks, and went up to the chain-link fence and yelled, "Tobey! You in there? Happy birthday! We have cupcakes for you!"

A completely gorgeous young woman strolled out. Not what we expected.

She could have been on the cover of a magazine. Her makeup was flawless, her body slender and well-proportioned. Her hair was pulled back as if a professional had done it. She wore a simple tee and shorts, and was shower-fresh clean … coming out of the SKM.

"I don't know Jason, but I know Tobey. I'll pass these along to him," she said without a smile. She was not interested in connecting. She spoke clearly, without a Southern accent. When she turned away from us, both Grant and I noticed the multiple syringes in her back pocket.

Who was this woman? A drug minion? Was she helping the SKM homeless shoot up? Was she selling? Why would she bother with those guys, who were obviously broke? We had no answers, because all the SKM homeless — all traces of them except the graffiti — disappeared.

Mental health deliberations were a point of contention in our community. A development offering permanent assisted housing was planned by the city, brought to the community's attention, and debated in December 2019. One community meeting and the following City Council meetings were heated. Ultimately, the proposed building was approved just as our homeless population exploded with COVID complications. (COVID increased the number of trafficking victims and drug addiction among our homeless community exponentially.) While we've always had the homeless and mentally ill near us in Parkridge, this group could be an entire neighborhood in itself.

~elles~

I had had a long day at work, one of those when you knew you were not going to finish your task list but you had given it your all. It looked like I was going to be working overtime at least one more day.

My days that week began with a brief visit to the NeoNatal Intensive Care Unit to visit with Baby O, on a ventilator, and her Mama, Ashley. Both were receiving excellent care. This particular day culminated in a sad visit to a former neighbor who was now in assisted living. He did not know me. Rescued life and imminent death were my work bookends.

Then on the way home my phone blew up with news of a verbal altercation between two of my neighbors. I tied up the loose ends of the workday, then (hands-free) began to return their calls. They both called, both were upset, both were blaming the other, both were swearing their version was the Absolute Truth. Sigh.

I came home and eagerly started organizing a room for our next guest arriving in two days. In the midst of needing to make up the bed for our newcomer, I sorted our laundry and started a load. I thought about dinner and doing the Whole 30; I went downstairs, started the dishwasher (why didn't someone else do that when they noticed it was full?), checked the chicken expiration date (today!), went to put the breasts in the freezer, and opened the door to *slosh*. Bad freezer sound! The ice was almost completely melted; the meats were softened but still quite cold; the ice cream was thickened cream; the shrimp was suspect; all my frozen strawberries and peaches were thawed. Damn. And 45 minutes till my favorite Hip Hop class started. Nothing in my house seemed settled. I looked outside; Wiley had just killed one of the rats that feasted on our chicken food. Good grief.

I scrambled and started cooking. Meats went into the crock pot and the skillet; thawing veggies went into a pot, mixed with the un-frozen and limp kale from our winter garden. I started mopping up the ice cream, the melted ice, and all the other unnamed leaky liquids ... a nasty, cloudy brew.

I made it to class, determined to dance away the stresses of the afternoon. The guest room was in a chaotic state, my kitchen was wild and wonky, but I really needed to shake off my stress. I got there and class was delayed. Sigh. No one had updated the website ... again.

Soon we jockeyed around the gym and found our places. Ten minutes later a large African American Mama with big, immaculate hair and long lashes came in with her son — to my delight, a special needs boy, probably about ten years old, glasses, big front teeth, a tablet in his hand. His chest seemed malformed somehow, his body just a bit out of 'typical' range. I smiled really big at him, given all I had experienced with volunteering with Joni and Friends, and his Mama noticed. She smiled back.

At the end of the next song, the boy approached me, eyebrows up, eyes bright. "Good job!" he exclaimed, looking right at me. I looked around, thinking he was talking to his Mama behind me. Oh my — no, he was actually talking to *me*! "Good job!" he repeated with the innocence and enthusiasm of a happy cheerleader. He flashed a strong thumbs up sign to me. I smiled back with a very sincere *thank you!*

When this precious boy gave me the thumbs up, my composure faltered. It was as if Jesus, with all of His glory packed into the broken body of that special needs boy, spoke words of love and affirmation to me. "Good job, daughter of Mine!" Thumbs up! Have fun! It was as innocent and glorious as if the words had come out of Jesus' mouth.

Add Joni and Friends + Hip Hop class in the gym at the Y + precious little brown person = tears rolling down my soul. I could barely keep the tears from spilling over. I couldn't decide whether to laugh or cry. So instead I just danced, a huge smile on my face, lost in the beat.

When I came home, Handsome was mowing, the neighbors had stopped yelling at each other, and the meat was browning. I made two peach pies and a blueberry tart from our un-frozen fruit, texted some friends, and we ended up having a lil' party with yummy sweet treats.

Handsome was exhausted. There was still so much to do ... too much in the kitchen, so much in the guest room, laundry to fold, mail to sort, showers, one more mopping, etc. I looked outside: Wiley had just assaulted a possum who was hoping to eat some chicken eggs (or chickens!). Good grief again! But there was no way we could do another thing. It would all wait till morning.

As I reviewed this day, dearths to zeniths, my favorite part of the day was the little boy and his beautiful, earnest, delightful, Christ-given "Good job!" I was so thankful for him. He was the focus of my prayers: his joy, his development, his Mama. It was the least I could do before I crashed into bed.

Fellini

The Fellini Kroger, our nearest grocery store, is like unloved, dirty Cinderella sleeping by the fire, aching from yesterday's work, aware that the stepsisters (the other shiny shops in town) look down on her. Haughtily despised as "ghetto." Rejected as unsafe.

But Fellini also has sass. They've got a mascot, a goose who frequents yearly during migration season, and her image is proudly printed on cloth shopping bags. They've got a Facebook page that always makes me laugh. The stories are hysterical; the best thread is "Decisions were made," usually showing cans of green beans deserted by the beer or lotion left by the Oreos. People have their priorities.

One of the most endearing (and frustrating) things about our homeless population was how they stole all but nine shopping carts from the Fellini. I went shopping in September of 2021 and there were no carts in Fellini. None. I went back to my car, grabbed two shopping bags, and went back in. There were other shoppers standing at the cart area looking bewildered.

As I went through the store, I counted six carts inside. My shopping filled my two bags and I left. On my way home I counted another six on the side of the road, near the bridges, and in the woods near the shopping center.

The Fellini is the roughest Kroger in town. The homeless hang out there in the shade, sometimes asking people with kind faces for a few bucks but mostly just hanging out and talking about their health and their situations. They are raggedy-looking with torn shirts and pants, usually braless, almost always missing teeth, always looking so tired, and often filthy dirty. They've had a tough go and it shows.

Occasionally I sent money using the Western Union stashed inside Fellini. The line there was often long because the poor and non-banking populations use a lot of the services there. A woman in front of me was paying her utility bill; another was getting a check cashed.

A gregarious older gentleman named Rick was in line directly in front of me. In a smokey voice he asked me how I was doing today, very kind of him, and I replied, "I'm doing well, how about you?" He had this sweetness about him that was winsome. I asked him to tell me about his tattoos; all but four were "prison tattoos; they don't cost you nothin' there, of course. It's expensive in a shop." I showed him one of mine and we talked about the high cost of colored ink (mine was burgundy-colored).

He mentioned something about his age; I rudely asked him how old he was: "67. I know I look it. This [he circled his face with his finger] is a roadmap." He smiled humbly. I knew he had many stories to tell.

God came up in our conversation and his eyes filled and leaked a bit. "Oh, you're gettin' me started," he choked. "God is *everything*. He is *awesome*." When he said *awesome*, I could tell he meant it in the real sense of the word, inspiring a sense of awe and humble admiration of someone more powerful, more marvelous, and great in every sense.

I asked Rick what his favorite part about knowing God was: "His grace and mercy. His grace and mercy. I wouldn't've made it without His grace and mercy." Again he teared up. "Oh, you got me goin' again. You can see on my roadmap that life has been tough. But His grace and mercy saved me."

The lady in front of him turned toward us, her face and legs a patchwork of white to brown. "He just saved me from cancer. I was a goner, stage four lymphoma, yet here I am."

"He picked me out of the pit and put me on solid ground," I quoted the psalmist, and they mmm-hmm'd, all of us humbled at the three-out-of-three testimonials of God's grace and mercy.

Rick told me he had been raised by his mother in a believing home and had had a real encounter with Jesus when he was young. Then he hung his head: "Since then, I'm ashamed to say, it's been off and on." He teared up again, leaking this time, and I put my hand on his shoulder. Rick called me by name when it was his turn to go up to the counter. "Suzanne, nice to meet you," he said as he gave me a little wave.

What a sweet gift it was to be in the Western Union line. I left Fellini with a changed heart, compassionately seeing the wounded and warring around me, wanting to love them better, wanting to be in relationship, wanting to listen and encourage.

My hair was simple and fresh, my clothes were clean and had a sense of style about them, my face had a bit of blush and my lips a bit of shine. I didn't look like the folks who were leaning their backs up against the Fellini brick wall. But Jesus moved me to love them, closing the (substantial) gap of class and experience; would they love me, or accept my love? Less us/them and more *us*. More love. I felt a sense of awe, recalling the Scriptures reminding us that "God has chosen the poor to have great faith" (James 2:5). I needed to be their student.

Our beloved Elder's Ace Hardware finally left the Fellini's shopping center because of the homeless. Apparently they were stealing and making the customers feel awkward. There was a local liquor store, Fellini for cigarettes, a Taco Bell, a locally-owned drug store, Goodwill, a vape/CBD shop, a Sav-a-Lot, a bullet-and-gun mart, and an Everything $10 store on that small strip of road. The homeless gathered there for hangout time together, got what they needed, then left for their evening spots. The police allowed those who slept in their cars to remain overnight.

There are lots of interstate bridges near the Fellini Kroger, and I imagine you have seen images of the homeless cramming their lives under the bridge's upper crook and cranny spaces out of the weather. When the homeless find a new spot, we see piles of clothing and trash strewn down like lava, constantly growing. It doesn't take much time — a few weeks maybe — and the police make them move on. Usually these were the folks who had disqualified themselves from the local shelter or just didn't want to be in those spaces for personal reasons. One man became the Bridge Guardian, greeting people as they came in and out of

Parkridge, a beer in his hand and a smile under his mustache. When the temperature dipped below freezing, we took Guardian Man old quilts, and he was kindly thankful. He had no interest in living indoors.

~ellee~

One morning I went outside to discover our little Honda push-mower had been stolen. Grant and I discussed this incident. Who would have the guts to come into our yard knowing Wiley would bark and be upset? Should we buy another mower? Where would we keep it safe?

We have no answers.
We have no mower.
We have a blower and weedeater and bike crammed into our dining room.

We also gained a deeper sense of what it feels like to be here on Woodbine. Some things don't work out. Some people have more and some have less and others steal. We didn't get our way; this was unjust and unfair. We were simply left in the lurch.

We know some of our neighbors have felt this and worse, so we entered into the feeling and the situation. We did not roll our eyes and quickly buy a new mower. So many of our neighbors could never just quickly buy a new mower because theirs was stolen. They would have to borrow one, pay some kid to take care of their yard till they could save up the money, or they would have to borrow from a loan shark (plenty around to take advantage of a situation). Here we entered into not being in control; to feeling taken advantage of; to feeling like we were robbed of the right and the good. It was a deeper initiation into Woodbine, and a formative one.

I complained to Rev Rena, who again went to the historic record. "History records white slave owners benefited from free enslaved labor. Systemic racism allowed this system to continue and as a result, throughout history Black families have not had the opportunities of their white counterpart to create generational wealth. The racial wealth gap has not only persisted but has widened. History bears witness to inequality in areas of housing, finance, business, education, healthcare, laws, policies and practices, and resources. Jim Crow laws, the practice of redlining by financial lending institutions, and other racists systems have caused generational Black wealth to suffer."

Learning about how the US government played a part in the financial hardships of black communities broke my heart. I had learned history from a white perspective, never from a minority perspective, which was quite different, even appalling. In my school, explorers and colonizers who wiped out civilizations and enslaved others were treated as heroes, not villains. They considered themselves "civilized," yet annihilated cultures; that, in my book, makes them *uncivilized*. But that was not what I was taught. Rather, I was taught they were victors, brave and courageous.

I can trace my own family's wealth. My grandfather was an orphan — he even performed as a clown in a traveling circus as a child — until he was adopted by awful people. He started with $0, literally, when he discovered that his adoptive father had spent all the money he'd saved from his high school job. He worked his way through college, then married and began building a life. A mentor, Mr Kellogg (yes, the cereal Mr. Kellogg), greatly influenced the trajectory of my grandfather's life. My grandmother, a second-generation American, put him through medical school; they had four children and raised them with very high expectations. As a country doctor, people paid my grandfather in quilts, eggs, jams, and vegetables, which he gladly accepted. My father went to medical school and benefitted from the oversight and resourcing of family, plus military and university systems. As white males, they had access to university resourcing, GI Bill benefits, housing opportunities, and societal networks. They were able to build a solid financial platform upon which our family prospered.

On my mom's side, there was more information. My grandmother was raised in a wealthy Southern family in Atlanta; she married a working class man who began an insurance company. They were solidly middle class, always had a bed for a stranger, had soldiers and less fortunate folks live with them off and on, and hung a branch of bananas in the kitchen for anyone in the neighborhood to eat. My grandfather came home after WWII and said he would never see another hungry child again.

I wondered, what had happened with the lawnmower thief? Where was the breakdown in prosperity and righteousness for him, for others? How would Jesus react to them and show them His way? What should we do? I pondered these questions as I sat on the porch swing, my mind swaying back and forth between more questions and possible answers.

The June 1st morning was cool, such a welcome gift. Soon after I settled onto the front porch swing, the rain began to pour. A couple was walking by, two tall, dark people who looked like they were in love. And they were not young ... I loved that about their mutual sweetness, how they looked at each other.

She had a small one-person umbrella, but he just shrugged deeper into his jacket and kept walking by her side. I jumped up and grabbed an umbrella we keep by the front door and ran it out to him. He took it gratefully and said, "I'll return it on the way home" in an accent laced with Spanish.

132

About 30 minutes later I went inside to brew some hot tea; when I came back out, the umbrella was in its spot, drip-marks fresh, wet tracks from the sidewalk to the porch.

I don't know why, but this moved me deeply, almost to tears. This was being a neighbor. I had no idea who that man was, but he kept his word and appeared kindly humble. Names weren't necessary; just one who had and one who needed. It was simple: *Give. I'll bring it back. You can trust me.* And it worked. My soul relaxed into Woodbine one degree deeper.

～ℓℓℓ～

Mid-July in our second year, my typical Wednesday began early to avoid the intense Tennessee heat and humidity. When I walked out of the door at 8 AM, I began to sweat: ugh, my least favorite time of the year. My 11-hour workday was capped off with Summer Study, a Bible Study I led at my church. I left there at 8:20 PM and headed east, dodging potholes on the interstate. I kept the car quiet and reflected on Summer Study ... what wonderful women, an army, a force, were at my church! Many were curious about why Handsome and I had moved to East Knox. I was just beginning to be able to put words to what was happening within me at a soul level, and they were rapt. "Tell me more ...." Woodbine was working its way into my lessons. I began to boldly confront my former West Knox lifestyle and limited exposure to other races and classes. They dug into my stories about the children and Parkridge as eagerly as they excavated Bible verses.

I spoke with some reservation: Did this feel like being a judgmental voyeur into a different class, race, or neighborhood? Was this just titillating gossip? Was I trying to look brave and daring in their eyes, mentioning how many times I'd heard gunfire that week? No. They proved their compassion as I began to get notes with a paper-clipped $10 bill or gift card with a quick scribble: "Use this next time you take the kids to Pete's Diner." "If they need any school supplies, please use this toward their total." "Just in case your neighbor needs groceries." "For an extra pair of gloves for the winter." "I'm volunteering at the school near your house." I mused aloud, "God, what are You up to?"

As I pulled down Woodbine Avenue, I counted six young men going hot and heavy at the basketball goal ... then I spotted Grant and two other tall young men having a beer on our front porch ... then Reyana and Marshay bounded up, laughing and sprinkling love and energy on everyone as they dashed by. A boy from Fifth Avenue, Zack-Attack, was walking his new Pit Bull, Gudder, to meet Wiley.

They stopped the game so I could crunch onto our side lot of grass and gravel.

133

This was being a neighbor. I loved it. God had changed me. I was not overwhelmed that night, even after continually being with so many people; I was delighted. In fact, the light within Reys and 'Shay sparked an idea: Let's burn some sparklers that were left over from a wedding! Yes, let's have some fun and shake off the demands of the day.

Dusk came gently in faded pinks and blues. We lit up the place, twirling and running with the elongated sparklers like condors soaring through the yard. To my surprise, Reys was scared — scared to hold the two-foot sparklers, even at the very tip. After we'd burned through several, she decided she *might* try to hold her own. She squealed in fear and determination, running then standing still in temporary terror. She was like a squirrel in the road, unsure of this whole thing, not unconvinced that she was going to die a sparkler-death right then and there.

I quietly took the basket of sparklers and retreated when Grant and all the fellows started throwing them, first at the ground … and then at each other. Silly boys, lighting up Woodbine.

These are the "wild creatures" God promised me at the beginning of this journey. I had said, "I'll miss all the wildness — the deer, the raccoons, the coyotes and their songs." In response, He had said: *"Trust Me, Child. I will bring you wild creatures beyond your imagination."*

Truly God had brought us wild, beautiful, extraordinary *people*. They were not the peaceful, elegant deer that used to grace our field; they were not the curious groundhog or the cautious foxes. There was no distance, no observing — we were *in it*. No one was more loud and happy and rowdy and wild than our new community: Reys and Cinco, Beels and Ray-Mee, Rocky and Deshawn, Zack-Attack and Gudder; more tempestuous than Thunderbolt and Freddy, or more distressing than the prostitutes and addicts. They were my new "wild creatures," and they were making me more wild and free too, more humble and more open, more like Jesus. This transformation was slow, incremental, beautiful, and painful for me, but so worth it. Yes to them. Yes to God.

134

Chapter Eight: Gifts, Fall/Winter 2018

FALL BEGAN TO CHANGE THE AMOUNT OF LIGHT, the temperatures ranges, and our attire. We shook out our jeans and stowed our shorts; we needed a jacket in the evenings. My calendar filled once again as school resumed. Kids left our home each evening as the streetlights blinked on, each day losing two to three minutes of sunlight.

During these days, Grant and I wrestled like Jacob (Genesis 32) to understand more about race, racism, culture, our neighborhood, our own expectations of ourselves, blackness, how to have conversations with people about all that we were learning, how we were changing … it felt like a lot. Like Jacob, we felt a bit wounded. Like Jacob, we were hearing God re-name us. Like Jacob, we named the place of our growth and new vision: our Peniel was Woodbine Ave.

One late afternoon I met with a group now named Marty and the Wild Women. Oh my goodness, I fell in love.

These women were likely to be in their very (very) late 60s, 70s, and 80s, and they were powerful. Cool. Strong. Firmly on their own two feet, even as their bodies were failing them. Don't be fooled by the wrinkles, the walker, or the swollen knee. These were warriors finishing well. They were planners, connected, resourced, and industrious. They were idea people and practical. They didn't mind theory and they appreciated pragmatism. My kind of women.

I told them all about Woodbine, filled them up with an hour of stories, and they listened intently. I could tell that the filter on their ears was (1) concerned, (2) loving, and (3) fierce. They were lions.

They asked questions, created verbal mini-proposals, linked resources city-wide, and cautioned me about voting issues related to my neighborhood. They talked about "The Foundation" as if It were a mysterious force for good that Must Be Informed.

Thank You, God, for women like these women. They are the lions who go before me, fearless and true to You and themselves, ready to rock the world until they leave it for Heaven.

May You make me like them and even double.
I love You. I'm exhausted. Protect Woodbine with Your grace and
peace. Goodnight, my beloved Father and Son and Holy Spirit. You
make life worth living.

While Marty and the Wild Women encouraged me greatly, I was also beginning
to get pushback and criticism:
"You're not going to change anything, *really*. People like you come and go.
Well-wishers and do-gooders. Good hearts but what can one family do?" In
other words, you're too small, too insignificant, and won't have a lasting impact.
"Some people are on the dole and not going to get off. They're just lazy and
used to getting their government check." In other words, *those* people won't
accept a different vision for their life. They don't know the value of work and
won't change. Once a taker, always a taker.
"People will just take advantage of you." In other words, you're a fool to be
generous.
"Why would you stop living like you did in West Knox for this, for these
people?" In other words, you're different, you deserve the good life, *those*
people aren't worth sacrifice.
"God said to enjoy His good gifts, but you've just sold your best gift — land and
a home. Don't you think He wanted you to have that? Don't you think your
safety and prosperity was part of His plan for your life, His blessing to you?" In
other words, God's gifts are material and material prosperity is a sign of His
affection. Selling our property was an affront to Him.

There was separation: *those* people, *that* area of town. It was obvious that we
needed bridges between cultures, classes, and parts of Knoxville that were based
on personal relationships and shared experiences.

Dream: I can't get through

My body stirred, my circadian rhythm set to the sun's rising. Even as I began to
fully awaken, I could tell I was agitated, frustrated, even starting to sweat. In my
dream I had been in the pulpit at a wealthy church — at times, surreal and
sleepy, it was my former church, but then it became any wealthy white
congregation — trying to communicate to people that the Church was called to
change the world through sacrificial love. I was asking them to be like Jesus in
their extravagance: "He gave up everything, *everything*. So shouldn't we? How
can we love and serve like Jesus did? As Christians, we are *followers*. Shouldn't
we take our lives into our hands and lift them up to our great Father and trust
that in His care, we will thrive, life will happen (the good and the bad), and He
will never leave us, as we give our lives to Him?" I was so full of the joy of the
Lord that I am beaming, telling people of His greatness and kindness, His
comfort, and His Presence. Any sacrifice for Him is worth it.

In my dream, I'm being ignored. Completely.

A man in a business suit turns his back to me and begins a schmoozy deal with another man in the pew behind him; they exchange business cards. A woman checks her nails, completely engrossed in every nick. One woman pulls out dental floss and begins with her upper left molars. One kid yells, "Ha! Go fish!" to the children around him, who are all holding cards. An older lady listens attentively, but says aloud, "I'm too old for that. This message is for young people." Another elderly man snorts, waking himself ... briefly.

And I'm at the pulpit, impassioned, exhorting: "Jesus chose — chose! — to give up the glories and beauties and honor of Heaven. He chose to release the authority He held as ruler there. He put aside all of His heavenly privileges in order to come to the earth to rescue us from sin and darkness. Let it sink in: you and I and all people of the earth are worth that loss to Him; *we are His gain*. His love called Him to us. That's *why* He came; now look at *how* He came:

"He chose to be born into a poor family in a no-account village into an oppressed people group rather than come as royalty, as 'leadership,' as a powerful person. Why did He choose to identify with the poor and powerless? He was a refugee — escaping murderous infanticidal rage in His home country, He and His family travelled to Egypt, then later moved back to disrespected Nazareth. This led Jesus to a dusty village and an obscure youth, to sacrifice, and a cross.

"There was a *cost*: His life. And, there was a relationship: continued intimacy with His Father. The same set-up applies to us. There is a cost for following Jesus: our lives. There is a relationship: His continued, abundant presence throughout this life, and then Heaven."

I pause. "Why do we think our stories should look different when we claim to follow Him? Why do we think our stories are all about the *benefits* of being God's sons and daughters without all the *sacrifices*? Jesus gave up His life; we must too. Jesus allowed God to intimately direct His days, His life, His death; we must too."

Someone yawns loudly, stretches out his arms, and stands. "Anybody ready for lunch?" he asks loudly, pivoting, looking at everyone in the church. Several people cheer, stand up, throw their hats into the air like it's graduation, and everyone begins gathering their purses, children, and papers.

I am distraught. "Wait, don't you hear? Can't you see? There is a different wealth from what you value. My life is covered in intangible sweetnesses: the peace and mutual honor that defines my home. Joy that flows through me and splashes onto everyone around me. Parents who deeply and dearly love me. Trust and hope and freedom. These intangibles are what make me wealthy."

A lady snickers at me as she walks past. "Well, *this* is what makes me wealthy, girlfriend," and flashes her many diamonds at me. All of a sudden I realize I am under-dressed for that church. I do not fit in: My hair is too long for my age, I'm not hip to the church's fashion culture, and people are rolling their eyes at me. Or worse, just politely ignoring me with a thin smile as they push their children toward the door. And all I want for them is greater intimacy with Jesus, to be with Jesus in a new, sacrificial way. They don't care.

Christmas Shopping with MeLissa

Along the journey of these past years we have consulted many sages. Our learning curve in some areas was an Everest climb, especially when it came to politically loaded concepts like white privilege, black embodiment, woke culture, policing, Critical Race Theory (CRT), and blackness and whiteness as cultures. Because the language of our American culture was getting increasingly flammable, I read about these ideas to self-educate but depended more on my black neighbors to enlighten me through their everyday encounters. My experiences with them meant much more to me than a politician's take on racial issues. I had no reason to question my neighbors' integrity; patterns emerged as many of them told me the same things.

I went shopping at our local mall with MeLissa; I needed measuring cups and new dishtowels, and she needed fish from Bonefish Grill. While we were at the mall, we window-shopped outside a fashion store. She leaned in and whispered, "Watch what happens. Let's go in together." We did; my curiosity was aroused.

The sales lady asked if she could help us find anything; *no, thanks, we're just looking*. Then MeLissa gave me a wink and we split: she went to scarves and belts, and I stayed at the shirts, watching her and wondering what was going on. Then I saw it: The sales lady was following MeLissa, not me.

When we exited the store, I asked her if we could do it again in another shop. We went to a boutique; same thing: nice greeting, left alone until we split, then they followed MeLissa. Again at a market. I was rattled.

At Bonefish, we discussed all that had happened over an appetizer of Bang-Bang shrimp.
"Does that happen frequently, MeLissa? It makes me so mad!"
She nodded. "Suzanne, have you ever *not* been trusted because you're a woman, or older, or dressed a certain way, or someone saw that tattoo on your wrist? Use that to relate to me. It's a terrible feeling to be treated with suspicion, to not be trusted, or for your integrity to be doubted because you appear a certain way that is inherent to you, such as race or gender."

138

"Yes, I've definitely felt that before. Terrible, awful feeling. In my job, I've been treated as lesser than because I'm a woman. I've walked into a meeting and heard a man sneer, 'Here's Gloria Steinem.' If I'm not in a healthy, God-centered place mentally, I can get reactive to the crap they're putting on me.

"I think I would likely feel defeated, defensive, or offended if someone treated me like I was already a criminal, especially if that behavior happened repeatedly. I imagine I would need to retreat to safe spaces to remember who I am; that I am not who they condemn me to be; that they were the one with the problem, not me. How do you feel when this happens?"

recessed into her memory; I could see it in her eyes.

"I can tell you every detail about my first understanding of racism. The shock of my first rejection, my first argument, the first slurs. The sound of people laughing at me for something that was essential to who I am. The disappointment, the hurt, the collapse, the distress, the confusion, the disturbing impact it had on my forming heart."

As I listened to her experiences, I was broken-hearted. Racism had happened to her without shame ... to *my neighbor*. My MeLissa, whom I am supposed to love and serve in the Name of Jesus. From her own lips she told me stories, and I felt such sorrow that I thought I could not stand.

A black friend of hers was pulled over by the police when he was driving a new, snappy car. "First, to be at the mercy of an authority who already views you with suspicion is scary. Has that ever happened to you with a teacher, professor, or officer?"

I had to think. Most teachers and professors loved me because I love to learn. But an officer: yes. Only once. I was pulled over on suspicion of outrunning a cop ... (c'mon, *me*, in a Honda Pilot?) but I had just gotten out of workout class. I did all I could to convince the officer that I was not the person he was looking for, and 20 minutes later he let me go with a grumble. No "Sorry for the inconvenience, ma'am, we'll keep looking. Have a nice day." I felt condemned but had done nothing wrong; my body was tense; I felt confused. Why was this happening?

She continued: "Second, to be perceived as someone who cannot earn something that represents the upper class or financially secure status is frustrating. People imposing such limitations on me can feel insulting and offensive, but if I say something or react a certain way, the situation can flare, and the other person is the one with power."

Our food arrived.

"MeLissa, have you noticed that you're the only black person in this room? You're the sole black patron tonight."

"Girl, I scanned the room before the hostess seated us. That's part of being a minority. You're always watchful. That's part of our collective exhaustion: always being on alert when we are in white spaces.

"It can feel relentless — even hopeless — to explain fundamental, essential information over and over, especially if that information involves painful memories. Constantly swimming upstream. More effort required to navigate two cultures."

"In my job, I scrape against the patriarchal culture. At times it feels like being in a container with walls that scratch me like sandpaper — not deadly, but painful. I am often the only woman at the table, bringing a different voice or view or tone, explaining … again."

"I know that scratch!" her eyes said to me. She continued: "When I left Woodbine, when my husband left me, I had to find housing. I was not considered first for my housing application because a white owner preferred and trusted what he already knew and trusted: whiteness. I may be making an assumption, but it looked like this, so you decide: I was struggling to make all of my deposits at once — utility deposit, safety deposit, and cleaning deposit — and asked for 36 hours. As I was leaving, a white woman, well-dressed, walked up. I stayed at a distance, looking at my phone, to hear if they made a deal. As they discussed the property, she disclosed she could sign the lease in four days. He shook her hand and she signed that lease, not me. I was better prepared with my paperwork; I had done all my bank work. But she looked like the landlord, and that probably felt safer to him."

"I'm sure that happens. Lin-Manuel Miranda wrote about a similar situation in his musical *In the Heights*, but it was a white-Hispanic tension."

"Have you heard Rev Rena's story about being treated as less smart or less capable? She transferred to a mixed-race school from a predominantly black school and was automatically put into low or average classes — no testing, no consultation, and we're talking about *Rena*, smart as a whip and able to run a city! She discovered the discrepancy in what she was learning during standardized testing, literally learning upper-level math in the hallway from her peers who were in higher level classes. It wasn't that she could not keep pace with more challenging classes; it was that assumptions were made about her abilities, motivation, and prior comprehension because she was black."

"Here's one thing that's been bugging me lately, MeLissa. A friend of mine's son was caught with drugs while he was wasted. His parents paid for an excellent lawyer. Their son became one more white boy who got community service, a stern rebuke, and required counseling. If that had happened to a black kid, they would've probably gone to jail and had more severe consequences. I was glad for my friend — she was torn up about her son — but it just reinforced the stereotypes I hear in our 'hood."

We prayed all the way home, MeLissa's hand out of the window, sprinkling prayers and love as we entered Parkridge. There was no other way to lift the weight, to find resolution and peace, other than prayer. When we pulled up, I whispered a silent, "*Cheers to You, Lord God Almighty*," and gave her a goodbye hug. I was so weary from the sorrow.

What did I do as a white woman as my neighbors told me their stories? I listened. Loved their broken hearts. Felt anger at lazy thinking and complacency. Friends have asked if I felt guilty: no. I accept God's design for me to be white. I felt *sad*, I felt the weight of their suffering. Their suffering inspired compassion within me, zeal to change and challenge injustice, and a desire to understand now what I have not understood before. That is my path: the East Side.

Pete Scazzero

Authors and speakers Pete and Geri Scazzero learned much about living out the Gospel as they planted and grew a church in New York City. Not only did Pete address the flagging emotional maturity of most Christians, but he also pressed into the spiritual realities of relationships between people in the Church. A theme emerged in his podcasts and interviews:

In the midst of a Roman Empire marked by severe prejudices and hatreds, the first Christians viewed themselves as part of a world-wide family that transcended national, class, cultural, and racial barriers. They understood Jesus, through His blood shed on the cross, had destroyed these barriers and created a "new human race," a new society, a new people, i.e. the Church (Ephesians 2:14-15).

I loved this. I wanted to live this … in a polarized, emotionally immature American climate.

Similar to our day, divisions abounded in Jesus' day: there were Hebrew Jews, Palestinians, and Greek Jews who were spread throughout the empire; Samaritans who had intermarried and worshipped differently from other Jews; pagans of all types of belief and unbelief, including Gentiles. How did Jesus bridge class and culture gaps? He tore down the "dividing wall of hostility through His blood" (Ephesians 2:14) to create a new society called the Church.

Jesus, my dearest love, wanted a multicultural church, and here I was for most of my life in a white world. True, my church sent me to other cultures (China, Mozambique, Ethiopia), but I always came home to a white congregation. Acts 13:1,2 opened my eyes.

"In the church at Antioch there were a number of prophets and teachers of the Word, including Barnabas, Simeon from Niger, Lucius the Libyan, Manean (the childhood companion of King Herod Antipas), and Saul. While they were worshiping as priests before the Lord in prayer and fasting, the Holy Spirit said...."

So for a time their leadership team included:
- **Barnabus**: a Jew, whose name meant "son of encouragement."
- **Simeon** from Niger: Jesus spoke colloquial Aramaic; the Aramaic word *niger* or *nagar* means "someone who works with wood, a carpenter," so Jesus was a *niger*. The Latin word *niger* means "black" or "dark in color." Nigerians today, as a race, are black, and I expect Simeon was a black man from Niger, just as **Lucius** was, since he was from Libya in northern Africa.
- **Manean**: Manean was likely a person of means since he was so closely connected with the highest leader in the region, "who was like a brother to Herod the tetrarch."
- **Saul/Paul**: a "Hebrew of Hebrews," a strict Pharisee from a highly legalistic sect, a zealot for who he perceived God to be. He even approved of the hunting of Christians like a terrorist, but was converted, then sent to tell Jews and Gentiles about Jesus. He was also a Roman citizen, an unusual hybrid of a man.

Consider Jesus' disciples:
- a Jewish zealot and a privileged Jewish tax collector for Roman occupiers, complete enemies;
- two sets of brothers, both in the same industry, but one set with higher class networks;
- at least one intellectual;
- a follower who raided the money bag for himself and later turned traitor;
- extroverts and introverts;
- women who helped fund Jesus' journey;
- a woman who had been demon-possessed but was healed by Jesus. She became Jesus' first "sent one," entrusted with the news that Jesus had risen from the dead. This was incredibly counter-cultural for that day.

It seems to be God's pleasure to mix His people together, but we keep clustering ourselves into like groups. Why are we like that? Why can't we celebrate difference? Why do we get so uncomfortable with people who are not like us? Pete asked, "Imagine yourself in a multi-cultural setting, a large meeting of all colors, shapes, sizes, abilities. How would you fill in this sentence? 'Hi, I'm from _____. One of the gifts I believe my culture brings to the larger Body of Christ is _____.'"

Pete and Geri Scazzero offered this advice: Transcending multi-racial issues and barriers is a long-suffering goal, so go slowly. Remember to pay attention to hires, staffing, and power differentials. Engage in difficult situations and conversations on race and power; be able to listen to uncomfortable things. Maturity is a commitment to loving well, to facing our own shadows, to being open to deep transformation. Racial reconciliation is a byproduct of loving Jesus.

The Scazzeros recommend the use of *genograms* for self-awareness and transformation, to explore if there is generational racism, classism, or sexism in your family of origin. For oppressed peoples, there is generational transmission of trauma, so show gentleness and respect if you do a genogram exercise with a historically oppressed person. I felt it revelatory when I did my first one. (@petescazzero, https://www.emotionallyhealthy.org; various podcasts, and www.youtube.com/watch?v=B43eLGFVFw4.)

Grief and loss can be a means to unite Christians in sacred spaces that are safe for all people — even on a simple back porch. I was reminded of several church services I attended. One black church lamented so authentically, pouring out their hearts and sorrows with gripping openness; one white church celebrated so joyfully, lifting their voices to the rooftop, hands waving and bodies bouncing. I wondered if they needed each other to find that yin-yang wholeness of human emotion, that balance of night-day, male-female, joy-sorrow. Dyads made for each other. Holy completion.

꒰꒱

Our third Christmas on Woodbine was so much more relational — and fun — than the first. Reyana and Beels had been waiting since Thanksgiving to do Christmas decorating with me and my daughter Marlie. I brought out several boxes with ornaments, nativities, and wreaths. We went through one box at a time (that was a discipline issue), and the girls' glee was invigorating and delightful. They flew to the tree with each ornament unless it was made by Marlie; if so, they ran to her, shouting and stomping and showing. "You did this one, Marlie! I love it!" Then they'd run back to the tree, place it with care, and come back for the next treasure.

After the girls set up the nativity, they voiced each character:
"Aw, my little Baby Jesus. You so cute! No cryin' today. Be quiet now."
"Hey, you angel, get back here. Quit payin' attention to the lamb and the Wise Men. And quit arguin' wit' me. You're about to go into time-out! Don't talk back to me, angel!"

Cinco came into the play: "We've got a mission, angels. Follow me. This is serious. If you can't take it, you need to stay here [heaven]."

Then the three Wise Men really starting bickering. Two ended up just going to bed. Most of the Nativity characters ended up in time-out at least a few times.

I learned a lot by listening. A lot of their play was full of dramatic, angry encounters. Sometimes these pretend encounters were about authority — who had it, who wanted it. Sometimes they were about who got what item. The common thread: drama, fighting, trying to get what you want, loud voices.

What I saw in the children, I see in our country.
What I want to see in the children, I want to see in our country:
Cooperation.
Less territorialism and bullying.
More collaboration.
More patience and discussion to reach win-win solutions.
Purpose. Play. Alliance. Goodness.

I felt the strong desire to do proximity better. Surely the Holy Spirit had given us the tools: love, joy, peace, patience, kindness, goodness, gentleness, faithfulness, and self-control (Galatians 5:22,23). How could I practice more?

God opened the door — actually, the door to our house — and gave me the opportunity to practice.

~elles

Reys came by, her hair done and her coat smelling like ashes. It was so good to hug her! We headed into the kitchen to do some holiday chef work; she donned her favorite red tulle apron (which she wears around her neck, not her waist), washed her hands, and asked what to do. She had grown accustomed to our routine.

We created a blueberry coffee cake. As usual, there were adjustments: buttermilk instead of low-fat milk *(of course)*; 1/2 teaspoon salt instead of 1/4; put pecans in part of the cake (for me); more blueberries and vanilla extract than the recipe called for. The result was over-the-top delicious.

When Cinco and Grant arrived home from a UT men's basketball game, kitchen time with Reys was never the same. The kids had been playing a long-term game of tag at our house; it had been going on for months! The kitchen island became the center of a fast and slightly violent effort to not simply tag each other, but to clobber each other. They finally had to come to a time-out so we could finish our next cooking tasks. Any bowl or implement with sugar, they wanted licks.

144

Then Reys opened her Christmas gifts. First, she opened the Pick-Up Sticks game she dearly loved … "Is it colored pencils? Is it … *IT'S PICK-UP STICKS!*" she exclaimed, lighting up more brightly than our Christmas tree. Then she enthusiastically opened the red egg full of Silly Putty, holding it to her chest and smiling her 1000-watt smile.

When we walked her home at dusk, Cinco carried her gifts. He said something very sweet to her as he crossed the street to go into his house, and that perked up Reys' ears. "Cinco, you like me!" she authoritatively yelled across the street. He yelled back, "I do not!" slamming the door as he went inside. Grant and I just smiled at them — they did seem to love each other in a very immature, childish, can't-admit-the-truth kind of way. Something was there.

⁓elle⁓

During the first few years on Woodbine, I kept hearing references to the themes of giving up your wealth for others, living generously, investing in the Kingdom, and humbling yourself. Across ideologies, we repeatedly heard the story of the Good Samaritan.

Though we are not Catholic, Grant and I went across town to the local artsy theater for the film "Pope Francis: a Man of His Word." From the film, I liked him: he seemed to be humble, be unaffected by the power and wealth available to him, and he was unafraid of differences. He hammered the wealthy, but his words were right: *"We could all be a little more poor for the sake of others."* He cited the classic commandment, **Do unto others as you would have them do unto you.** Then the film applied that to refugees, homosexuals, victims of abuse by clergy, and more. It was simple. Straightforward. Challenging. Humbling.

The following Sunday Grant and I visited Hope Church in Austin-East High School, a predominantly black school that rates two out of ten stars in our local educational network. It was a small gathering of millennials with black and white leadership in worship. It felt so good to worship with a black sister behind me who boldly declared *yes* and *JESUS!* and *You made a way*. Her cultural, out-loud love was encouraging. It felt honest and authentic, and it reminded me of how MeLissa prayed.

Dominic, the African-American teaching pastor, spoke powerfully on the parable of the Good Samaritan (Luke 10). In short and *in vernacular*, a (presumably) *Jewish dude got jacked up* on the dangerous, narrow road *where thieves used to chill* and wait for loners and vulnerable people. After they robbed and beat him, they left him half-dead. Two religious men passed the needy man, unwilling to help, but a bi-racial man, a Samaritan (whose race was despised by the Jews), *did the hurt man a solid* by binding and cleansing his wounds. He hefted the weak Jew up onto his donkey, got him to a safe hotel, *shelled out for his room*, arranged for the innkeeper to help him, and left with the promise that they would square financially when he returned in a few days.

Dominic was exploring social justice and the role of the Body of Christ with his flock, pushing them to live honestly with needs and resources like the church in Acts 4. His main message:

Share. Don't clique up, don't hoard; open up, be willing to give. Give what you can. Like the Good Samaritan, your spending may change; you may allocate your money differently than you expected. Take care of each other. Like the Samaritan, be willing to say, "I'll take the cost of helping this person. Put it on me." It's costly to care.

If you have a way to meet someone's need, do it. Whose burden do I see? Stop walking past people. Don't turn away. Be inconvenienced, give up your time and money for a neighbor. Slow down. Listen. Watch. We're accountable to God for how we respond.

A neighbor is anyone who crosses our path whom we can tangibly show the love of Jesus.

Stop standing around discussing help; do it. Don't turn away; get involved. God wants to pour out His love through you, so stop walking by and stop talking and do something.

"Not all people are my brothers, but every person is my neighbor." I loved that quote adapted from Tim Keller. Pope Francis agreed completely: every person, every race, every religion. We are all *human* neighbors. This was the consistent message: we need to act lovingly toward each other regardless of country, tradition, or faith preference. We need to *see* each other. We need to not just be willing to help, but actually do it, right in our own cities.

146

Chapter Nine: Living With Us, Early 2019

AFTER HANDSOME AND I WATCHED "*I Am Not Your Negro*" by James Baldwin and *13th*, an account of racial inequality in our nation's prisons, I awakened with a soul hangover: sluggish, unsettled, emotions and thoughts mixed and muddled. I was a muddy river after a rain, heavy with the sediment of brutality and racism. Like a river, I was still rumbling along, but I needed to sift some soul-silt and get clear again. But I wasn't even sure where to begin.

In times like this, I go out to my garden. I prune and pick and process, all the while seeing that I am a garden, and God is simultaneously clipping off the dead places, refining me, and making me abound and blossom and flourish. Pruning is a painful and necessary procedure but ultimately brings growth and beauty.

The movies renewed my sorrow at the inhumanity of my race. All the things I have feared in my life —torture, rape, violence at the hands of insane men — and more, lynching, even burning black bodies after they were dead, just for spite and satisfaction — it's bizarre to me, unfathomable, satanic, hellish. Black people were harmed by generations of white terrorists. Why did whites feel and act so exclusively, or think they were so superior? Where did that lie begin, and why?

Historically, white American hands are covered with the blood of Native Americans and African Americans. So why are we not the most humble and most helpful race in the United States? "Here, let me speak to you honestly. I want to apologize for all of the wicked horror, the violence and harm my ancestors did to your ancestors. I want to apologize to you, face to face, eye to eye. Look at me; see that I am serious. Hear me; I am a simple white woman who is absolutely ashamed of the prejudice and bloodshed perpetrated by my white people against your people. As a show of good faith, what can I do for you? How can I pray for you? How can I help you advance? How can I serve you through my networks and prosperity? I am asking for a Biblical, beautiful chance at restitution."

I felt the silt settling out as I morphed my thoughts into written words.

I do not despise my own skin … that doesn't work either. It's just me here, a simple lover of Jesus and people, a person of light and hope. But I still need more; the ache is not gone. Perhaps it will never leave. So I turn to the Scriptures, which is what I do and how I live, and I search for guidance.

I compiled Scriptures from all over the Bible and created a sequence for me to use in prayer. (See Appendix A for The Woodbine Confession and Appendix B for Scriptures that Smacked Us Around.) I had in mind what I see on Woodbine: poverty, disruption, racism, beauty, strength, resilience, happy children, broken things, joy, play.

I prayed God would use my prayer of confession and repentance to wash me clean. But not only me: the Old Testament prophets prayed on behalf of their nation. "Father, forgive us, we have sinned," they would say, when the prophet was actually a very righteous person. Jeremiah prayed over Grant with the "we" pronoun: **We acknowledge, O Lord, our wickedness, and the iniquity of our fathers: for we have sinned against thee (Jeremiah 14:20).** In a famous prayer for his nation, righteous Daniel prayed, **"Lord, in keeping with all your righteous acts, turn away your anger and your wrath from Jerusalem, your city, your holy hill. Our sins and the iniquities of our ancestors have made Jerusalem and your people an object of scorn to all those around us"** (Daniel 9:16, NIV). **"... Let your ear be attentive and your eyes open to hear the prayer your servant is praying before you day and night for your servants, the people of Israel. I confess the sins we Israelites, including myself and my father's family, have committed against you,"** prayed courageous, righteous Nehemiah (1:6, NIV). I wanted my prayer to cover more than just me; I wanted it to cover white generations.

I remembered my dream. It was Jesus' blood that would make things right: **"If we confess our sin, He is faithful and just to forgive us our sin and cleanse us of all unrighteousness"** (1 John 1:9). **"Brought near by the blood of Christ"** (Ephesians 2:13). I journaled an evening prayer:

"Wash me, dear Jesus, and wash my people. I acknowledge our wickedness, our sin, in using and abusing people of color. I think of Native Americans. I think of black Africans. Of mistreated Asian Americans. I recoil at the horror of what these races experienced at the hands of white people — white, as I am white. Cleanse us from our sins, Lord God Almighty. Remake us. I humbly ask You to change our hearts. May we serve people of color, lifting them up, to show our repentance. May we be appalled at racism of all kinds. May we learn to see people as You see people. I ask this, God, for Your glory, the good of the world, and the healing of the nations. In Jesus' Name, amen."

As a forgiven, humbled believer, what am I — we — to do now? In my job, I am constantly aware of what my next steps should or could be. So in my 'hood,

148

what now? In our cities, what are our next steps? As American citizens, what should we do next?

These questions are my prayers. I sleep trusting You will guide me and move me forward, dearest Father. Thank You for Your patience with me. I love You deeply.

~elles~

When I speak with my white friends about race and class, systems in my city, and American history, their earnest reply is, "I'm not racist." They quickly make references to friends and co-workers of color or minorities or organizations they financially support. Some feel like they are not racist/classist because they engage in what many cynics call "drive-by compassion." "I helped feed the workers at [name an organization] who work with the poor." "I give money to the marginalized through [name an organization]." "I donate a Thanksgiving box every year and even tuck in a devotional." "We go feed the poor and sing Christmas carols around Christmas." Older people reference the progress they perceive over the past five decades. I don't want to minimize such efforts or put a limiting label on them. I understand that for some folks, that is the best way they know to enter into this complex situation.

Through these conversations, I find there is a split: Some people, both black and white, are done with racism and are moving on. In personal conversations, I find these people are collectively in the upper middle/upper class, or generally very young. In *my* neighborhood, however, race and class are still the filters used to interpret almost all facets of life. There is active anger. There is frustration. There is exhaustion.

One way to find out if you are who you say you are is to share your life. Open it up. Unlock the doors, welcome someone in for a meal, and then sit with them. Talk and listen. Notice each other's quirks. It's more than your Myers-Briggs score or being a "blue" or a certain personality animal or an Enneagram 3 with a strong 2-wing. No: Take off the bandages and show the wounds, as Jesus invited Thomas (John 20:24-29). Live honestly and fully in the presence of another person. Who are you? Who are they?

God's challenge to us was not just to move to Woodbine; it was to love our neighbor. To do that wholly, we took the risk, opened our home, and welcomed the stranger. Following are two glacial stories that have re-formed the landscapes of our lives as we've risked being in proximity with others. Glaciers scrape, shove, move, and break. These stories are not pretty.

An Open House

When Grant and I were thinking through leaving the 6.6, we needed a very strong WHY. God provided that with His own voice and some challenging, encouraging, disturbing books about the more leathery parts of living out sacrificial faith. Enter *Strangers at My Door*. The book challenged us to look beyond our own comfort, introversion, privacy, and control, and to open our home to complete strangers. What could that look like on Woodbine? It might be someone knocking on the door and looking for a place to bed down for the night, or friends of friends needing a spot to land for a while. The Bible confirmed hospitality as a sign of faith, so we decided to open up. After all, a bud is beautiful, but an open, fully developed flower is sublimely lovely.

We've welcomed people who were ...
passing through town;
attending a wedding;
teaching a weekend seminar;
doing a residency at the University;
effecting a short job stint;
photographing a wedding;
hiking in the Smoky Mountains the next day;
visiting friends or family.

Opening our home, extending generous hospitality, and creating community are such important Kingdom principles that we chose to purchase a large house with two extra bedrooms for people passing through. I was excited about Acts-style hospitality. Sure enough, we had people stay with us for as little as a weekend and as long as two years.

Yes, doing this put us at risk. Heartache, theft, harm, misunderstanding, mistreatment — all of those were possibilities. We did it anyway, relying on the Spirit to help us and sometimes floundering our way through it. What should we expect from our guests? What did they expect from us? We usually began with a good foundational conversation, then handed them a key.

~elllee

Jo Saxton on Hospitality

Grant and I were part of Q Commons, an effort led by Gabe and Rebecca Lyons out of Nashville, on the topic of neighboring. (This event was not related to Q Anon or conspiracy theories.) They were trying to establish space for people to ask questions and talk about faith in a noncombative, open environment, and keep faith and current issues connected.

We were given nine minutes in an interview format. Our convener, Steve Moldrup, asked me, "So Suzanne, why did you move?" In two minutes I condensed our discomfort and restlessness, our conviction about safety, wealth, and comfort, and my sense of challenge and loss. Whew. Then over to Grant for two brief questions about living on Woodbine, then back to me for the final question about praying for Woodbine Avenue.

Nine minutes for two years, loads of lessons, new friendships and faces, tension and money, settling into a new house and hood … it all felt too fast and too small. But what a privilege. What fun to encourage others to take risk, make a leap of faith, leave their familiar comforts, and open up their lives in a new way.

My favorite part of the evening was hearing the origins of the word "hospitality" (φιλοξενία) from Jo Saxton, a dynamic woman originally from Africa. Her intoxicating accent made her sacrificial hospitality even more beautiful.

She taught us that two Greek words combine to transliterate into "hospitality": philo (brotherly love, warm affection, friendly) and xenos (stranger, guest, "other"). Philoxenia connotes an accepting love of strangers and extends a moral code of hospitality to foreigners. It implies showing warmth and readiness while generously extending hospitality to a stranger. This same word and its modifications are utilized in Romans 12:13 **("Share with the Lord's people who are in need. Practice hospitality")** and Hebrews 13:2 **("Do not neglect to show hospitality to strangers, for by so doing some people have entertained angels without knowing it")**.

Jo Sexton's words resounded in my head: "Who in your life is 'other'? Are you moving toward them or away from them?" It was a question to keep, to mindfully ponder about Parkridge. I collected verses to consider:

1 Peter 4:9 Offer hospitality to one another without grumbling.

Romans 12:13 Share with the Lord's people who are in need. Practice hospitality.

Romans 16:23 Gaius, whose hospitality I and the whole church here enjoy, sends you his greetings.

1 Timothy 5:10 …. and is well known for her good deeds, such as bringing up children, showing hospitality, washing the feet of the Lord's people, helping those in trouble and devoting herself to all kinds of good deeds.

3 John 1:8 We ought therefore to show hospitality to such people so that we may work together for the truth.

Each verse was like a connecting vertebrae in my backbone, strengthening me to show the hospitality God loves so dearly. I began to feel sturdy in my offerings to people: here are flowers for your room. Wipes for your glasses. A map of the city. Some local places we enjoy. A safe gas station. Join us for beef stew and fresh bread at 6. Red or white or water or beer or juice? Oatmeal or eggs or yogurt? Peaches or figs?

My former pastor, John Miles Wood, preached directly to me about this engaged love of community and hospitality:

"We are not saved individuals. It's not just *Jesus and me*.... We don't have an exclusively personal relationship with Jesus. We have an interpersonal relationship with Jesus.... And we can only be healthy and function and know of God's grace in its fullness and richness as we are plugged in deeply to other believers.... God is supposed to have a body here in the world, and it's you and me *together* being the church, being the body of Christ.... And the world should be able to look at how we love each other and how we lay down our lives for them and know who God is...."

Two of our guests changed us forever: Collins and Njalla. I might as well rename them fire and water. Collins wanted to bring people together; Njalla just wanted to be left alone. Collins wanted everything to converge and be open; Njalla wanted everything to diverge and be closed. Collins craved harmony; Njalla only knew cacophony. Collins wanted us to take hold; Njalla wanted us to let go. And in the middle of the months they were with us, Grant and I felt simultaneously lost and found ... and always on our knees.

Collins

At age 28, Collins appeared to the eye as a lanky, lush-lashed young man with a quick laugh and a quizzical gaze. Through friends, he found out about our open home and reached out to Handsome. He came to live with us for a few months and stayed two years.

Collins had diagnoses for anxiety, depression, and OCD (especially regarding cleanliness) in a house with an emotional, shedding dog, a snuggly cat, and two people who love to be in the dirt. I prayed for him literally every night as I watched rolling hairballs either accumulate under the chairs or get expelled from our fluffy cat. I tried to get to the tufts before he would notice them balling up under tables and behind doors. Not to mention our shoes, the mud, and our generally relaxed approach to housekeeping.

We divided up rotating chores on our kitchen chalk board. For a while, Collins took the kitchen, but it took him hours; he was slow, meticulous, and thorough, as one would expect. He changed to windows; that helped. He labored to do a perfect, precise job.

For a short season in January 2019, Collins' OCD, depression, and anxiety put their claws into him and tried to reduce him to nothingness. He felt like he was trying to climb his way out of a muddy pit and kept sliding back in, horrified that grime was in his hair and under his nails and in his nose and staining his clothes. Like he was hiding so many secrets, and each was the size of an elephant, and each weighed in heavy like the sea and sticky like honey, and each one had a darkness that masqueraded as light. Like he had never gotten all the odors off of him, especially in all those cracks and crevices that come with a human form. His efforts were never enough, no matter how much hot water he used, no matter how many bars of soap he used, no matter how often he cleaned his nose. The bath mat was perpetually new, never a footprint. Never a water droplet on his bathroom mirror. Bed always made. Even the dirty clothes in his hamper were neatly folded.

In a mall retail store, Collins folded and refolded, unstacked and re-stacked, sorted and placed, fluffed and pressed and starched till all the towels and the shirts and the rows of shoes and the skinny jeans met his painstaking, rigorous, relentless demand of perfection. His work colleagues began to distance from him.

His OCD life was stringent, burdensome, taxing, and critical. He had either chosen to leave or had been fired from numerous jobs because of his OCD. And the voices! The voices told him to do the same thing over and over and over again, never letting him rest, driving him to repeat behaviors until something within him broke.

It was heartbreaking, whether it was his incessant, extensive hot-water hand washing that left his hands chapped and red ...
or his extraordinarily long sniffs, nose twitches, and mouth movements ...
or his minute, painstaking photography edits ...
or his showers that we had to limit to eight minutes because they were taking all the hot water ....

He did not want to inconvenience me or Grant, so he sometimes began his hygiene routine at 4:00 in the morning in order to shower until the hot water ran out. That way by 5:15 AM, when Grant got in the shower, the hot water was refueling. With a 4 AM start, Collins could get to work by 9 AM.

But there was more to Collins than his OCD life.

Collins began to reveal more about his inner conflict and exhausting exertion to us. I think even speaking it — the action of getting the words outside of his own mouth and mind — was a relief. We started to list ways we're all a bit OCD: Handsome checking his zipper over and over, or his ears — any wax? Me, obsessing over the hairs that grow out of the mole by my lip till I pluck them.

Me, trying to 'reduce, reuse, recycle' *everything*. Me, loving that all my clothes hangers match.

Yet I saw God Himself in the particular, punctilious, precise specifications of temple worship in Leviticus. It brought up a question: How did Collins, in his OCD, reflect his good heavenly Father?

To Collins, the answer to the question was unfathomable, even ridiculous, like thinking you were in Caribbean blue water yet in reality you were really in a mudslide. Collins felt awful. Dirty. Self-loathing. What he did was never adequate or acceptable.

Yet in Scripture we were left with this verdict in the sanctified, consecrated courts of our omniscient God: In the screenplay of lives, *we are not enough*. Our good deeds are like filthy rags under the brilliant examination of the light of God's judgment (Isaiah 64:6). The Holy One has every right to reject us because *we are* dirty with sin, awful with harm, sick with independence and opposition.

I think it surprised Collins when we agreed with him that we are dirty before God: Wait, aren't you guys Christians? Aren't you going to talk me out of this? What to do? What disheartening news. How do we proceed? What do we do as we sit in our sin, totaled by transgression, filthy with fear, humbled by harm, full of flaws and faithlessness?

Ah, the good news about Jesus: His unexplainable, supernatural, even magical love saw us as we were and deliberately moved to make us clean. Mercy ... it was mercy that silenced the judgments, the accusations, the condemnation, with a finger across His lips. No more of that, now. All is made new. God made a way.

My beloved spoke and said to me,
   "Arise, my darling,
   my beautiful one, come with me.
You are altogether beautiful, my darling;
   there is no flaw in you." (Song of Songs 2:10, 4:7)

Jesus put God's truth into action. Synapses and sinews, fingertips and follicles, bones and balance, pupils and pituitary: He showed mercy to all of us, all who despaired at our inadequacy and reached out for rescue.

In Jesus, God committed to take our sin-stains and bleach them white.
In Jesus, God, like a tender mother, stooped to scrub the soot of opposition off of our faces, and we smiled back up at His gentle face, unpolluted and relieved and radiant.

154

Jesus freed us from our hard-heartedness and transformed us into malleable, breathing works of clay. Works of His art.

We came to Him blemished; we stay with Him white as snow, free and washed.

How does this happen? By Jesus' meticulous adherence to all God required. Not a jot of a requirement, not a tittle of a Scripture, failed. Held by Jesus, every word — *every* word — was fulfilled, even to the most bitter moment of His dying:

Later, knowing that everything had now been finished, and so that Scripture would be fulfilled, Jesus said, "I am thirsty." John 19:28.

Details, details. Just read Psalm 22: Jesus quoted it on the cross to make sure we read through it. He fulfilled every detail, every point. Could we describe that as obsessive?

This led our conversation to the cross: By Jesus' blood we were made clean and new. His blood was a disinfectant of the soul. Meet Collins, spotless. Meet me, meet you, with the clean glow of a person recreated. As we continue to live and fail and pray and try, daily He scrubs us. That was good news for all of us.

~elle~

Weeks passed. Even as I prayed that Collins could experience the beauty of the Lord, the refreshment of a clean soul, and the security of forgiveness, he had a full-blown panic attack.

From crouching in his room against the wall, hands over his head, crying and feeling frozen, somehow he made it downstairs where Grant was. Grant came and got me.

Collins sat in the chair looking like a bent elderly person, like a folded flower that had gone without water and was about to die. He told us how he was struggling: it was the cleaning, it was germs, it was the voices. His mind had gotten caught in a turbulent mental whirlpool and he was sucked down into it, unable to swim out of it by himself.

Grant is the first to say he has had zero training in mental health care, but he is also an observant guy, and blunt. I hugged Collins as he sobbed, thinking firm physical touch would help anchor and comfort him, but Grant simply steered the conversation away from where Collins was mentally stuck — and it worked. Collins's body began to ascend, just like a plant does when it straightens up out of dehydration.

I looked up OCD Residency programs, but Grant talked about basketball and photography. Pretty soon Collins's tears dried.

Remarkable.

At one point in the conversation, Grant looked directly into Collins's red eyes and simply said, "I accept you. Right in the middle of this, right now, I accept you. This is part of your journey, this thing, this OCD. I'm in it to walk it with you."

That was meaningful to Collins and so beautiful to me (I write this in tears). Acceptance has been one of the sweetest gifts Grant continues to give to me in our marriage: real, raw, sinner acceptance.

Four days later Collins texted 12 friends and family to meet at our house punctually at 8 PM. He placed a bottle of red wine on the counter. "It's the least I could do," he smiled wryly. "They're coming here for me." I loved his vulnerability and grateful heart.

We stuffed chairs of all sorts into the family room, Wiley weaving his way through the legs to find Grant and me. Collins sat on one side of the room; the chairs made an awkward circle so we could all hear and see him.

"Thanks for comin', um, I want to get started and let you know, like, that I've been really strugglin' lately with my OCD. Like, *really* struggling." He did not go into the minute details of scrubbing his hands till they were raw-red, or his constant worrying about his nose, but he did touch on his excessive cleaning, his long showers, and the voices. People sat respectfully, concern on their faces.

Collins turned to his friend and informal counselor David, asking him to explain more about OCD. Without hesitation, David stated with authority, "The root of OCD is trauma."

People pledged their support to Collins, and he thanked them for coming. He felt their love and was buoyed by warm and loving attention, honesty, and vulnerability. Just as he could look through his camera lens and find beauty in brokenness, he began to see it in himself and his community that evening.

Community is a word that has marked Collins' life. Collins, the one who will listen. Collins, who asks good questions. Collins, who wants to know you and be known by you. He taught us many things about *seeing*, about connecting people, and about appreciating the reality and beauty of brokenness. His photography was stunning, and he brought this keen, reflective, questioning eye into our home. How do we really *see* each other? How do we heal each other? How do we stay vulnerable?

156

When Collins lived with us he was also testing another part of who he was: a gatherer. He longed to see and live authentic faith, especially among artists, so several times he invited musicians and singers to our porch or foyer to have a worship night. People would stack in, sitting on the steps and singing while a keyboardist led us. Harmonies were sweet and strong, especially when singers came from a University of Tennessee group — so skilled, so tuned in to how to pace into the next musical movement.

Collins decided to host a Friendsgiving his last year with us, and it was classic Collins. "I don't know who's coming, but I've invited a ton of people. We'll just see who shows up!" Collins felt insecure about asking people to Friendsgiving, but at his first pass through Facebook, he had invited 158 people and was still adding (!) when we helped him understand that our house couldn't hold that many friends. He cut it down to 12.

At 29, his life training had many gaping holes. He did not know how to cook, but he wanted everyone to come for a meal. His parents asked him about the details of the Woodbine Friendsgiving: "So, Collins, are you going to cook the turkey?" This had not occurred to him, even though it was his party. His eyes grew wide when he relayed the story to me as he saw my head nodding "Yes." "Yes, Collins, this is your party. You cook the turkey. Everyone else is bringing side dishes." "Oh no," he exclaimed, body language backing up as rapidly as a cat realizing it's been spotted by a running dog. "That's a lot of pressure!" he said slowly. "What if it's dry?" His eyes expressed primordial fear. Beloved neighbor Tall George stepped in to cook the turkey.

We cleared counters, emptied out the fridge, made sure the garbage and recycling cans were empty, and then … I rested, while Collins fretted. He stayed on his phone constantly, unsure whether anyone would show up.

We lit the candles, watched the clock, and … friends came! Scrumptious dishes from many traditions filled up the counter spaces. It felt like Revelation 7:9, every nation, every tribe, every tongue, every type of food. Spaghetti salad, two macaroni and cheeses (heaven!), fruit, potato salad, roasted broccoli and carrots, green beans made with bacon, squash casserole, mashed potatoes, other foreign dishes I could not name … a carb-lovers dream! Tall George's turkey was moist and tender, and his gravy was the best stuff we'd ever tasted. He'd never done it before, but he sprinkled in flour, added some onion scraps, a few leftover carrots, some of the herbs that were still on the counter … perfection! We stirred in the leftover turkey and ate it for dinner for the next two days. Lemon cookies and snickerdoodles topped off the meal.

When we all crammed toward the kitchen, overflowing into the family room and dining room, it was time to pray. I looked at Grant, Grant looked at Collins, and

Collins stammered, "It's me? Well, okay." And he blessed the gathering and our food.

When the house was filled with people — about 30 came — it was lovely. The UT worship band came and had a good meal; they were exhausted from doing so many performances. Miz Janet came from next door and waved her way through a few worship songs. A new neighbor, Genevieve, came over and happily formed new connections.

Collins cued everyone to move from dinner to singing; later, he made the call to close with a final song. Look at our Collins lead!

~elles

Collins and his girlfriend came to **DropBy Church** before they moved to Waco. was a simple, back porch gathering with several couples from our neighborhood during the initial year and a half of COVID-19. It was a small, sweet haven of rest for the de-churched who wanted to pursue deeper life fueled by the Holy Spirit. People would walk over on Sundays at 5 PM to share a meal and conversation. We shared stories of work, what God was doing, what we were reading, and how we were feeling about life, the world, the nation, racism, Parkridge, COVID-19, and anything else that was brewing. The children would check to see if there were any eggs in the coop or try to pet the hens (which the hens never once allowed). The littles played with puzzles or fidgeted as the adults talked. We started to know each other well, able to ask about family members by name, keeping histories and stories in mind while listening to each other. Usually there was an informal transition to discussion of Scripture, readings, or whatever the Holy Spirit was prompting within. There was no specified leader or teacher, although someone always seemed to lead naturally. There was no set agenda, yet the wisdom of the Spirit always moved us. It was "unforced rhythms of grace" (see Eugene Peterson's translation of Matthew 11:28) in a simple setting of low stress. Wear your jeans. Bring the kids and a side salad. Don't expect us to have all the answers.

I always loved to see what we would eat at DropBy Church. Typically I would have a main course and a side, and everyone else would add in. It was always such a feast — something to celebrate. In the heat of 2021's summer, we provided a choice of three small cold salads, and that was all we had. But by the time we ate, there was sliced cantaloupe on the table, a rosy pile of fresh strawberries, golden-toasted-buttered bread, and two desserts. We had cold wine, water, and peach slushies with gingerale. It was glorious, a picture of the heavenly feast when we all sit down together with Jesus to celebrate. There was always enough.

We found that we were surrounded by people who had left the church but had not left faith in Jesus. At one point, we were all lamenting the direction of institutional church, "big" church. I asked Collins what he was thinking.

"To be honest, I'm done. After my experiences with institutional church, I'm just done. I don't see it as trustworthy. There's behind-the-scenes changes, there's no transparency. It doesn't feel honest to me. I just don't want to be there. I'd rather be here at a meal with friends and talk about things that matter in a context of being known." That sounded like the house churches of Acts to me. It wasn't that Collins was done with God; not at all. I heard that from so many of the people around the table that day. They loved God; they didn't trust the church. Lord, have mercy on us, we just want to find You.

When our oldest contributors spoke, we listened attentively. Tammie wove stories, images, and musings into profound non-religious Christian truths. Glen was wise, circumspect, and gentle, slim as a reed and a loving servant to his wife. He was showing the younger couples how to be married well, and a good thing, too: We had two weddings and one "get together" among us.

We began missing Communion, so someone brought red wine and I made challah bread. If you've never done this, picture in your mind one of those golden loaves shining from an egg wash, woven together with six strands. My loaves were never perfect, but that was typical of DropBy, Woodbine, and Parkridge. We were weaving our lives together in a messy, friendly, loving way. It was holy and sacramental, a taste of the divine in the center of the ordinary.

At DropBy Church, there was no denominational fighting, no stiff forms to follow, no hierarchy, no judgment of gifting. It was friends coming together to talk through what it meant to live by faith.

But it was also goofy. There were times when the awkward silence went beyond awkward. (My husband can stand *minutes* of such silence.) Then there was the night we drank all the red wine we had intended for Communion, so we brought out the bourbon and the cranberry juice instead. There were times when we tried to sing, but that didn't go well — at all.

Our group, however awkwardly authentic, was on the move. One biracial couple moved to Miami and is currently helping Haitian refugees. Another of our biracial couples moved to Waco to work with Magnolia magazine. Another couple had to frequently isolate due to health concerns and COVID. We found ourselves wondering how to best proceed. After some discussion, in the cool fall of '21, we wrapped up DropBy and began visiting other local, small churches.

Over time, our relationship with Collins evolved. We began to think it would be better for him to learn to manage his own household, so at the two-year mark, Collins moved to his own house a street over and several blocks down. We packed him a care box of paper towels, various cleaners, toilet paper, and a few favorite foods. He left, stronger and loved.

I wish we could have extolled the leaving of our next guest as joyfully, but the Woodbine glacier smashed and crushed too cataclysmically for celebration.

With Collins: "Go get 'em!"
With Njalla: "What the hell just happened?"

Njalla

It was my birthday, October 18, 2018, and apparently my gift from God was a 23-year-old homeless girl named Njalla.

One afternoon I was working beside Britton, a bearded, burly man who works with University of Tennessee faculty, when he received a call from the Director of the Multicultural Center. There was a girl, a student, who had been living in her car at a truck stop (so she could use the showers) since July. *July!* Did he know anyone who could house her? He whispered this information to me in the coffee shop where we were working. The answer was easy: She could take our extra room and be there this evening. Safe, in a *bed*. I felt the Mama Bear within me rise up: No girl was going to be sleeping in a car on my watch when there was an extra bed in my house. Just let me change the pillow case with all the cat hair on it.

I began to pray. "God, what is her mind like after living in her car for months? Will she be fearful?" I sensed Him alerting me to "PTSD," post-traumatic stress syndrome. Of course. But what were her stressors? I hoped that over time, she would let me know.

The UT lady also said her mother had died about one year ago; that Njalla was a senior at UT. Njalla's work shift (at a gas station) went till 12:30 AM, so she would arrive at our house around 1 AM. Wow. Then she had class all day. Wow again. She was obviously carrying so much weight in her young life.

But Njalla never made it to our house. This brown girl was speeding and got pulled over by a white policeman, automatically a tense situation at this time in the United States. He was kind but ticketed her for speeding and driving with a suspended license. He took her license away.

Transportation for the marginalized is *epic*. Without a way to get to a job, to earn, they are quickly banished to the streets. No license? This was major.

She was near the truck stop where she had been spending her nights, so she stayed there instead of our home. It made me angry that the policeman did not follow her to my house and get her safely to Woodbine, where she could then make appropriate decisions about her driving situation. Basically he left her in a situation in which she would *have* to break the law.

When Njalla arrived, she was nervous, understandably. She wept as she told me the story of her mom's battle with breast cancer; of the tensions in their relationship; of the decision left to her to remove all life support. Such pressure on a young person! She felt guilt and shame, as if she had personally killed her mother.

She said she was "slow." I didn't believe her, and I have good instincts about such things. After listening, I concluded she had been in survival mode for years and had not been able to be intellectually dextrous. Because her circumstances were tumultuous and tenuous, I think it was just enough to make it through the day.

I prayed she felt safe.
I prayed she could feel God's love through us, though I didn't think she knew much about Him.
I prayed she could get to a point of soul rest so she could heal. There was no "*post-*" to her PTSD.

Offended, November 1, 2018

It didn't take long for difficulties to surface. Just two weeks in I realized I'd offended Njalla. Dang. When I had arrived home, I asked her about school: Did she go today? No. But she did go to Disability Services and got some accommodations to fit her situation; good news for her.

Then she brought up her dad, that he had called and wanted to travel to Knoxville for Thanksgiving weekend for a visit. Njalla had strong suspicion of his motives: She thought he was just needing money and she didn't want him to come. I called out her assumptions, and that ended in her getting out of her chair and leaving the room, right in the middle of the conversation, literally mid-sentence. As she slid past me, I said, "Wait, are we done?" "Yeah, sorry," she said softly, and she was gone, first to her room, then out the door. Sigh.

Handsome said I pressed too hard, that this was a time for compassion, not teaching. Ugh.

I texted her later, apologizing for upsetting her. She texted back, saying she just needed to cry. Oh, precious woman. I prayed for mending: her heart, our relationship, whatever the truth was about her dad. She gave me another chance, and we texted about school. As Njalla stabilized, she realized how far behind she was academically and doubted her ability to pass her classes. I made some suggestions, but she identified her greatest need: lack of structure. She was working, attending classes, and needed restorative sleep; she was struggling with all three scenarios. How could she organize her waking hours?

～ₐₗₗₑₛ

Plump tears ran down her cheeks as she related some of her story to us, and then linked her choices and reactions back to trauma. There was so much that was unsettled in her life.

She was depressed.
She was not taking her medicine.
She had no friends.
She did not like the way she looked: her hair was not done, her eyebrows were bushy, she had gained a lot of weight. When she showed us a picture of what she looked like two years ago, I never would have known it was Njalla. There was light in her countenance, and I had not seen that light … yet.
At school, Njalla was taking the same classes she took when she pulled her mom off life support.

She wanted to keep her mom's vehicle for sentimental reasons and needed a place to park it, but couldn't pay anything for storage. She missed a payment of her storage unit in Memphis … and then another … and the owners were going to put her stuff out for sale. That broke her heart. We tried to release some of her stress by paying several months rent for her unit.

Njalla was obviously astute but couldn't even reach that part of her brain at that time. There was a poet in there, waiting to blaze. There was a passionate voice about social justice issues waiting to speak out. I wished she was not in school and could simply, daily, focus on her mental and emotional health.

She was suspicious around Collins. At one time, Collins closed and locked the front door, not realizing Njalla had briefly stepped out to her car. She was furious, thought it was intentional and racist, and got very bitter. I could imagine that happening elsewhere, but Collins was a meek man — gentle, kind, unassuming. Her accusations didn't fit. A palpable tension began to grow in the house.

She cooked a massive meal for us, taking an entire day to shop and cook. We helped out with paying for groceries so she could "do it right," following her grandmother's recipes. It was really spectacular. The entire kitchen was her domain, and I saw an energy flame up that I had only imagined within her. It was beautiful. She moved like a dancer, tapping spoons on pots here, gracefully removing lids there, twirling from the kitchen island to the counter to the sink, bowing to taste and sample. Scents of creole and oil filled the bottom floor. We were transported back two generations through fried chicken, jambalaya, and side dishes galore. I was scared of some of her hot spices; even just smelling the orange-red shakers made my nose run.

When we all came into the kitchen, we blessed the food, blessed Njalla, and had the best fried chicken ever. Ever. But, curiously, nothing was good enough for her. She pushed back from her seat with a full plate and disgust on her face. Too hot, too mild; "it's just not right." Clearly this was part of the inner work that was ahead for her; the food was authentic and scrumptious, but in her mouth, it was gravel. I prayed for her as it became more and more clear that she had a very difficult road ahead of her. Mental health is such an important, primary pursuit.

Three weeks after moving in, Njalla moved out. Grant listened to my cracking voice, shocked.

"It's Njalla. She's leaving. I don't understand why, and I'm broken-hearted."

Oh, I was so sad. Njalla politely informed me via text that "today was her last day with us." She would not answer my call, but would respond to my texts. When I asked her why she was leaving, she wrote, "Just don't think I'm a good fit here." I was deeply grieved.

She left so kindly: returned her key, stripped her sheets and put them in the washing machine, took down her trash. But she lashed out verbally at Collins, intentionally hurting his feelings.

I offered her the names of two other women with whom she could stay, but she declined. It hurt to realize that Njalla would rather be in her car, alone, than with us in our house. Sigh. My burgeoning philoxenia had not gone well with Njalla. Being alone felt safer for her; interactions with people brought up hurt or caused new injury, so how to create an impervious environment? Control it all by staying in the car. Alone.

But I was convinced that isolation was detrimental to Njalla. I could hear therapist Marla DeLong in my head: "We are wounded in community, and we are healed in community." While to her the world outside of her car seemed perilous and poisonous and formidable, disengaging could also have adverse affects, especially on her mental health.

We had so many thoughts:
We (I) pushed too hard.
We (I) asked too much of her.
We (I) overwhelmed her with "our kind of love" which involves forward motion, conversation, engagement, and expectations.

163

We should've left her alone. Well, no, we shouldn't've.
We should've … what?

Should our home be a bed and kitchen, solely? No real relationship? Neither of us were comfortable with that. I believe we are made to love and be loved and that God can direct us to love if we will listen to Him. I think we didn't know enough about how to be with people who have been through the types of trauma Njalla had been through. And I don't think I listened well to the Holy Spirit; I think I relied on my own training and past experience, my own expectations. I thought my motherly, kind encouragement of her would be enough, and I was completely wrong.

So I missed her. I felt like I failed her. She was my birthday gift, the best kind — a person.

I heard Hallerin Hilton Hill tell a story. In his address, he explained that emeralds are found deep in the earth and take great time, energy, and resources to unearth; you have to move a lot of dirt to get to them. They are lovely, to be sure, even in their raw state, but when they are given form and facet, they become radiant, luminous, prized.

Njalla was an emerald. My prayer became that in the right time, in the right way, someone would reveal the glory in her, the radiant jewel she was, that she would one day dazzle the world with her thoughtful theories about racism, homelessness, and womanhood.

~elles~

Njalla and I kept texting, but she kept her distance.

Four months after she had left us, she had decided that she had been wrong about Collins and needed to apologize to him. She was as nervous as an antelope that smelled a leopard on the breeze. Eyes alert, neck staring to see her opponent, fear and adrenaline on the rise. Humility? Apology? Oh, anything but that! This was an extremely uncomfortable situation for her; apologies were not part of her family culture.

Njalla was ready to face Collins to apologize for her rude comments to him when she left our house. 10:30 AM was their talk time. When she arrived, we cleared the room so they could talk. After a long while, I went in to see if they were verbally stuck, and it seemed they were.

She was not connecting at all with Collins' feelings. He was being honest — such a risk and an accomplishment for him, such a miss for her. I stepped in as a processing mediator.

Shame caused tears to run down Njalla's cheeks. She did not see herself as worthy of love, a happy home, of friendship. When we said, "Njalla, you are forgiven and loved and welcome here," the voices in her head countered with, "They're playing you right now. Don't believe them. This is not true. You're not worthy of forgiveness."

Collins picked up on this easily. "I know about those voices. You've got to quiet them by telling yourself the truth. You know about my OCD and anxiety, right?" What growth, what vulnerability! Go Collins! Njalla nodded and kept listening.

We concluded about an hour later. She was agreeable to visiting with us a bit more, but not quite ready to move back in. Njalla carried "home" (car) a paper with several truths written in bold letters:

You are worthy of love
You are worthy of a good home
You are worthy of peace
The Truth will set you free
Fight to live your life in the truth, not the lies
You will not live according to paranoid thoughts; you will live in the truth
Forgive others and forgive yourself
Give yourself grace
Keep battling
We love you!

Chapter Ten: Moves, Summer 2019

Dream: the Committed

AS I FELL ASLEEP THAT NIGHT, I drifted into a dream: I was on my back porch. I was meeting with over a dozen young men and women at night, and we had a Bible open on the floor. Cross-legged, we were gathered around it, about three concentric circles of us, seated and kneeling until broad-shouldered young men were standing at the edge of light, angling forward to see the Word. My hand was on the old Bible — my wrinkled, spotted hand, soil staining my nails. There were candles lighting up the Scriptures and small candles here and there so people could see, but their faces weren't strongly illuminated. I spoke, and they listened intently.

"As Christians we believe God is our comforter, healer, provider, shepherd, and hope, a consuming fire. He feels; He is the author of emotion and intellect and decision and spirit and soul and body and mind. He is always previous, always good, always opposes evil. We can agree on this, can't we? It's all there, in Scripture, no tricks, no contortions."

The small crowd "mmmm-hmmm'd" and I continued.

"God calls *all* of His followers to *follow* Him. This call isn't just for the few: Do you see it? Search the Scriptures and it's there; look at Jesus' life and it's there. *God* is your Lord, not your wealth, your properties, your job, your family, your safety, your school system, or your traditions. When He tells you to go, what do you say? 'Yes, Sir.' Even if it feels like we're leaving beauty in order to embrace ashes, the exact opposite of what He promises in Isaiah 61:3, we do it. *Maybe our concept of what beauty is needs to change.* Maybe He's going to put us in the middle of ashes in order to bring beauty to a place and a people. Jesus did it: He left the beauty of Heaven to embrace the ashes of people, sin, and earth, and He brought beauty here.

"Biblical *shalom* is the concept of total wellness, a fullness of life physically, economically, and spiritually, lived in healthy community. God is held in the highest esteem; all people are regarded with the celebration and integrity due to one created in His image. Resources are available, not cut off or limited by skin color or class. People share, extend a hand, celebrate together. Power

166

differentials are gone. Race is carefully and gently considered, as are culture and ethnicity, because history and community matter; but race is not a definer of treatment, class, or opportunity. Here's my question to you: What would it look like for you to *live shalom* in your neighborhood? What sacrifices would it take? Are you willing? Are you ready?"

Everyone earnestly conferred, maybe even for hours, then knelt to pray. As they began to sing spontaneously, Heaven opened above our tin roof, and I saw a group of serious angelic warriors observing the group. In a massive tome, one of the angels drew a lengthy feather pen and wrote down who was present, and how they honored the Lord and His sacrificial love. (I was the only one who saw the angels.) Then the young people quietly left, commissioned by their own worship. As they went to the streets, warrior angels flew above them, and there was just enough light for them to know how to take their next step. A long, white pennaceous feather settled on the sidewalk in front of my house.

I wept. I wept for the beauty of their hearts, for the protection of the angels, for the kindness of God as He honored the young people. I wept because I knew some would die for their faith: not abandoned by God, but rather, determined by Him, a holy and yielded death that would change a culture and rattle the darkness. I knew some would willingly suffer, from economic disadvantage to the loss of children. I wept until I could weep no more, and then I sang an exhausted song of love to my sovereign Father. I sang softly at first, then fiercely, my heart swelling with belief and surrender. And the spirits of the dead-but-living-in-Christ cheered me — that great cloud of witnesses from Hebrews 11 — and I found peace.

"The sacrifice is worth it! Worthy is the Lamb! Our God's love is real, more real than they will ever know on earth. To live is Christ, and to die is gain. Do not be afraid, Suzanne. Shhhh, be still. Be refreshed, and sleep."

And I did.

Our "Project", July 2019

"How's your project going in East Knoxville?"

I must have looked puzzled. The well-meaning, bright blond, highly educated doctor was engaging me in conversation at a receiving of friends.

"You know, with the kids and everything?"
I clued in.

"It's not really a project, it's more, *our life*. We're so glad to be there, it's where we want to be. Our relationships with the kids are doing really well but we have lots of challenges."

Grant and I had begun to notice that some people wanted to categorize our move in a certain way: "It's mission work." "That project." "Your ministry." They mentally separated us from my neighbors — *those* people." "*That* part of town." Ugh: The implication of favoritism was *you're a better person going to lesser people*. But they are *my* community, and I see their humanity; they are not my *project*. Because words can get in the way, we needed to put words around this.

When we got in the car, Grant cringed: "*Project?* How unrelational! People are not projects! We are not above them, like WestKnox royals who feel a social obligation to do good things — *noblesse oblige*. It's the same thing with the word 'ministry', like someone is above me and has all the answers," he opined. "It's really an upsetting way to talk about Woodbine. This is local *living*, not 'local ministry' or 'home missions'. It's just loving our neighbor. It is just living here and knowing our block."

One evening I was a speaker at a women's conference on prayer. The woman who introduced me did not know me personally, and it showed in her introduction of me: "Suzanne Standing has heard the call of God and moved where no one else will go — you know, over in *that* part of Knoxville with people who are *different*, where it's *difficult*." She paused. "No one else wants to go there," she said beaming at me, "but Suzanne *lives* there. And she gives God all the glory."

I was speechless. I had no idea how to respond to that. She made me sound like a hero when all we were doing was loving our neighbors, which all Christians are supposed to do wherever they live. And she made my neighbors sound awful, like they were living on the streets and had no sense of God or beauty or morals or empowerment. I squirmed. How many times had Miz Janet or Rev Rena or the children ministered to me? These were not one-sided pseudo-relationships; these were friendships, these were my sisters in Christ. Rev Rena encouraged me to become a stronger, more informed ambassador for the love of God in a hurting world, a soldier for justice, and more aware of historical black-white dynamics. She would quote Martin Luther King: "Injustice anywhere is a threat to justice everywhere. We are caught in an inescapable network of mutuality, tied in a single garment of destiny. Whatever affects one directly, affects all indirectly." My life was being woven into the tapestry of my street by God's own hand.

We are here to love our neighbor in the Name of Jesus. To serve our neighbors and 'hood with love and grace and truth … that is our entire hope. We needed to figure out how to talk about our move to East Knoxville in such a way that the privileged class could comprehend our motives: a loving approach as opposed to thinking we have all the answers and can 'fix' our neighbors or neighborhood.

We came here as learners. We came with the meekness we saw in Jesus' demeanor with the poor and the repentant, and the boldness we saw in His demeanor with the upper class religious folk. We have so much to learn about class, race, dignity, drugs, American history, welfare, mass incarceration, white supremacy, and alternative family systems. The only 'fix' we know is relationship with Jesus and His people.

So we open our door to the stranger. We listen to our black and brown and gay and straight and white and poor and financially stable and unstable neighbors. We bake cookies and share dinners and color with children and feed chickens and offer lots of cold water at the basketball goal. We are present. As I look at this life, perhaps a better way to look at it is *we* are *their* project. They are our teachers, we the students. We're both taking risks to be friends. We're both trying to learn each others' languages and cultures.

We reached one conclusion within the first year of living on Woodbine: If people want to change a neighborhood, they need to live in that neighborhood. Real relationship was primary.

Bob Lupton agreed in his book *Toxic Charity*. So did Gregory Boyle in *Tattoos on the Heart* and Jonathan Wilson-Hartgrove in *Strangers at My Door.* Mother Teresa too: Go live with the poor. Pay attention to the one, the one, the one, not the masses. Bono too: God is with the poor.

As I spoke at churches and met with women I began to ask,
Are you bored with your faith or experience with God? Go live with the poor.
Are you wondering where He is, where He is at work? Go be with the poor.
Are you longing for His joy? Go be with the poor.
Are you looking for Jesus? Go be with the poor.

God cares deeply about justice (Hebrew, *mishpat*) and the care of the poor. He watches; He knows who is advocating for the poor and who is consuming them. Watch *thebibleproject.com*'s insightful illustration of justice. It is visually profound and intellectually impactful.

I hope my neighbors can see our intentions are good and our love is real;
that we don't look at them as projects, but as people to know and love and understand and hear;
that we delight in them (most of the time, ha!) and are glad we're all here, together;
that we're not here because we're heroes or weirdos;

that we want to be good influences, strong reconcilers, and stable voices; that we choose them because Jesus said to love, give, clothe, feed, visit, tend, and care. He did it. So can we, through His strength and love.

~elles

Sweet Reys was at our house daily lately, and she was hungry.

"What does your Mama do when you tell her you're hungry?"
"She just say, 'I ain't got no money.'"
"Is there food in the house?"
"Yeah."
"Do you or your sisters make your own meals?"
"Not really."
We cooked as we continued our conversation.

Cinco joined us. We turned our attention to creating a healthy salad. She chopped colorful peppers while I chopped up radishes. Collins and Handsome came into the kitchen and told us of their day's adventures.

"Grant, I dare you to take a bite of that jalapeño pepper," she giggled. Reys had a strong streak of playful mischief that showed her dimples.

"You do it!" he responded, reading her mind. That was the invitation she was looking for: a cup full of attention, a measure of intrigue, and the spice of crazy drew Reys in. "Okay."

She held the pepper up to her mouth and paused, looking at everyone looking at her. She loved it; more giggles. She put her teeth on the pepper, closed her eyes ... and couldn't do it. Then could. Then couldn't. Finally she did.

"It's fine, it's not hot," she considered. Then, an explosion. "Oh my gosh, oh oh **OH**," she erupted, and her waving hand flew to her mouth, and she ran to the trash can, unceremonially ejecting all of the pepper into the garbage. "Water, water! Milk! Help!" she demanded, half laughing, half crying.

Later, as Reys and I were about to serve dinner, I asked her about school. "I hate school," she replied glumly.
"What?! It's just the third full week of classes, and last week you loved it. What happened?"
"I dunno. I don' even know if I will go tomorrow. No one can get me there."
"Wait, Reys, I thought you were taking the bus."
"No one will walk me to the bus stop."
"I can. What time?"
"6:40."
"So early!"

170

"Yep."

"Do you eat breakfast before the bus?"

"No, my Mama usually wakes me up at 6:15 or 6:20."

"Wow, so you literally roll out of bed, brush your teeth, and get out the door for the bus stop."

"Yep."

We talked about the virtues of a good breakfast as we populated the dining table. "I don't wanna eat what they serve at school. It nasty," she proved with a wrinkled nose.

I thought about a conversation I'd had with Njalla. She was concerned about the safety of the girls on the street. "The bad shit happens when kids move around a lot. Somebody starts messin', and then it can get bad. When they Mamas and Daddys and Aunties aren't watchin', people take advantage." Clearly she was speaking from either her own experience or the word of friends. While I was glad to see her feel affinity for the girls, the look on her face chilled me to the bone.

Njalla: Meetings at KLF

Two days later, I piled in quarter after quarter, feeding the parking meter. It was almost time, and I was hopeful: Njalla and I were meeting with Chris, director of Knoxville Leadership Foundation. He has a heart for the homeless, has exceptional knowledge about nonprofits in the city, and is well-connected. I hoped he could give us some direction.

Njalla had ideas about how to help the homeless, since she had been homeless for about a year. For example, laundry: Njalla needed to have laundry done so she could look and smell presentable for work, but there were inherent challenges for a homeless person in being clean and wearing clean clothes.

When she got out of her car, I could tell she was nervous. "Do I smell alright?" she queried, leaning into me as she passed by. "Absolutely fine," I assured her. Her relief was visible.

The meeting with Chris was really about two things: networking and affirming Njalla. Chris told us to connect with Gina at Compassion Coalition, and the two directors/case workers at Flenniken Landing, a converted school that offers permanent housing to the formerly homeless. Chris encouraged Njalla so tenderly; I was amazed at his gentle kindness in his choice of words and his facial expressions. This white, powerful, male authority figure was genuinely lifting up this searching, black, homeless woman.

Calendars opened, appointments made.

We had to celebrate, of course! We went to Cru Bistro, one of our absolute favorite places on Gay Street, and toasted to Njalla's future. She let me know her birthday was just days away, so we even got dessert.

Njalla was back!

～ⅇⅇⅇ～

It did not take long for Collins and Njalla to have an altercation. They are yin and yang, opposites that could bring life or death to each other. This time was death.

She was overly tough, he was overly tender;
She tended to be aggressive with him, he tended to be passive with her;
She burned over him, he crumbled before her.
She made assumptions that damned and condemned him, he did not stand up and rest confidently in the truth.
They both operated out of their trauma.

She wanted to simply live in the same house and not interact, but that was not how we live in community. We had a household meeting; I had the feeling this would not be the last one.

Njalla had cast the enemy suit on Collins, and he did not deserve it. My prayer was that in time, she would lower her own prejudices and trauma-guard and see him for who he was. The thrust of our household meeting was how to live in community. This was difficult without trust, and Njalla flat-out stated that she did not trust Collins or Grant. Wow. Two of the most trustworthy, gentle men in the world were here with her, and she could not see their virtue. *Yet*. I didn't know what her man-wounds were, but perhaps in time she would tell me more about her life. This was a time for patience, steady love, and hope.

That was easier for me to say than for Collins to live. As she sat on her couch accusing him of racism and meanness, his tall frame literally shrank as his head bowed down low. "All I can say is, I didn't do that and I don't think that." He could barely get out the words. They were soft as a whisper, a feather floating on the hurricane force of her fury.

Handsome and I were consistent with Njalla: "That is not Collins' character. You are misreading him. This is a misunderstanding." But there was absolutely zero grace or kindness from Njalla; she was defending her territory and trusted only herself, her thoughts, and her feelings. It was, in a way, frightening.

～ⅇⅇⅇ～

I observed that the darkness of trauma coupled with the complexity of homelessness was like a steep climb. I was asking Njalla to put in the effort,

172

make the time, and have vision for something greater for her life. The climb out was difficult but there was a worthy summit in her future. I believed in her; didn't that make it easier for her to believe in herself? Flat out, no.

Step by step, Njalla's inner dialogue, unlike mine, sounded like this: "I'm getting somewhere … she says I am, anyway … but where? What the hell am I doing? This climb is not worth the energy. I feel like I'm dying. The pain is loud and keeps shouting, STOP. It's easier to give up than go on. I just want to be alone. I look terrible. I'm not worthy to climb.

"Watch your step, girl. Don't do something wrong and fail. Then what would happen to you? You can't go to the hospital. No one cares about you. You're on your own. You can't pay for it.
You think you're so important, trying to work on yourself. Here, take this pill and wash it down with something that stings. That'll remind you that you are alive."

And I? I was repeating, "Do not reduce someone to their worst moments." The mountain of mental health seemed higher and more technically demanding than Everest.

But then there would be an encouraging vista on the trail, and I would see life in her eyes again.
After the low of the unresolved conflict with Collins, she had a high — a glimpse, an encouragement. February 22, 2019, was a monumental day for Njalla.

We both parked on the street, fed the meters and tried to skip puddles so we would not mess up our "nice" shoes. I could tell by the way Njalla's smile flickered on and off her face quickly that she was nervous. She had ironed her good blouse and looked lovely.

She breezed by me and turned slightly, then leaned close and whispered, "Do I smell okay?"

Before meeting Njalla, I did not realize what an issue smells were for a homeless woman. But think about it: *that* time of the month, oh my. Unpredictable shower availability. Products for nappy hair. And in hot weather, the constant sweating. Normal body odors added one more layer to Njalla's feelings of insecurity about her femininity, worth, and beauty.

As people came and went, we waited for the meeting in a hallway.

First we met with Gina. What a remarkable woman! She explained the Compassion Coalition to us. Njalla was wondering if there were any jobs

173

available there, but as she listened, she became more interested in a program called "Getting Ahead in a Just Gettin' By World." Njalla decided to apply.

Then we met with the two directors of Flenniken Landing, Trey and Del. Trey captured more of Njalla's attention (he too had been homeless). After the meeting, Njalla and I drove past Flenniken Landing to see it for ourselves. It was lovely! The thought of living in an encouraging community was so appealing to Njalla … perhaps she could work there? Cook for everyone? Live there eventually too?

But as the day matured into night, she began back-pedaling and became much more reserved and fearful about it. She never inquired about Flenniken. In fact, her trajectory turned south, and fast.

~~~~

It was leap year, and on February 29th I came home after a long day of intense work to find Njalla in her room, a little smiley and watching a movie. There was a tenderness to her, a softness. She even let me turn on her light and sit on the edge of her bed.

Then I saw the signs: the elongated paper bag … the cork tinged with red on one end lying beside her bed. And oh, some red wine stains on the comforter.

She was drunk.

Why? Four years ago, Njalla's grandmother died on February 29. All Njalla wanted to do was to medicate, to forget, to continue on her movie roll. But when I walked in, the glow from the screen on her phone lit her face; she wasn't even paying attention to the film.

"I'm sorry," she said, smiling shyly, realizing I comprehended her state.

The next day Njalla wanted to know if the wine above the fridge was off-limits. That was a yes.

I had given her a $20 bill so she could get black electrical tape to temporarily fix the sagging front of her car … did she buy the Swisher Sweets and wine with the rest? Where was my change? I wrestled: The righteous judge in me wanted to say, "Hey! I worked hard for that money and gave it to you in good faith, and you're getting drunk on it? Seriously?" The compassionate forgiven sinner in me just wanted to hug her and tell her it would be alright and I knew she was sad and tomorrow was a new day.

174

The Bible says, "Mercy triumphs over judgment" (James 2:13). I landed there: Mercy is what I want too, when I'm falling apart, so that was what I extended to Njalla. "Do not reduce someone to their worst moments." Yes.

~~~~

God gave me an analogy for trauma … it felt deep and profound and yes, disturbing.

Picture a lovely orange. In your mind, hold it in your hands. This orange represents your heart.

Now switch on your intellectual imagination. Divide trauma into two categories, A and B. Type A traumas are things like not being cherished or treasured; not being allowed to develop and face difficult things; not being dearly loved and known. Type B traumas are all-out abuse and neglect, abandonment and harm.

During childhood, depending on your family and culture of origin, you may experience both types of traumas. As a child, you are a keen observer, but do not necessarily know how to interpret and judge what you see. I am no expert, but I think Njalla experienced both A and B.

Back to the orange: As you experience trauma, you naturally protect your heart. In imagining our analogy, you might illustrate this by wrapping up the orange in a paper towel; but that's not enough. It feels too thin when the traumas continue. You try a thicker paper bag, brown and sturdy, and wrap it around your heart. The walls and protections help you feel better.

But type B traumas are violent in nature, and when they come, they are sharp and wound viscerally. Picture a knife jabbing into your orange, your heart; this is type B trauma. Oh, the pain! The shock! The fear, the disbelief, the confusion! And if the trauma is by close family or sexual in nature, when that knife rips through the thick bag, the paper towel, and the skin of the orange, the perpetrator gives it a twist. And, horror of horrors, they walk away, appetite sated, while you are left in shambles, shredded.

Then the bewilderment of life continuing to move forward hits. You still have to function. Go to school, go to work, eat, try to sleep. How? You're in pieces, crushed and bruised and no longer whole and dripping with trauma. So you grab a baggie, put your heart together as much as you can, and zip it tight. There, you're contained and can function without leaking all over people and work and society. But you feel unsafe, so perhaps a storage container would be better. The isolation feels better. You can breathe again; no one can hurt you in there.

But just as we were wounded in relationship, we must be healed in relationship. It is not human to be completely alone, or even completely safe. God's first

175

intervention into His creation was when He saw that Adam was alone (Genesis 2). Relationships require risk and vulnerability. People can live for decades locked away, full of fear and hidden rage. But that orange will decay.

This is where Jesus' promise comes in: He will give us a new heart. He will reshape our damaged, pained hearts into something beautiful — He will bring beauty from ashes.

He will create life where there was death,
hope where there was none,
joy where there was no prospect.
He alone can do this.

In early March, I realized I needed to have an intervention with myself. I was making myself crazy.

When Njalla never came out of her room except to smoke or go grab booze …
When Njalla was getting drunk at night in her room or drinking to while away the day …
When Njalla wouldn't answer a knock on her door …
When Njalla kept to herself in the darkness of her room, curtains closed …
When Njalla left dishes in the sink …
When Njalla didn't clean off the stovetop …
When Njalla changed the house temperature …
When Njalla didn't do anything around the house to help even though she was there all day …
When Njalla was surly …
When Njalla's movie was really loud in her room (which was beside ours) …
When Njalla left lights on and the tv on …
When Njalla asked for money …

… I was to love sacrificially. That was my call. That was my highest priority with her. *But what did love look like?* Patience. Conversation. Step-by-step accountability. Another knock at her door. Another invitation into the light. Patient understanding. Higher standards communicated kindly.

I wrote,
God, I'm so unlike You. I'm so impatient. I want her to be better NOW, stronger NOW, less prejudiced NOW, wiser and kinder and more helpful NOW. Sigh. I've got to change. I can't point the finger at her all the time; some of this is about me.

You're patient with me, and generous with me, and kind with me even as You convict me of sin,

176

even as You raise the standards of my life toward holiness and love.
I have so far to go. Especially today. Help. Amen."

~ellee~

Home from work, I knocked on her door, entered her room, and sat down on the corner of her bed. Njalla was burrowed under her blanket, bonnet on, movie blaring and fan blowing.

I was confused. Was she cold? Then why was her fan on? I asked.

"Noooo, this is the setup," she grinned. She waved her hand just above the comforter. I was still confused. Had she been there all day? Was she creating cold air so she could snuggle? What about getting a job? I could feel myself tense.

I moved on. "So what did you do today?"
"Nothin', nothin' really."
"Did you apply anywhere? How is the job hunt going?"
"I applied to two places online."

I could feel Mama Bear inside of me wanting to claw her way out, begin to roar, and rip that comforter off the bed. I swallowed. "Njalla, I'm worried about you. This is not a life. There's more for you than this [I waved my hand above the comforter]. But you've got to move."

I could tell I was making Njalla very uncomfortable. But this time, I did not stop.

"You've said you are passive. Njalla, you've got to *own your life*, you've got to make it happen. And it's not going to happen in here. You've got to get out of this room. You've got to move.

"On the scale from passive [left hand] to aggressive [right hand], there's a really healthy space in the middle that's *assertive*. You've got to get assertive; passive is not serving you well."

At this point, Collins knocked on the door. "Want to see some of my photos?" Njalla agreed quickly; I'm sure it was to get away from Emerging Mama Bear.

After we looked at Collins' photos, Njalla went into her room and shut the door. Any time I knocked, she did not reply. When Njalla came downstairs I asked for a moment.

"Here's the bottom line. I want you to thrive! I see so much for your life! But you are settling for less than who you are. You've got to get a job and participate

177

in life. Do you trust that I want what is best for you? Do you believe me?" Njalla nodded yes as tears fell.

The next day, she was softer. We even cut up vegetables for dinner together, talking at the counter as we made kabobs. At Household Dinner, Grant asked the question, "How important is privacy to you?"

Njalla responded immediately: "Very." She followed up: "It always surprises me that you live with your curtains open and your shades up. I'm always wonderin' 'why do they live like this?' Reyana mentioned to me that she didn't understand why Lu [who was visiting for her birthday] is in a downstairs room; what if there was a drive-by? And couldn't somebody see in the windows?"

We described to Njalla the changes we've seen on Woodbine: gunfire 3-4 times a week to currently once every month or two; less crime; more friendliness between neighbors. She agreed that matters.

"Njalla, do you think you've changed? I think you've changed since you've been here this second time."
Njalla agreed with Grant, nodding slowly with her eyebrows up.
"I'm less guarded. Less tense, more relaxed. I know y'all better," she said softly.

Our conversation continued, floating from person to person and topic to topic. Then she really let us in.

"When I was a sophomore, I was on food stamps, and I got dropped from the program. So I had $80 to last for two months. I went out and bought lots of Ramen Noodles, vegetables and staples, then froze a lot of it. At the end of the two months I was stirring up flour and salt and pepper on bread and frying that. It's all I had.

"In fact, I still keep a bag of rice in the trunk of my car. Still to this day." And as she said that, I believed she would fight someone for it. She looked fierce and her tone was factual and grim. I told her a story I'd read. A woman who had lived through the Nazi concentration camps kept dinner rolls in her coat pockets at all times. She had starved in the camps and would never allow herself to be without food.

The rest of dinner and clean-up went well, and Grant and I settled into watching March Madness. Collins sat with us for a while. We heard Njalla softly pad down the steps: "Are y'all doin' waffles in the mornin'?" Affirmative. "Can I have a chocolate waffle? I noticed the hot chocolate mix in the pantry ... what if you stirred that into the batter? But no chocolate chips [gasp!], I don't want to overdo it." ... and she told us goodnight. Progress!

"More," she directed. One more teaspoon of Private Selection (Kroger) dark chocolate hot chocolate mix. Handsome stirred it into the Krusteaz Belgian waffle mix under her watchful eye. I dipped my finger into the batter: it tasted exactly like rich brownies. Oh my!

That was how our morning began: a household wafflefest. Lu came in and joined Collins, Njalla, Grant, and I in trying chocolate Belgian waffles with heated organic maple syrup, melted butter, Suzanne-whipped heavy cream (that means lots of vanilla), and pecans. It was scrumptious!

Conversation was easy. I'm always thankful for such times. We stood in the kitchen, plates near our mouths trying to avoid syrup dripping down our t-shirts. Brunch bliss, kitchen connection.

I worked in the yard, hoping to create a corner of flowery beauty now that the chickens are fenced in. Njalla eventually came out. We talked about Ray-Mee, Cinco's mom, who was getting ten teeth pulled on Monday and immediately getting dentures. I was worried about her; she was going to lose a lot of weight and be in quite a bit of pain. I told Njalla about stocking her up with soups for the next month, just to help. The lights in her eyes fired up.

About an hour later, she came back outside with a soup list — all she could make for Ray-Mee. On her Kroger app, the cost would be $51 and change. The light in her eyes had spread to her whole self— she seemed giddy, happy to help. Now *that* was the real Njalla.

House Slave

Maybe someday because of her interactions here at Woodbine, Njalla's filter about slavery will not be her first thought. But not today.

"Have you ever thought of being a house manager? You love to cook," I said, imitating her cooking semi-dance and broad smile. "You could run a household. I think you'd be good at it."

She paused, but didn't flinch. "You mean be a house slave?"
Njalla's answer slapped me in the face, stinging.
"No, I mean a *manager*." I struggled with getting my words together after such a remark. "I've always taken such pride in being able to manage my household well." I staggered out of the room.

It was just months ago that we asked Tall George (a white young man, 6'6", very community-minded, a gentle giant) if we bought a large house, would he be the manager for it? He prayed and said yes, he'd love to.

I still had to fight back tears. *House slave? Are you kidding me?* Part of what hurt me was that Njalla would think that I would say or think such a horrible thing. Didn't she know me by now? I guess not.

~~~~~

We were positioned on the stairs, Njalla several steps higher than I. It was a good angle, because I was bringing confrontation today.

"Njalla, how are you feeling? Better?" She had cancelled volunteering with me today.
"Ummm, yeah … I am."
"So what did you do today?"
"Nuthin really. I just woke up an hour ago." And I had just gotten home from work. What?!?
Njalla had gotten drunk last night and slept off her hangover today. That knowledge lit me up.
"Do you need a rehab facility?"
"No! It's not that big of a deal."
"You just slept away a day of your life. You can't seem to stop. It *is* a big deal. I don't think you're seeing yourself well. We all need someone to help us see sometimes — for me it's Grant, usually, who will get in my face and say, 'Um, no Babe, you're not seeing this correctly.' Njalla. Your room is a wreck, and it's an indicator of how you live on the inside. Your life is worth more than this. Sleeping all day is beneath your gifting. You need a job. You have bills. How are you going to pay for your storage unit next month? We're not giving you any more money, period."
"I know, I'm hoping I'll slide by with being late. Once I have that job I think I'll be fine."
"You're banking everything on that job, but you just learned a lesson about that. You were banking on CVS and they chose not to hire you. You've got to be smarter than that."
I was getting very agitated with her blasé, passive approach to her issues.
"Njalla, this is what caring and loving looks like. It looks like tears in my eyes. It looks like me upset when you're settling for staying in your room in the dark getting drunk. Staying in your room is not helping you. You've got to get out of your room! You need a job and a productive life!" I could feel my forehead furrow and buckle under the strain of tears, and my chin quivered as I spoke forcefully.
"Oh no, if you're gonna cry, I'm gonna cry," she softened.
"That's okay, that's good!"

We talked a bit more, then parted ways. I had some chores to do and needed to breathe outside. Simply feeding our chickens sounded relaxing. Their simple lives, their beautiful feathers, their funny mannerisms — just being with them

180

seemed to ground me a bit. I sat down in the sunshine at our hightop on the back porch, thinking.

She came outside and joined me, bringing up several things she was learning in her class, "Getting Ahead in a Just Gettin' By World." She asked me about who I was when I was her age, 22. "'Cause we seem to be coming at things from very different viewpoints." I appreciated her question. At her age I was married to a professional athlete and traveling the world through sport. We were in completely different worlds, yes.

"And you keep talking about doing things and being productive and living a productive life. What does that look like, for me, Njalla, young African American, daughter of a mechanic? Identity is what I'm struggling with. My life does not look like the plan I used to have. I have no friends, no job, I'm not a social worker, I haven't graduated from college.

"And I don't know how to do the things you're talking about, like writing Senators about homelessness and telling them my story and navigating those systems. I need you to show me [step-by-step hands] how to do these things. And I need you to tell me the unwritten rules about being in that world."

Awesome girl, applying her class like that. She was 100% right.

She continued. "And I'm not stable. I'm better, but I'm not stable."
I was so surprised when she said that. "What do you mean? What more could you want here?"

"This could all be taken away tomorrow. I could do something stupid and you could put me out tomorrow. Or I could just leave. Something could happen. Everything could change."
I didn't realize she felt this way.

"Njalla, do you see that house across the street? It will be up for rent soon. If you had a job, you could live there. And Reyana could come spend time with you, and you could continue to love her like I know you do. I see it. I see you care for her. I think you know she's like you when you were little. She's nine. Who's reading to her? Who's guiding her?"

At this point Njalla looked distant, reaching back into her own childhood, and I saw it: Little Njalla, bored, needing an adult to open doors of knowledge and relationship, but no one was there. No one offered her that. "My house was boring too." Her tears began to tumble.

We talked more, and then she called it — she was on overload. We switched and kept our conversation light, enjoying the sunshine and each other's company.

I've put in so many house slave hours today:
Grocery shopping.
Cooking. Cleaning up the kitchen. Again.
Starting the laundry. Switching the laundry. Folding the laundry. Putting it away.
Sweeping. Collecting all the dog hair and dust and dirt and putting it into the garbage.
Mopping with vinegar and water while listening to "You are My Joy" by United Pursuit.
Bringing order to our family room.
Collecting the glasses and mugs from the family room, loading the dishwasher, starting it.
Emptying the dishwasher. And it's 8:30 at night and I worked a normal job too; I'm tired now.

As I've done these chores, I've mulled over "house slave hours."

What does that kind of language do to my spirit? How does my labor shift, my attitude change?

Everything changes when I think of myself as a house slave: I hate it. I hate everything I do. I hate my life. I get mad easily. Resentment settles into my soul like ashes below a fire, hot and gray and paper-thin.

"This will be true in our pursuit of reconciliation, and we must learn to see the confusion and discomfort as part of the change process that will eventually move us toward transformation."
- Brenda Salter McNeil, *The Roadmap to Reconciliation*, p48

Having Njalla and Collins in our home was definitely a catalytic event in our lives.

Collins' OCD, his artistry, his openness, his creativity, his longing to connect with the marginalized, his difficulty with work, self-care, finding church, and verbal expression;

Njalla's fiercely guarded heart, her deep and intense sense of black womanhood, her secrecy, her complex shame and heartaches, her experience with homelessness, her occasional, crisp articulation about her passions, her glorious — and rare — sparkle.

We were faced with discomfort daily. We were confused daily. Sometimes we were uncomfortable and confused by them; sometimes by our reactions to them;

often by their reactions to us; sometimes we were confused by ourselves. Lord, have mercy.

I saw the Genesis 3 Adam and Eve sequence playing out: fear, cover, hide, and blame. I saw the Kingdom calling us out: love, serve, and walk out the tensions of grace and truth.

~eellee~

Two weeks went by and there were more bumps in our relational road. Njalla kept leaving her dishes in the sink and not cleaning the stove or pots. She completely disrespected our rules for common spaces. Handsome found himself doing her dishes, praying as he scrubbed. We had to have another talk.

Handsome asked, "Njalla, why aren't you doing your own dishes?"
"I don't want to."
"But that's rude to everyone else in the house."
"I don't care, I don't want to do them. I don't want to be a house slave."

Ugh, that phrase again — I hate it! I have rarely felt anything turn up the dial of disgust within me like that phrase.

I said, "You are not a house slave. You are free! With freedom comes responsibility. You have the freedom to be here, AND you have the responsibility to care for common spaces like the kitchen. We ask that you be responsible for yourself and your own life." No comment.

Handsome asked, "Why do you think it's okay for me to do your dishes? You want me to be your house slave? I don't like to wash the dishes either, but I still do it."
"I don't care," she said more vehemently. "I don't want to wash the dishes!" Clearly this was a major blockage.

I elaborated, "Njalla, when you willfully don't do your responsibilities and expect other people to pick up after you, it makes me feel used. Like you're intentionally trying to take advantage of me or Grant or Collins." She said nothing in response.

Handsome said, "Njalla, to stay here you have to take responsibility for your own actions."
"Are we done here?" she asked.

The gray inside the house went darker.

~eellee~

I spoke out of town at a women's retreat and came back exhilarated, high as a kite. It was April 6th and spring was at maximum momentum: new buds and blossoms covered most of the outdoors, birds filled the blue skies, floral fragrances mixed in the air … all my favorite things.

On the way into Knoxville, Handsome met me on Market Square for a meal and conversation. We caught up, which was mostly me beaming and him listening. Once I finished my lively comments about the retreat, he smiled, bent in closely, and said, "Babe, I've got some rough news."

Uh-oh.

"I brought you here because I wanted to talk to you before you got home. You know that Collins and I were not home Friday night. Well, Njalla had some major problems over the weekend and our house is damaged. There's a hole in the wall. Actually, make that two."

I was wide-eyed as he told the story. I couldn't wait to get home and hear from Njalla what in the world had happened. Would she tell me the truth? When I walked in, I put my duffel down and heard Njalla make her way down the stairs immediately.

"C'mere, I want to show you something. I damaged the bathroom."

There was a hole in the sheetrock *and* a fleecy circle where she had slammed the door handle into the wall. The antique glass, wavy and beautifully imperfect from the 1920s, was shattered down low; I looked out of the hole and there in the yard was one of my favorite vases with a few dead flowers scattered close by.

"I drank too much when you were gone. I was alone that night and I got really mad, but I don't remember it all. I think I hyperventilated and passed out on the downstairs floor. I did some stuff in my room too."

I looked at her and was flooded with emotions. I wanted to hold her and bless her and rock her in my arms. I wanted to yell, "What are you doing?!?" I wanted to lock her eyes with mine and tell her we weren't going anywhere, and she didn't have to either. I wanted to ask her why … why was she making these choices and doing these things?

"Njalla, I've just walked in the door. Let's all meet downstairs in 30 minutes. I need to think and pray and take a deep breath."

We gathered, triangulated in our family room. It was obvious from her body that, as usual, she felt more comfortable with me than with Grant. White man.

184

I began, speaking slowly, savoring the syllables of her African name: "Njalla, dear one: what happened?"

"I know y'all are gonna kick me out, but I wanted to confess it all to you. I'll repair it. I'll pay you back. I'll fix the sheetrock and pay for the supplies." She began to cry. "I hate this talking." She fidgeted and I wondered if she was going to bolt.

Handsome acknowledged how uncomfortable she was. When he began to speak, Njalla stiffened as if waiting for a verbal assault, trying to be like a board to withstand his verbal blast. She still did not know or trust him. "Do you not trust that we are *for* you, Njalla?" he offered. For the first time, Grant got emotional, tearing up as he spoke to her. "I'm sorry you've never had a trustworthy man in your life."

It was the last thing she expected: Grant Standing, white man, being gentle after all she did. She was speechless. We decided to rest from it; there were so many emotions rattling around the house, ribcages of wonderings expanding and contracting against each other.

Sometimes a person has a sense that trouble is coming; sometimes we walk blindly into it like it's a wall we didn't expect or a step that we missed. Neither Handsome nor I realized the trouble that was coming the next day.

We had gathered again to revisit how to live in community, how to be together in one household, and be at peace. Njalla voiced a complaint: "I never have my own space." I was completely shocked. She was almost always in her room, door shut. How could that be her perception?

The house manager vs house slave conversation came up again, and Njalla was defiant about chores. I asserted that it wasn't fair for me to clean the house alone; I worked full-time and had after-hours obligations. I needed help and asked for it. I suggested dividing up the chores among all the people in the house to get them done. Collins was agreeable about "owning" another chore besides the windows each Saturday.

Handsome: "We would like for all of us to work together to run this house. We want to work *with*, to work *together*. Everyone needs to do something. You can pick your chores, but everyone needs to contribute. We all use this house."

Njalla said a flat, angry no. Grant said, "If you're going to stay here, you need to help and do your part. If you won't do any chores, you can leave if you choose to."

She rose up, turned, and went upstairs. We could hear her starting to pack. She came down and grabbed two garbage bags, then kept packing. Grant and I were completely stunned.

I called out to her, "This is a misunderstanding, Njalla, please come back down and talk this out." No response, just the creaking of stepping sounds, elephant-feet on my heart, reverberating from the upstairs. Grant and I went to the front porch to breathe. I was dazed, astonished, incredulous. I whispered so to Grant; he responded that he was sad. What should we do? Not do?

She came out with two large garbage bags and dragged them to her car, sacks that weighed on my gut and twisted it into a knot. As she left, Grant said firmly but gently, "We *want* to work with you. You don't want to work with us."

Njalla, equally as firm and gentle, agreed: "I accept that." And drove off.

Handsome and I were just staring at each other, mouths open, at a loss for words, in wonder and confusion. What the heck just happened?

~elles

There is nothing like failure to inject massive energy into a learning curve.

We called our neighbor friends from DropBy, the Wettstones. They were half our age and doubly wise. We respected their cross-cultural journey: when they were in their young 20s, they had fostered-to-adopt three local black middle school girls. They had loved fiercely and had won the trust of the girls, who now called them Mom and Dad.

Carolyn, all of age 27 but so astute, said simply, "You have to fail at this to get wisdom." That was good to hear. I felt like a miserable failure, but an angry one, too.

Carolyn and Joel had excellent challenges for us:

Some of what was happening within Njalla was unhealthy. Njalla's actions were saying, *I don't want to "get better." I just want to be in my room alone. I'm going to ask for money. I'm not going to be responsible for my car or belongings or health.* Njalla ran from emotional difficulty: *"I'm not going to learn to deal with sorrow; I'm going to self-medicate with alcohol and drugs, and I'm going to hide most of it, especially the drugs."* There were words that triggered Njalla, and we didn't know them until we said them. "Consequences." "House manager." "Chores." From these months with her, "house slave" had become a trigger for me.

I knew the adage, *hurting people hurt people*. Got it. But she was refusing to get help with her hurts. Njalla felt, *"I want a hotel-type experience, not accountability or community. Relationships are too hard, too scary. I don't trust anyone except myself ... and I'm not that great."* The Wettstones wondered if Njalla's attitude was, "I'm willing to stay till y'all give up." We hadn't thought of it that way.

There were vital *power dynamics* at play. In this scenario, Grant and I were the ones who culturally had the power. We had a home, jobs, transportation, order, relational skills, love, friendship, and success under our belts. We were white middle class people operating in a white world and a mixed neighborhood. We felt we had laid down much of our power by asking her into our home, sharing our resources with her, helping her, living with her, opening to her, embracing her, and learning from her. We did not feel like we dehumanized or lessened her in any way. We were careful to encourage and lift her up.

Njalla, on the other hand, felt her only "power" was her choice to stay or to leave. She took that choice seriously, and left when our relationship felt too threatening to maintain. Leaving said, "I'm in control." Leaving (in her past) was an act of violence. She had zero imagination that leaving could be done in a healthy way; it usually involved verbal abuse.

We needed to be more clear with our *expectations*. At the Wettstones' instruction, we created a house rules document so if a person stayed longer than a weekend, they could read them and choose to agree or disagree. We could always offer to help them find a different place if needed. "We'd love for you to be here, and here are the house expectations. Take a day and think about it."

The Wettstones asked us some good questions:
- What does love look like in this situation? *We didn't know.*
- If there was no outcome to our love, was our love enough? *Yes. But I still wanted outcome. Sigh.*
- For Njalla, what would consequences be? *Neither of us were used to or comfortable with enforcing consequences with an adult.* Kids, sure — but a woman in her 20s? That felt so awkward. It also emphasized any cultural and class differences we had. We strongly felt that we wanted to stay away from "power over," and move more in "power to" and "power with." Those dynamics felt healthier to us.

They asked us to think from Njalla's point of view. To her, there was no positive reinforcement for *relationship*: Relationship was a threat to independence and was not necessarily beneficial. If someone took care of Njalla, she felt she owed them yet couldn't repay them. That created dissonance, a debt of gratitude that was impossible or at best improbable to reciprocate. Carolyn encouraged me to try to stay in relationship with Njalla, to keep texting with her, to think, "You can move out, but I am still with you, I am still for you."

Growing up, if I had trouble, my parents would sit me down, lovingly talk through my issue with me, provide support and firm guidance, and expect me to get my shit together. They had every expectation that my life would be strong, fruitful, healthy, productive, and beneficial to others. That was not Njalla's experience. Carolyn reminded us that we couldn't project our image of a good life onto *her* life. She also taught us to not take Njalla's meanness deep into our hearts (I did take a lot personally), for this might be the first time she was able to hurt someone else and not BE hurt (very powerful!). To keep our own hearts stable, we needed the Holy Spirit to give us moment-by-moment wisdom. In fact, she encouraged us to have the attitude of, "Bring it on. We can take it, in the Spirit. We are going to love you *no matter what*." Carolyn was such a warrior!

The Wettstones observed that both of us were trying to prove our truths:

Us: Love matters, relationship is crucial, God is for us,
vs
Njalla: Work doesn't matter, love doesn't matter, I don't matter,
you don't matter.

Their insight was that Njalla needed to find a safe place to open her pain with people who would not hurt her. Njalla's fear made this a life-threatening challenge. She was terrified that if she revealed her worst fears, they would completely control her. So to survive, she cut off relationship, she cut off emotion … she dehumanized herself.

They left us with this thought: There was a sweet tenderness within Njalla. We had all seen it. We couldn't forget the beauty of that.

⁓ₑₗₗₑₑₛ

The following day, Njalla, through Carolyn, said she might stop by after work — after all of our fireworks the previous day, this was her first day of a new job. It should have been a day to celebrate her, but now I just hoped she wouldn't come when I was here alone.

As I rubbed the sleep out of my eyes, I wondered if that would happen; if she would actually come by. I still felt raw with anger, sadness, and even a tinge of bitterness, something I have never allowed myself to wallow in. Bitterness is like acid to the soul; I wanted none of it. And yet … it felt real. Honest. Energizing, tantalizing, justifying. It was a carrier for my anger, adding in the spice that began an instant, subtle decay of my soul.

I know of two mandatory things to do when I feel bitter: forgive and confront. Both are equally important. Both help heal and debride the corrosive effect of bitterness.

Because of the retreat I had just co-led, I had taken the day off. I knew I needed time to process physically, mentally, emotionally, and spiritually what had happened over the past week with Njalla, especially the last two days, so that's what I did. It felt like moving from the Mount of Celebration to the Valley of Chaos and Betrayal.

I went into Njalla's room to observe the fallout:
Garbage bags full of beer cans and liquor bottles [recycle bins, filled twice!]
Blue pills under the bed, some crushed in a yellow paper [Oh Father. Oh Father. Oh no, not pills too.]
A large red wine stain on the pillow top of the mattress [Damn, that's probably ruined.]
Two bowls of old food, crusted and nasty-nasty [One of the few house rules I did state: no food in the room. Because, mice.]
Dirty glasses [So that's where all the glasses are!]
I inspected the bathroom she damaged and cleaned up the glass [Speechless.]

It hit me: here I was again, her house slave, cleaning up after her, dealing with her trash and mess. Bitterness washed over me. Just as a snarl was forming inside my soul, I cried out to God for help.

I opened the windows in her room to clear out an unsavory, strong scent.
I cleared out her part of the pantry and threw away some of her old food in the fridge.
I washed her sheets, comforter, and quilts.

During a mid-day phone call with Grant, I vented: "She took my retreat joy and shattered it like she shattered the antique window. Why did I give her that type of power over me? Because I cared for her. I let her in my home and my heart. I lived honestly with her and she did not live honestly with me."

I explained myself: I felt a touch of relief that she was gone, but that day I just felt angry, disrespected, used, hurt, and betrayed. I felt a bit guilty that I felt this relief; Grant felt concern, care, and was upset that she was alone. I didn't, and I felt like a lesser Christian, muddied and muddled where he was clear. I didn't want to invite her back into our home. An oppression had lifted and I was glad. Yet I felt that if I didn't invite Njalla back into our home, I'd be judged by Grant as weak: not able to shake my fist at Satan and yell, "Bring it on!" like Carolyn did, like Grant was ready to do.

I HATED the house slave thing. It was really digging at me. I needed to deal with that: I felt most bitterness there. She had the gall to say I was suggesting she be a house slave (which was offensively ridiculous to me), when *she* treated *me* like the house slave. I wanted to lift her up and strengthen her, not treat her as a house slave! Deep breath, dispel the bitterness. But then it would race back in: I wanted relationship, not to feel used, and I plainly saw her hypocrisy.

So, Christ in me, what would You do? How would You handle this? What does love look like in this case? I know You are quick to forgive. Make me like You, Lord Jesus. I'm a mess.

Anne Lamott's quote echoed in my head: "Earth is forgiveness school." Today I was flunking.

By the time Njalla did get to our house, Grant was home. She said, "I would like a relationship with you and Grant, just not under the constraints of this house. I won't ask for anything, anything at all (hands waving; meaning money). I will repair the sheetrock on the wall [Suzanne: Actually, there are two walls. N: Yeah, I know] after I get a paycheck [not holding my breath, heard this type of thing before with her]."

Njalla: "Do you have anything you want to say to me?"
Us: "No, not tonight."
Njalla: "Okay. Well, I'm going to clean up stuff in my room."
We hadn't realize she would come back to clean her room. We had done the bulk of it already.
"Hey, what do I do with this trash?" she yelled.
"You can bring it down and finish sorting through it for recycling. Grant said he didn't finish."

She was dismayed that we had seen the contents of her trash. She explained the dozens of cans and bottles: "This IPA I drank for pleasure, but this, *this* I drank to get to the edge." She quickly deposited the rest of the glass rum bottles into the glass recycling.

It made me feel sad for her — *finally, I felt a kindness warming me.* She was sleeping in her car in the Kroger parking lot with other homeless folks and some truckers nearby. She felt safe with them; she did not fear getting harassed by authorities there. Besides, she had her big cooking knife if she felt threatened. Her phone was off till she got paid on the 25th, 17 days away.

"Did you throw away my food?" she asked.
"Only the old stuff. The rest I packed up into the bags in the foyer."

Njalla was lucid and engaging, the Njalla that I felt hope for. I hoped she would maintain this healthier self. As she exited the front door, bags in hand, she said over her shoulder, "I really do care about you." Then she said something else we could not hear, and the screen door slammed, and I closed the door.

For the next week I vacillated between feeling sad, confused, angry, tender, understanding, bitter, and frustrated. My anger and my humility were taking turns bobbing upward in the sea of my emotions, splashing me in the face, hard.

We conferred again with the Wettstones to create our House Rules. Here's where we landed.

House Rules
for 2330 Woodbine Avenue

1. **Loving each other** is the most important thing.
2. **Outserve each other.** Be kind, not "fake nice." Do conflict with patience and expect the best of each other. If you have expectations of someone, talk about them; never assume someone knows what you're thinking.
3. **Alcohol**: no alcohol upstairs or in individual rooms. Alcohol is welcome in social settings (at dinner, talking with friends, watching a ball game, etc.). Practice moderation please.
4. Do your own **dishes**, and take care of your "mess" *immediately*. Don't wait or expect others to clean up after you. We do not have a maid service.
5. Keep the left side of the **kitchen sink** clear. It has the disposal and is the "working side" of the sink. Keep the **laundry door** closed (no insulation up there!).
6. **Your room** is your own space. Please respect anything that is part of the house, but know we are not going to "police" your room. Keep in mind some of our furniture is decades old.
7. We occasionally have **mice**, so please do not keep food in your room.
8. If this applies: We practice a **two-month grace period**, after which we expect you to be employed and there will be a rent fee.
9. We expect you to **help** around the house. We'll decide together what chores you will choose to do. If you have preferences or dislikes, by all means, let us know. Examples are: taking out the trash & recycling; sweeping & mopping the downstairs flooring; mowing; helping in the garden; cooking meals for the house once a week, etc.
10. We practice a Sabbath rest on **Sundays** … we nap, we don't do housework, we chill, we read, we might watch a movie. We love it. Join us.
11. We try to **eat dinner together** once a week so we'll coordinate with your schedule. There is a calendar in the kitchen; go ahead and write your hours/plans.
12. If this applies: We would rather **empower you** by paying you for work on house projects than let you borrow money.

13. We **recycle**. We have three containers in the kitchen: landfill, plastic/paper/cans, and glass. Please use them accordingly. Remember all plastic must be rinsed and paper must be "clean-ish."
14. **Having friends over:** Bring them! Once people go to bed, please kindly keep the noise down.

We're so glad you're here! Please remember to sign our guest book in the front hall.

Joel gently reminded us that rules never work perfectly.

We asked them about money, jobs, getting taken advantage of, how to address offense and forgiveness, how to create a home culture of grace and truth. They patiently answered our questions, often with stories of their own. Truly, we are wounded in community and we are healed in community.

~~~~~

Journal Entry: May 11, 2019

It's the Saturday before Mother's Day, and who gave me a call? Njalla.

We've not talked in about a week and a half; along with her malfunctioning phone, she was working on getting a new phone number, so I was out of touch.

We chatted. It was easy and honest. She sounded so good: strong-minded and clear, expressive and even hopeful. She likes her new job … celebration!

At first I didn't make the connection that she was acknowledging me as a mother figure, but it slowly became clear, ultimately culminating in a card, a glorious, generous, over-the-top card. She extolled me. What?!? With all our mistakes and head-butting and differences, she reached out to me as a special person. I was speechless, treasuring the moment.

~~~~~

Summer came.
Since Njalla wasn't answering texts …
since her phone was giving me a weird message and wasn't working …
since she hadn't contacted me about grabbing some pans I had for her …
since she "lost her car to TitleMax" …
since she hadn't connected with us about the celebration dinner for getting an apartment …

I was really concerned.

I emailed the two addresses I had for her with a message forwarded from the Knoxville Office of Neighborhoods about the *Next Step Initiative*, a non-profit focused on providing services to those who are homeless or addicted. The organization was hosting a collaboration to talk about services, food, entertainment, and art; I thought it sounded amazing. In the past, on her good days, she would have been interested, even intrigued, by this effort.

I received a terse reply:
"i'm fine.
I don't want to be made aware of things like this.
I don't want to participate in anything."

Dang. That felt like it came from a very dark place. I fervently prayed that she would let God's light into the dark place inside, that she would cooperate with Him to dispel the thick gloom, and that she would not believe the lies in her head.

~elles

Thunderbolt at the Gathering

Intermittently and informally, some neighbors got together, shared a meal, talked about God and culture, and prayed. We volunteered to host one evening.

Reys helped me chop up veggies for a colorful rainbow salad — so healthy! The chickens and the compost pile got the scraps of red, yellow, and orange bell peppers; carrots; cucumbers; radishes; and purple onions. We readied avocados as Grant placed pork chops and pineapple slices on the grill, organized like houses in a neighborhood. Forks? Check. Knives? Yes. Napkins? Loads!

Thunderbolt happened by and I invited her to come. I knew she had a bit of experience with God, but didn't really know much about her faith.

She came drunk and scared.

As I stood in the foyer, her slight figure caught my eye. I saw her outside the screen door, hesitating and wobbling like an egg on a counter. Her hand reached for the doorknob, then fell to her side; another reach, more hesitation. A precipice moment. "Poor thing," I thought. "It's got to be scary coming up here, feeling alone." I opened the door and saw that her eyes were filled with tears; she was scared to come in and meet new people, to be seen and known. I gave her an enormous hug, which she returned like a trusting child.

Everyone made a place for her at the table. She reeked of alcohol and cigarettes. When she opened her mouth, it was downright unpleasant, an old onion that had been soaked in liquor.

Thunderbolt had a voice like a trombone, sliding and loud when she wanted it to be. There were times when she was a bit too aggressive and repetitious with her voice, but then she would put her hand over her mouth and slur softly, "Oh sorry, I'm being too loud." Obviously being rebuked for that before had made a fixed impression.

She never ended up eating the plate I fixed for her. Instead, she just listened and marveled at the young people around the table, appreciating their beauties and gifts. Little Amari, less than two years old, made Thunderbolt smile. Some of her hard shell melted. Cinco watched with worried eyes, and Reyana stiffened under the discomfort of Thunderbolt's nearness; she didn't trust her.

When we moved into the family room, she and I sat side by side. She took my hand and never let go. The room felt open; people were happy to be present. Everyone relaxed into the couches and we crammed more chairs into the room. We were disheveled in a family kind of way, glad to hear from each other, and speculating — with part tension, part curiosity — about what Thunderbolt would do in this setting. These folks were so accepting and so generous; they benevolently entered into this situation with kindness and sensitivity to a stranger. Present to this moment, tender toward her humanity, there was no spirit of judgment.

As she listened to prayers and wonderings, she alternately jumped in or teared up. After Collins played a moving song by Common Hymnal ("Refugee"), something shifted inside of her.

"I'm forgiven," Thunderbolt wept. "I know it's true. Forgiven ... forgiven ... forgiven," she repeated. She had a snotty cry, her nose buried in my hair, repentance and alcohol oozing from her pores. I just held her, reassuring her that Jesus' forgiveness was real. I had a mental picture of Jesus lovingly holding me, encouraging me that His outrageous love was authentic and genuine. That's what I wanted to do for her.

Thunderbolt prayed out loud. It was as if she lost all sense of shame and just let herself be emotionally honest. (Maybe that was a bonus from the alcohol? Maybe it was the moment?) She leaned her head on my shoulder and I leaned my head on hers. We had a sweet moment of peace, and others spoke up.

Then she remembered the group and refocused. "That man" (pointing to Tall George, our Scandinavian neighbor) "has Jesus in him!" she exclaimed. "I can see Jesus in him," she said at least two dozen times, marveling at Tall George, who handled her attention gracefully, his smile serene. She was intrigued by him.

I sensed it was time to pull her out of the room, so she and I went and sat on the porch swing. We talked about perhaps moving to the local women's Serenity Shelter to address her increasingly tentative situation with Freddy.

We talked about her hard life. She told me her age (53) and I gulped; I thought she was near 70.
We talked about how she wanted to leave Freddy but didn't want to leave the dog with him; he was calloused right now because of drugs. I reflected quickly on how I had not seen him at all this summer. Isolation — one of the worst parts of addiction that can be traced to the original sin (see Genesis 3). Fear, cover, hide and blame. So many relationships are somewhere in that sequence.

"I drink too much sometimes," she noted. "And I do crazy things." She stated it factually and firmly, eyes dry, resigned to the truth about her behavior. I knew the police had visited her house recently but didn't know why, if it was about her or about Freddy or both.

"I done Jesus so wrong," she grieved, her gravel voice scraping the bottom. Her heart seemed to break when she said it. "But He forgives me. It's true! He forgives me," she repeated, her head back on my shoulder.

Eventually Thunderbolt walked home, wanting to be alone. When I returned indoors, we all split a bottle of red and prayed for her. Precious, precious woman.

~eelee~

Thunderbolt texted me: "Hey sorry was working day labor but could use your help he been using bad and I been drinking to hide this needs to stop."

About an hour later I texted back: "Sorry to hear that. What do you think your next steps should be?" I wanted to see where a knock on the door would lead — I felt the need to check on her in person. I couldn't NOT go to her house; I had to see her with my own eyes. I wanted to see if Freddy was lucid, to claim them both for Jesus, to open up a big can of His light and spray it into their darkness.

I asked Grant to go with me; that felt safer. I reasoned that their house might be smelly, dirty, have some pet filth because of the neglect that comes with addiction. I imagined washing their dishes, caring for the dog, cleaning up, sitting with Thunderbolt as her tears fell, and seeing Freddy high and incapacitated.

195

After Grant and I talked about expectations — we cannot save anyone, fix anyone, but we can love on them — we walked over and knocked on the door. Freddy kindly and warmly let us in. He was clear-headed, "jus' havin' a few beers, na doin' anythin' bad, watching a movie. You see fuh yuh-self."

The dog barked at us like we'd just robbed them. As I hugged Thunderbolt, she shook. Tears began to fall. We didn't let go of each other for a bit. I felt her take a deep breath.

The house was immaculate. The order of the house surprised me; *I have so much to learn.*

We chatted as they made room for us on their couches: "We wanted to come by and check on you," Grant said. "We haven't seen you in a while."

Freddy immediately began quoting the Bible. It was uncanny how many Scriptures he strung together, each verse like a pearl on a necklace adorning a queen. But why did it all feel like a coverup, just incessant talk, the most powerful verbiage on earth suddenly powerless?

Thunderbolt broke in: "We're not doing well," she contrasted. "They know. I'm going to tell the truth," she said as we sat in the darkness. The most light was coming from the TV, which was showing a scary suspense film. I had to look away.

"Freddy knows his Bible, but he doesn't live it, so he's a liar. *You're a liar!*" she accused loudly. "But I'm drinkin' too. I couldn't make it through the day without this drink. I need to detox somewhere but it can't be here. He's out back smokin' crack. It can't be here." Grant agreed and said he'd ask around.

At one point she turned on the light. I felt relief; I am like a cat, chasing the sunshine through the house as it moves during the day. Light felt safer to me.

We had friendly conversation, then a time of prayer on our knees. Freddy was quick to say he had messed up and needed God's forgiveness; so was Thunderbolt. We left feeling hopeful.

As evening began her texts started lighting up my phone: Could we get her to northern Indiana, to her people?

She texted that after we left: he hit her and dumped out her purse … there was a feeling of much alarm in her writing. Now she just wanted to leave with her dog and cat.

196

"Ministry is messy," my friend Kathy used to say. This life — what some would call ministry, but we call neighboring — was definitely messy.

So was a dental loan with Ray-Mee,
ballin' with boys who yell *fuck* and *nigga* constantly,
learning from my neighbors,
having people live with us.
It was crazy and messy and we were full of dependence on God, clueless but willing.

Thunderbolt tried to find a way to get to the YWCA. I asked on Facebook if anyone could foster her pets ... she had two offers. We saw the couple once from our front porch; they walked into their house from a friend's car with groceries in their hands. We waved and they waved back ... Freddy waved large and long, purposefully connecting.

~elle~

Her voice was once a hazy stream, but now was a clear brook. She spoke her words quickly and definitely, with more authority and assurance and less gravel and booze and smoke. Thunderbolt informed me that she was leaving — actually, she was already gone.

I listened to her voicemail, ear crammed to my phone so I wouldn't fail to notice her every tone.

Freddy knew she was leaving him.
She didn't want me to know so I wouldn't lie.
She would be back tomorrow to quickly pick up a few things.
She said she was taking very little with her.

I felt that familiar sorrow again — that loss from her leaving. On Woodbine people came and went much more frequently than I was used to. Relationships felt more choppy, like short sentences, when what I longed for was lyrical poetry with lots of commas.

When I came across a list of helpful organizations at work, I thought, "I need to make a copy of that for her. I need to put that in my bag so I won't forget."
There would be more general musings during the workday:
"I wonder how her search is going."
"I wonder if she found a home for her cat, and if she's going to travel with her dog."
"I wonder if she heard back from her people."
"I wonder if she's sober, if he's lit up on crack, what is happening inside her house...."

The last time I saw her, she was walking at a fast clip down Woodbine — the fastest I've ever seen her move. Kids had come up to my car, so I did not get to say hello directly. She waved, her cardigan's big sleeves flapping. I wish I had run to her and given her a huge hug and prayed for her.

Freedom for you, my sister.
Freedom and joy, ease and hope and healing for you.
Shalom-style, all-encompassing peace and wellness for you.

And for Freddy ... prayers for him too. Prayers that he and I could be friends, that he would put down his glass crack pipe, that the warmth of Jesus would envelope him again, that all that Scripture he knew would come alive in him. Rescue and release for all that was bent and broken in him. I longed to see him in God's arms at the end of his life, smiling, at home, and clear.

A few days later Thunderbolt filled me in: She was being loved generously by her new church in a tough neighborhood in South Knox. They had found her a place to share a fairly low rent; she could keep her support dog; she could smoke outside; and she had instant community. Now she just needed to figure out how the bus system could get her to her job or see if she needed to find a new place of work. She was optimistic and encouraged, praising God for taking such good care of her. What a story. What a woman.

Chapter Eleven: Home, Fall 2019

REYS CAME BY, TEARS IN HER EYES. She and her family were moving. "It's not too far, so we'll still see each other, right?"

"Absolutely, sweet girl, absolutely!" I promised. "You've been part of our home. We love you. I can't imagine our house without you."

An image floated into my mind: Grant was dancing in the kitchen. We had always sung in our kitchen, but Reys took us to a new level, trilling her high notes so purely that wolfen Wiley would turn his head. We sang with wooden spoons as our microphones, and Reys would execute all the dance moves perfectly. Grant danced as Grant danced: shoulders up, hands closed, making his familiar jerky movements and smiling shyly. We had a family hand clap we used when we triumphantly finished a song, proud of ourselves for our moves and grooves: bumping Reys hip to hip, hand to hand, fingertips to fingertips, roll your shoulders with an "Ahhhhh" at the end, as you're taking off fake sunglasses with flair.

Reality set in, though, and we saw Reys much less. She was not old enough to walk the many blocks to our house, and our neighborhood was not safe enough for her to walk alone. As per the 'hood code, when we walked by her new house, we would yell — not go on the actual grounds — but we rarely got a response.

~~~~~

Grant, the Cinco family, and I were on an adventure to get a set of bunks from a cabin in the countryside. "Who wants to ride in the back of the truck the rest of the way?" I cheered. Cinco, Terrell and I loaded up; Cinco was very cautious. I put Terrell in the front right corner of the truck bed and showed her how to put one hand on the front of the bed, and the other on the side; Cinco did the same on the left side. I snugged up behind Terrell so she would feel safe.

"I wish you were over here with me, Suzy," he worried.

"You'll be fine! This is so fun. You're going to love it!" I was all smiles, for I had grown up doing this from the time I was a little girl. The wind in my hair, the sun on my face, dodging branches and spiderwebs, singing if I felt like it, taking in nature's beauty … sheer bliss to me.

199

Grant put the truck into gear and we began to move slowly, s-l-o-w-l-y. Terrell smiled, but Cinco began screaming, then leaned down toward Grant's window on the driver's side. "You're going too fast, Grant! Slow down!"

"He's going to go faster, Cinco, hold on!"

"Faster?!? No way! You done this before? When you were my age?"

"Absolutely, a million times! We're going to go faster! You're fine! Have fun!" I couldn't help but bubble up with happiness. Cinco, wide-eyed, began to smile too.

By the time we made it the mile to the cabin, Cinco was a pro. He could dodge branches and bounce along with bent knees as springs just like me, exclaiming about what he saw as we went, loving the bumping and swaying. But jumping off the back … now that was a challenge.

My parents took over once we arrived. Mama gave a quick house tour, then the men set to work on dismantling the bunks.

There were several *firsts* that day at the cabin. I demonstrated our rope swing. Urban folks aren't used to rope swings, and ours was a doozy. It was the kind where you had one of two reactions: You screamed like a woman giving birth or you froze, breathing in and holding your breath in sheer fear. Cinco wanted to swing but was filled with fright. The second time we walked past the swing, Grant decided it was time. It was one of those 'man moments.' He went first. Cinco, really scared but wanting desperately to go, crawled up the launchpad base (although I had to help him take the final steps), positioned his body on the small sitting board, launched off the platform, and screamed in utter panic for several full arcs, face distorted with abject terror, screams coming from the core of his being. Then he wanted to do it again. Of course.

We strolled down to the lake. Our fiberglass dock was very plain, just a postage stamp rectangle of white lying on the water's surface, slightly bouncing with the wind and waves. To get out to the dock, we had to walk on a narrow wooden gangplank, which terrified the family, but they eventually braved it. Ray-Mee took "cheese" pictures to document the moment.

After Henry took a swing (he yelled on the first arc, then held on for dear life), we all helped to load up the bunks. Then the unthinkable happened: the big truck ran out of diesel. We told the other family to go on, but Henry warmed us with a sweet comment: "We came *together*." That was special, coming from quiet, strong Henry. The guys siphoned diesel from the tractor and we headed home.

Grant made it back to Woodbine with the beds at sunset, victorious and worn out. The kids were so excited to get their "new rooms." I was actually allowed into the house (such an honor!) as Terrell showed me around. Sigh of happiness.

I sent Ray-Mee a message and was so moved when she sent back what I always do: three yellow hearts.

~elles

Just after they had set up the new bunks, the family was slammed with devastating news: They were required by their landlord to move, and fast. Because of the gentrification tsunami gathering force in our neighborhood, the poor began to be turned out, including Cinco's family. Let me give you, Dear Reader, a bit of background on Parkridge's gentrification before proceeding with Cinco.

Gentrification and Renting to Others

Quickly after moving to Woodbine, Grant and I realized we needed a vision for affordable housing and lifting up younger, entrepreneurial minority brothers and sisters. Where were the affordable houses for the working poor? Why were so many people of all races struggling with housing issues? Why were there so few black business owners with employees in Knoxville?

When we moved to Woodbine Avenue in 2016, according to others' research, Parkridge was 66% rental or blight (*blight* is when a house is crumbling in on itself from neglect, weathering, and deterioration). Healthy communities hope to stay below 50%. Research indicates that in communities where the scale tips over 50% rental, drugs and crime move in partnered with quicker turnover and the neighborhood destabilizes. Just as our Smoky Mountains need strong trees with deep roots to stabilize a mountainside, as well as underbrush and a growing understory, communities need people with deep roots and longevity. Who were Parkridge's oak and maple trees? What advice did they have for us?

When Grant and I sold the 6.6, we made a tidy sum. We asked God and each other what to do with that money. Neither of us were comfortable with it sitting in an account of some kind. This money was meant for Kingdom work: but what? How?

Our hope was to buy a rental place or two or three so we could ensure affordable housing for our renting neighbors, especially if they were historically from the Parkridge area. Many of them were black, young, and searching for a good place to settle, but because of gentrification, property values, property taxes, and rent rates rose, so they were being forced out of their home neighborhood. This is classic negative gentrification.

Our questions became, How can we help our neighbors stay in Parkridge? How can we provide affordable housing to young black entrepreneurs? Where is the movable mountainous tsunami of gentrification going to course next?

As we pondered, our neighborhood was becoming gentrified before our very eyes. Starting on the end nearest downtown, Parkridge was upscaling, becoming

201

home to many professors, downtown professionals, and white hipsters. The wave was moving in our direction, but it was littered with three major problems: flippers, remote investors, and corrupt landlords. I wanted to metaphorically fight all three.

"*Flippers*, your cheap buck makes me absolutely crazy. It's obvious you don't care about our neighborhood or the beauty of an old home; you just care about wrapping around the vinyl siding (even over old windows? Are you kidding me?) as quickly as possible. Your shoddy patchwork is detestable. It's below, less than, ugly. Do better.

"*Remote investors*, wake up. This is my neighborhood you've put your money into, and that house you own looks like crap. You don't know the stories of the people who live here, and it appears you don't care — because you live in Miami or Ohio. Change that. Get involved. Don't just invest to make a profit; invest to elevate your renters, to be profitable to the neighborhood.

"*Corrupt landlords*. You're sneaky, slippery beasts and I deplore how you continue to wound the ones you take advantage of. How dare you neglect your homes like that! How dare you launder your drug money through your rentals! How dare you take advantage of the powerless! You make me so angry. When you die and those properties are released, I want to buy those houses and fix them and offer humane spaces for real people with real stories and real ambition." (Dear Reader, could you do that in your city?)

You feel my passion, outraged like Jesus when He flipped tables in the temple.

Dumpsters started appearing on almost every street in our 'hood. Dirty insulation, old wood, broken windows, and old firebrick started piling up. Big trucks pulling trailers of equipment and supplies filled our streets. Each week we began to get one, then two, then a handful of "We'd like to buy your property" postcards and unwanted texts.

On the street there was talk about a drug lord who owned over 80 houses. He used the houses as a front to hide his drug money. I began to do a bit of research; I began to get angry.

"These houses are being bought by the drug lord guy, rented out at medium-high rates, and then neglected. They're deteriorating right under the poor, who won't mess with the drug lord. It's not right or fair. We've got a great opportunity right here to use our 6.6 profit. Let's buy a house, rent it at a fair rate, and stake a claim here, in God's Name."

With Realtor Tom, we found another house on Woodbine that was already stripped to the studs. The crew was looking for a local investor to help finish the job. It was $52,000, and we jumped in. Cabinets, appliances, paint — all the simple details — and within a few months we had a beautiful home we were really proud of. One of the workmen, Dustin, asked if he could rent from us; we were thrilled. Dustin was just the type of person we were looking for. At 6'6" he is not easily missed. He is a young, entrepreneurial black man with a proven work ethic, strong ties to the community, an active faith, and a gentle nature. God had connected us with the very man we were looking for.

Doug Winter was an energetic man of clout and command in the Knoxville entrepreneurial scene. He was an African American international business coach for those who were striving to create, sustain, and build companies, and he was focused on those who were on the outskirts trying to break into the risk-ringed world of accomplishment.

Doug called them "strivers": the kind of kid who is holding down three jobs so they can realize a dream. The kind of kid who has no back-up or parental money or much in the form of networks, but who has a dream so real they can taste it. The kid who needs $10,000 to patent and manufacture a genius idea, create a website, and find his or her niche. The kind of kid who needs a lift, a mentor, and some working capital. Doug was looking for the kid who was working hard to just get through school while maintaining two jobs and checking on Grandma, who knew there was no way a bank would lend them the money. Doug told us to be in "observation mode," looking for minority people who were hustling hard. Restaurants, bars, stores: It turned out Dustin was right here already, striving to create the very house he would later rent and ultimately own.

Our next house was on Jefferson Avenue. The JeffAve house, as I called it, was purchased with a large black family in mind. The father was a former pastor, the mom held various jobs at non-profits, and between natural children, adoption, and legal guardianships, they were 18 strong. Six were currently living with them, and they were going to have to split up the family because they couldn't find a house large enough to rent. It broke our hearts.

Unlike the JeffAve house, our next home purchased on Linden Avenue was a mighty 900-square feet, a two-bedroom, one-bathroom sweet space with a shaded back yard. Two weeks after we bought it, someone was murdered just across the street. Grant and I wondered if we should move there; the other side of our main roadway, Magnolia Avenue, was experiencing more and more crime, whereas our neighborhood was calming down. We were open to the risk but did not feel God's "yes."

Out of all of our rental experience (which was minimal), we had only one nightmare. (I say that as the maid who goes in and brings back the openness and the shine and the good smells.) When I went in to clean, I realized the tub wasn't draining. I spent 35 minutes pulling other peoples' hair and soggy, packed-in gunk out of a long drain. I had to put on Jenn Johnson's "You're Gonna Be Okay" and sing it out loud so I wouldn't throw up. It took us over $30,000 to get it back to where it was when we bought it. We learned some painful, awkward lessons.

A young couple bought a house three doors down from us in March, 2018 for $40,000, put in sweat and expertise, time, and some money, made substantial improvements, and in August (same year) listed it at $150,000. It was a two-bedroom, one bathroom. It sold for $143,000 the following spring. Two years later it was estimated on Zillow at $215,000, $167/square foot. For Knoxville, this was outrageous. But by 2022, some houses around here were above $200/square foot.

This brought up a philosophical conversation between us and Realtor Tom. He said that because of gentrification, Parkridge was whitening up fast. The black population was generally and slowly migrating to the other side of Magnolia Avenue.

Where did I turn when I needed a strong black female voice to educate me, to lead me? To Rev Rena.

"What do you teach over and over? When people come to you for counsel, what do you find yourself repeating?"

"I talk a lot about money. The struggle is real for many families. While you and I have sufficient money to live in other communities, I choose to stay in our neighborhood; I grew up here; I could leave if I wanted to, but I stay. I have the privilege of knowing I could leave at any time. There is a freedom to that. But some of our neighbors, don't have that choice. Their choices are often limited. Our houses are right beside each other, but because our options are different, one household has freedom while the other households are free to struggle.

"People who come to me sometimes say, 'I'm gonna do what I have to do, ya know?' They've got to pay their bills, care for their kids. Sometimes that leads to making poor choices, and those poor choices can lead to bad choices. They're just trying to survive. I share my faith and encourage them to not lose hope. Likewise, I use my influence to connect families with resources that are available."

I told Rena about our plan to buy a few small houses, keep the rent low, and lift up African American entrepreneurs.

204

"Rena," I said forcefully, "Talk to me about how race and racism plays into all this. Tell me the truth, don't hold back. I want to hear you."

"I don't talk so much about racism as I do history," she responded. "That's heard more easily." Then she took a deep breath. "You can expect suspicion. In our African American Knoxville history, whites have come into historically black neighborhoods that have been underinvested bought up properties at a low cost and rented to low-income families. Over time as investment is made in these neighborhoods, the property values begin to increase, higher income families move into the neighborhood and poor families are displaced. Rents are no longer affordable and homeownership is no longer a reality."

Rev Rena was totally correct. Appropriate caution noted. Handsome and I determined to keep her wisdom in mind as we navigated the rental world.

What Gentrification Looked Like on Woodbine

Imagine a gorgeous old dame of a house with faltering paint, neglect and time degrading her beauty, the glorious now sagging, only a few strengths left. Then a container appears, and it is filled with old wood and bad smells and rotted parts. Sometimes it is spray-painted by gangs while waiting to be filled. Stickers appear declaring new windows, signs appear on doorways, and loose wires are tucked away. Boards are replaced, fresh paint brightens the exterior, and the porches are bolstered.

The price increases by $100,000, someone who looks similar to us buys it, and poof, property values and taxes rise. Flowers appear near the front porch. A dog barks from the inside.

Then our poor neighbors ask if their vouchers will still be accepted, but their landlord decides to sell their house to someone for a substantial profit, and the cars on the street upgrade a bit. Everyone is very excited to have moved here … what a great neighborhood, what a reasonable price, what a great deal!

That scenario was literally happening all around us. And the voucher people? Several of our neighbors, including our beloved Ray-Mee, Cinco, Jerrell, Terrell, and Henry were out.

In October of 2019, our beloved neighbors got the word. Their house was going to be sold. The family of five had to be out by the beginning of December, about 35 days away. Ray-Mee was extremely stressed, pursuing housing options and not finding anything her voucher could cover. This was gentrification at its worst.

I think we participated in this system without even realizing it when we bought our house; gentrification can be similar to systemic racism in that way. Until we gained new understanding, we didn't discern that the systems that benefitted us were harming others. For us, the price of our house was terrific; in other parts of the city, this house would cost double, literally hundreds of thousands more. But as we watched the gentrification tsunami roll through, we became sure that our purchase of 2330 began the increase of our block's real estate prospects and prices.

So how do we gentrify with justice? How do we speak with Ray-Mee's house owner when they don't live here, don't want to be contacted (we tried), don't want to be personal — they're just ready for their check? Perhaps gentrifying with justice was more about fixing Ms Janet's awning and helping Ray-Mee get a loan for her dentures … but what about the economics of our neighbors?

Back to Cinco: Moving, End of November, 2019

After weeks of bringing home all the empty boxes I could find, it finally happened. Ray-Mee finalized her packing just as Thunderbolt also moved off the street.

It was so sad to think of life on Woodbine without these priceless people! I could hear their voices in my mind:
"Suzay, I want some peanut butter. It's the best thing in the whole world, except maybe orange juice."
"That is LIT."
"Those shoes are *fresh*."
"C'mon, bruh, let's go ballin'. I'm gonna take you to school, old man."
"May I pat the chickens and check for eggs?"

I had to brush the tears away as I helped them load boxes.

Grant got Blue, the stick-shift flatbed Ford, so I could help them move. They needed a truck for their beds and mattresses, those same bunks we had helped them move from the cabin. We loaded up Blue while Grant and the men of my extended family helped Miz Janet with fixing her porch awning and cleaning her gutters.

Cinco was a subdued version of himself. He was trying to be helpful when asked, but I could tell he was simply and irrevocably sad. In another circumstance, I think he could have shed a few tears, but not while we were lifting and loading, "taking care of business."

The new house was smaller, especially the bedrooms, but it was cozy and had everything they needed. The yard was extensive. It sat on a downward slope with a view of the Smoky Mountains that anyone would envy.

As I left his new house, Cinco's caramel eyes seemed so sad, but I could tell he was trying to put on a brave face. "Bye, Suzy," he said a bit too softly. I blew him kisses and hoisted myself up into Blue, mashing down the clutch and feeling the sorrow of distance. I remembered:

"Can I use your phone, Suzy? I wanna call my mom."
"Sync, why don't you just walk across the street and ask her permission? She's just *right there.*"
"It's too far to walk and I can just use your phone," he would insist.

Now *across the street* was a simple and beautiful thing of our past. I felt keenly the loss of our proximity, the sound of the bounce of the basketball as he walked to our goal, the crash of his bike on our front steps.

Since they left Woodbine, our families have stayed in touch. Cinco has continued to be a part of our family, drinking more orange juice than I can swim in, loving Doritos, yelling one foot from the TV when the Vols play, and challenging Grant to arm-wrestling matches every time he comes over (Grant still wins *every time*). When his voice changed, we freaked out: *Cinco, the young man.* He passed me up in height at 5'7" in 2022; by 2026, I imagined him at 6'3", a wire of a young man, determined to fill out his slender frame with muscles and gold.

～ecccc～

"Home begins with love and safety," Hamilton said with tears in his eyes. "The basics. The foundation for connection. I didn't have that as a kid, and then, to my growing dismay, I didn't experience it in my marriage."

Hamilton stayed with us as he awaited a divorce settlement. "During these last three months, you've provided the home for me that I've never had … never in my whole life. It's been amazing to be here," he smiled, eyes sparkling. "You and Grant actually *like* each other. You hike and laugh and manage the house together. You can be quiet together. You trust each other, defer to each other. You want the other to succeed, to be well. You build each other up and speak kindly, even though you are so different. You're attentive to each other. You make space for others and value people." He rubbed his eyes. "I've never seen that modeled, ever, and I didn't experience that freedom or oneness in my own marriage. There was none of the general ease and happiness and nurturing I've experienced here. This is the first time in my life — ever — that I've really felt *at home.*"

Grant and I remained silent, holding a sense of spaciousness so Hamilton could continue to speak at his own pace. This unhurried listening and revealing was a gift to all of us.

"You don't try to control each other." His eyes misted again. "I've never known that freedom. I've been managed and manipulated and controlled more than I even comprehend. I'm coming out of my former life with new eyes. Thank God for therapy. Thank God for friends." He drew a deep breath. "Without basic safety in my family of origin, my childhood hope for connection and affection withdrew deep into my soul's caverns. But you know," he said with a quivering chin, "I *wanted* to completely open up within my marriage. I *know* God made me to be deeply connected with people, especially my wife and my children." He sighed. "But that didn't work in my marriage."

Grant and I looked at each other, humbled. We weren't doing anything strange or special ... we were just living. In a home. With Hamilton. For us, that looked like Hamilton having space to do his laundry twice a week and being in charge of dinner once a week. It was Wiley warming to him and quickly trusting him enough to snug up next to him on the couch. It was deep conversations after dinner and outrageous football uproar on the weekends. It was Wordle-ing in the family room when the dishes were done and movie nights with Grant's famous popcorn shared out of a massive wooden bowl made by artist and friend Tyler Jamison. It was asking Hamilton to help me move heavy things and set up space heaters and feed the hens when we were gone. It was the comedy of watching Hamilton, Grant, and Wiley chase a few small rats out of our grill. It was welcoming him into our very simple lifestyle and helping him see that though we lived in an uncomplicated way, we lived like kings and queens, lacking nothing, rich in food and friendship. We would clink brown bottles above the candlelit table, toasting the Lord and His provision, feasting on a sumptuous meal and even richer after-dinner discussion. "Kings and Queens of Woodbine!" he declared, acknowledging the kindness of the Lord's good gifts.

"And now I get the privilege of creating a new home for me and my children," he said, simultaneously looking excited and frightened. "What kind of home culture do we want to create? Around what ideas will we form our home — what are our words, our values, what will we rally to? And how will I manage?" His eyes moved downward. When he raised his head, tears splashing from his nose, he quietly asserted, "God will help us. God will help *me*."

Yes to that, as we add another prince to the glorious royal street of Woodbine Avenue.

The Princess

In the fall, Njalla drove by to check in with me and her appearance took my breath away. No bonnet, no frizz, no nap: her hair was *DID*. It was a stunning African pattern reserved for African princesses and was gorgeous on her. Her eyebrows were manicured to perfection, as were her nails. Her clothes were clean, right down to her shoes. She was lucid and erudite, and wanted me to see her like this. While on one hand I wanted her to know we loved her in her darkest times, it was so good to see her walking in more healthy light. She looked beautiful in it.

God, I thought. *I am so moved by her beauty. It points to a wellness, a wholeness, that she was destined for. I want this for more people. I want to see others truly reflecting Your regal glory, princes and princesses, full of Your dignity and shimmering with Your light. I imagine You sitting on Your throne, royal and resplendent, a smile on Your face as they approach to curtsy and bow. We will all proclaim that You have won the battles for our hearts and spirits. And we will feast together, toasting Your goodness and power, regaling each other with dramatic stories of Your rescue and singing songs of victory.*

My imagination ignited. A dream came to mind, a scene from the future, unknown but perhaps someday, true:

It is my birthday, October 18th, 2039, twenty years after I'd last seen Njalla. I hear her voice: *Njalla!* She is streaming on a news site, an authority, interviewed for her expertise on homelessness. She is chairing a government task force … doing research … I could hardly hear the content because the blood rushing through my ears is so loud. Njalla!

She looks like an expert: poised, assured, passionate. I feel the fire in her again, channeled and burning brightly for the cause of homelessness.

Our local station, WBIR, has ideas about how to get her contact information. We meet on her secure app three days later.

"Njalla! I don't know if you even remember me. Our paths crossed in Knoxville, Tennessee, on Woodbine Avenue. You briefly lived with us."

"Oh Miz Suzanne, is that you? Oh my goodness." Njalla's hand flies to her mouth.
"I know, dear one, I've aged. I was well into my fifties when you were with us, and twenty years have passed. But I knew you from the sound of your voice — the recent news segment. You've grown into a beautiful woman, Njalla. You present yourself so well! I always knew you had the promise and ability to go so far. Look at you!"
"Miz Suzanne! You saw it! Oh, we have so much to catch up on, but my assistant has me meeting with another caller in four minutes."
"Njalla, are you ever near Knoxville? Could we meet?"
"No, I'm mostly in Washington now. The President heard my story, Miz Suzanne, and appointed me to head the task force. It's a miracle, and I feel so inadequate. What am I doing here? But I keep going. I just keep trying. Oh!"
She got up and walked to the red purse that was hanging on the back of the plain white office door. I could see her figure now — she looked sturdy and solid and

feminine, more in control of her body than when she lived with us. She quickly returned to the screen.

"Miz Suzanne, do you remember this?"
She presses a worn piece of paper to the screen. I can just read the handwriting — her handwriting. I read it aloud:

You are worthy of love
You are worthy of a good home
You are worthy of peace
The Truth will set you free

My voice cracks, and I both laugh and cry.
"Njalla! You saved it!"
"Keep reading, Miz Suzanne, please. Out loud."

Fight to live your life in the truth, not the lies
You will not live according to paranoid thoughts; you will live in the truth
Forgive others and forgive yourself
Give yourself grace
Keep battling
We love you!

"Miz Suzanne. You were right, you and your husband were right. And I fought, Miz Suzanne. Damn, I have fought for my life."
"Njalla, look where you are. You're doing it! You're doing it right now! I'm so proud of you."
"I've got to go. Would you give my assistant Rachel your contact information? I want to talk more and tell you … oh, so much to say. But later."
"I will. Thank you for your time. And we still love you. Big hugs. Go get 'em!"

I cried and cried on my knees, just saying, "Thank You, God, for her life." I had to get up twice for tissues, and my aging joints did not appreciate that, but I was so thankful and elated it did not matter.

~~~~~

Njalla moved out of Tennessee and eventually ended up in rehab in Texas. Njalla's mother's car had been locked, dead, and parked at our house for about two years when she gave us permission to junk it. One of the windows had slipped into its socket and couldn't be reinstated, so I tried to reach in and retrieve all I could before it was towed. It felt so intimate to get into her things. "Njalla," I thought, "how are you? I wish I could see you face to face." I decided that what I could save, I would send to her in Texas.

210

Much of one box was soiled pots and pans. I took them into our kitchen and washed them. She had clothing strewn in the front seat; I washed some of it, but the rest, mildewed and victim to the weather of the past two years, went straight into the trash bag.

It was strange. Here I was, her house slave again, but this time I had a different feeling: I loved her compassionately, tenderly. I felt deeply for her pains, her trauma, her family. I respected her brave attempt to make her car her home, a small, safe, and intimate space filled with treasures that defined her young life. *Oh, Njalla, you have worked so hard to live and yet not live, to be safe externally while internally, you didn't know how to stop the emotional chaos echoing in the chambers of your heart, the synapses of your mind. You have fiercely guarded your life while running from the harm of it. I'm so glad you are a survivor ... but I want more for you than just surviving.*

~ellee~

In the back two-thirds of the 2003 Ford Explorer, Njalla had organized her life into bins. I hesitated to touch any of them. They felt holy, personal, intimate. It took me a few days to decide to open them.

One bin contained information about her mother's death. I flashed back to the first time Njalla and I had a serious talk. We were on the back porch at the high top table, and tears were rolling down her cheeks as she explained why she felt she had killed her beloved mom. Her family had left it up to 20-year-old Njalla to decide when to pull the plug on her cancer-ridden mother; she died shortly after Njalla gave the doctors her consent. To me it was compassion, but to Njalla it felt like medical murder. There were pictures from her youth; Njalla was such a cute little girl! Photos of her mother, her family, and people I did not know had been tucked here and there in another bin. Njalla had also kept her mother's history of work badges. How hard she had worked to manage her life and preserve the memory of her mother!

In a medium-sized container were clothes and personal care items, a variety of nail polishes, and a gorgeous wig. It made me miss her so much. Elegant, stately statues of shapely black women were tucked in another bin, but a few had been broken. With regret I put the broken things into the trash bag. There was so much dignity in those statues. I reflected that as a girl I only saw statues and paintings of black women if I was in another country.

The treasures in a large bin related to food: a dozen bottles of spices, old and sticky oil that had leaked out, food tools and baggies, a can opener and, was this the knife she told me about ("If anyone comes at me...")? Shuddering, I remembered the feeling of praying for her safety, and when it was so cold, texting her to come stay with us, and always getting a reply of, "I'm okay, thank you, don't worry about me, really I'm okay." The final container had thick blankets, wraps, and scarves. Njalla, wrapped in her car when I dearly wanted her to be wrapped in our love at home.

I sent her one box. Two boxes. A third, then a fourth, and a fifth. She was delighted to see her wig, to receive anything from the car. I was concerned that it might be too emotionally heavy, especially after rehab, but she seemed grateful to reconnect with her old things. I got into the routine of going to the local postal service twice a week, lugging the heavy parcels. "It's going to Dallas, please." Never had Texas seemed so far away, yet with such a near heartache.

And then, suddenly, I didn't have the correct phone number for Njalla. My heart ached to know that she was alright. When I said my prayers at night, as she came to mind, I lifted her up, hoping that Texas held life and light for her. Productivity. Meaning. Relationships. Healing.

When I worked on my masters in ethics and leadership, I wrote about Plato's Cave. It is a famous story which I will tell minimalistically here using female pronouns. Imagine people imprisoned in a cave, only able to look forward, and in the dark. Behind them is a fire that casts shadows and light onto the cave wall in front of those imprisoned there. Since they cannot look around, in their limitation, they perceive and process reality according to what they see playing out on the cave wall.

One day, a person escapes, makes her way out of the cave, and lives in reality for a time. Adjusting to reality is a process. At some point, she remembers the others in the cave, and turns, giving up her freedom in order to return to the cave and rescue the others. She guides them out of the cave and helps them adjust to the real world.

I see Njalla as a character in this story. I can imagine her in the noble position of guide, using the freedom and wisdom she finds outside the cave to return to help others who are still caught up in the world of shadows and fire. She is fierce enough; she has endured her own shadows and fire; she has earned much knowledge through pain and trauma. Oh God, where is she?

The legacy Collins and Njalla left with us guides us to this day. I'll never look at trauma or OCD the same, ever, ever, ever. Collins's vulnerability was transformational to all of us: he is so courageous. His love for gathering people has marked me; knowing others deeply has marked Grant. Those values are now woven into how we live.

Njalla's destructive crashing, her intensity, and the fallout of racism and family trauma have directly changed how I listen and enter into the lives of others. All that defined her — trauma, racism, and family — seemed set to crush her; yet I believe within her there is a bold and mighty woman who can change the course of this society with her voice and experience, if she can maturely weaponize her trauma for good.

Njalla could be a wounded healer.

Njalla could become a light in the dark caves of homelessness, depression, and substance abuse.

May it be so, Lord.

~elles~

I found that in opening my life to others in my own home, my spiritual immaturities and distortions came to light. With the help of my podcast mentor Pete Scazzero, I made this list of what I needed to unlearn/learn and practice for the rest of my days.

Unlearn	Learn and Practice
Shallow spirituality: Church and Jesus don't really affect change or form my life. (A Southern struggle for sure.)	Intimate spirituality based on rhythms that open me up to God like silence, solitude, sabbath, Scripture, listening
Ignore my blind spots	It's my responsibility to pursue new understanding where I have blind spots
Emotional immaturity; poor skills	Emotional depth and maturity; practicing strong relational and emotional skills
Defining success as money, power, privilege, likes, followers; world- and self-driven measures of prosperity	Defining success as maturity, loving others, serving well, wisdom; God-measured prosperity
"Safe" love that still serves me	Sacrificial love that honors God and people
Impressing others; others' opinions of me are ultra-important	Obeying God; God is my first love and His opinion of me is primary
Conforming to the norm of the world or a church	Conforming to the norm of the Kingdom

Not allowing God to interfere in my ambitions, my money, my soul	Letting God into my motives, defensiveness, bank accounts, ambitions, dreams … my soul!
Ignore my soul's pathology (and my family's too)	Dive into my soul's pathology (recognize my family's pathology with grace and truth)
Be cynical or simply ignore social issues that make me uncomfortable, like racism or abortion	Confront racism or any difficult issues with grace and truth; be a learner
Do. Do more. Don't slow down.	Be. Be more. Slow down.
Closed doors, territorial with space, guardedness	Open doors, hospitable home, living honestly
Individuality	Neighboring
My heritage's point of view; defensive	Open to others' point of view; listening
A politicized church	A kingdom-oriented church
Church aligned with politics; church used by politicians	Church aligned with Jesus and the Kingdom
First pursuit: self-centered success	First pursuit: Jesus.
Combine the American dream with the prosperity gospel to justify what I want or have	Wisely assess the American church vs global church of the ages
Get to more stuff, happiness, don't deal with feelings, accumulate, ignore anger, jealousy, envy	Grow my daily relationship with the Holy Spirit, embrace simplicity, deal with ALL the feelings

Church: Crowd, entertainment, programs flowing out of technicians' expertise and marketing	Church: Transformative community flowing out of inner life with Jesus
Keep wealth for yourself and your family; dam up the flow of wealth to pool around you	Invest wealth into others' well-being, steward wealth's flow to benefit others and God's world
Do life the way the culture does life	Do life the way Jesus calls us to do life
Avoid grief and loss; stay numb, live in denial, keep moving and don't feel, the past is past	Search for the treasures found in the grief and loss of my neighbors, their cultures, their histories
Repeat the sins of my family because that's what they taught me	Break the power of the sins of my family by relearning from Jesus how to live and love
Filled with stuff, clinging to the world	Filled with the Holy Spirit, letting go of the world
Stay so busy and full that I don't have to deal with inner growth. Speed up so I can't contemplate my immaturities, challenges, and wounds.	Make space to renew my self, to listen to God, to heal, to be challenged. Slow down to stay in step with the Spirit.
Dominate my body. It's full of crazy. Compare it to others' bodies and my 20-something fitness level.	Appreciate my body. It's been redeemed and is doing the best it can to serve me well. I'm a soul in a temporary body.

Chapter Twelve: the Pandemic(s), 2020-2021

2020 WAS SUPPOSED TO BE the year of perfect vision. People were celebrating the gift of sight: 20-20 eyesight is exacting, clear, sharp. So what did we see for 2020? People were hoping for overall prosperity, strong business networking, personal happiness, positive activity, stronger relationships. Gain and growth and goodness. But, as the saying goes, it's *hindsight* that is 20-20.

In my neighborhood, the complexity of two pandemics — racism and COVID-19 — intertwined like the double helix of DNA and staggered the United States.

When I spoke with black friends, they told me that US citizens were able to view a more accurate experience of racism through the video of George Floyd's murder. They told me that *finally*, Americans saw more deeply into corrupt, racist systems of power, and this time, more Americans reacted and acted. My friends lamented that this pandemic of racism had been raging unchecked for years, even centuries, in some areas of our nation, and the sickness was destroying not only black lives, but the truths of our country: *Let freedom ring. One nation, under God, indivisible. Liberty and justice for all.* Racism, like violence, often acted like a virus, spreading from person to person, generation to generation. The virus of racism had to stop.

COVID-19 encircled the globe like a reaper's hand, silently at first, then with voracious vigor. It disregarded station or class, location or border. It felt like the books of Exodus and Revelation came to life, a plague similar to Pharaoh's day. Rather than prosperity, 2020 became a year of crisis relationally, economically, personally, corporately, and globally. The world felt like it was rolling off course, as if a nightmare had become reality, our blue marble rolling off into an unseen micro-verse of harm and chaos and sickness and death.

The winter chill gave way to spring's rebirth of pre-March Madness enthusiasm and high competition at the goal. One evening I arrived home to a weary husband. He had found out some bad news. Today was a day of fights. He and Ray-Mee filled me in.

The kids were off from school to accommodate our county's voting schedule. Home all day, 80+ degree weather … a foretaste of summer, right? Bliss to have a break, right?

Yet the basketball court had become a site of contention: cussing, threats, bullying, and domination, according to one side of the story. As they say around here, some of the boys were "showin' their ass." Ray-Mee said it got aggressive enough for her to pull Cinco off the court.

I sighed: What were we going to do about the aggression at the basketball goal? More and more it was a place of anger and bullying. One male neighbor indicated *that's just the way it is*. It was a battle that some boys win and others lose. They had to toughen up and show the drive and skills to compete on the court. I thought, "Tell that to a fourth-grader who is accosted on the court by an eighth-grader."

Sometimes talking didn't solve much.
Sometimes fights were useless.
Sometimes kids were hurt and worn out and frazzled because of their own home situations.
Sometimes they exploded on the outside because the inside was raw with need.

Then there were the days that were incredible at the goal. Dunking contest days were always my favorite. I'd take my Sony a7 camera and get photo after photo of the boys doing their best to slam the ball through the rim, mimicking the fancy stunts of their favorite NBA players.

The kids at the Loud House were also starting to play. They were little kiddos, ages three through five, and did not know to get out of the street as quickly as the big kids. Sometimes it felt dangerous; several of our older neighbors were getting very nervous about it.

One afternoon Handsome and I drove home and noticed all the city goals had no nets. What was that about? Then we realized: COVID-19, which was permeating every global border, a virus cleverly penetrating the cell of the world, with uncanny speed. And our goal? Touching the ball, passing the ball — oh no.

With kids beginning to engage remote learning, the goal was one of their greatest reliefs; being home doing school was not "fun" or "comfortable" for any of the players. Should we follow the city's example and move our goal when it was giving them a vent for their remote learning steam?

No one came into our house. People wore masks, even alone in their own cars. What was happening? Proximity became a fearful thing, a possible precursor to illness (even death), an exposure, a contraction, a hazard, a risk, a liability. I missed hugs.

During COVID-19's lockdowns and warnings, our home filled with three consistent relationships as water fills a glass. Handsome and I welcomed our daughter Lu as she fled Brooklyn just before it blew open with the virus. We adjusted to a new normal: family dinners at 6:30pm. Tasks till 7:45pm. Grant popped popcorn just before our evening show at 8:00pm. We read till around 10pm, then arose early for our strange, limited, home-bound days. Lu and I transitioned to sitting in front of screens, using Zoom, and coping with being fidgety. Thank goodness for the loving closeness of Wiley and Ninja Bear and the hysterical entertainment of the chickens. As I worked from home I found I needed them: the touch of their cool fur. Their even temperaments and accepting love. The comfort of their nearness, and their honest requests for affection. Wiley's bark-alert when the mailman came (the big social event of the day).

The End of an Era, May 2020

Standing outside in open air, we relaxed our masks.
"Rev Rena, what am I missing? Is there a code, some unwritten rule about how to deal with neighbors who don't care about late-night noise?" The Loud House was on a roll. A painfully abrasive aural roll.

"Yes, there is a code. You never complain; you suck it up. You can't change them so you change yourself. You adapt. As a white person the police are your first line of defense. For the black person, that's never our first line of defense.

"Part of being in an urban neighborhood is the closeness of houses. We're all stacked on top of each other, so we're used to hearing each other. On every block there's a party house; it's just the way it is. There's always one within hearing. They're young and they don't care and that's it. So suck it up. Adapt. Change yourself; you aren't gonna change them! Can you imagine from their point of view how ridiculous it would look for you to walk over there and ask them to be quiet?" She burst out laughing, each giggle a wasp sting. She continued:

"Let me give you an example. I hate your basketball goal. I have hated it from the very first day and every day since. The position of the goal is right in front of my house. You can't control who shows up with a ball ready to play. I hate the foul language that is used. I hate their trash that I pick up all the time. Their balls hit our cars. They put their clothes on our cars. I hate that when I get home from church on Sunday, I can't take a nap because they're so loud. Sunday is *my* day. All I want is to relax and rest, but they're out there. So I turn my soft music up a little louder and try to rest. I can't change them, so I change me. I suck it up. I don't say anything even though the front of the house has turned into a full-on basketball court."

218

I had a meeting so I had to end our quick conversation, but I was really disturbed. The only time she'd ever mentioned anything about the goal to me was at the start of COVID-19; her concern was for the kids being in such close contact with each other. Rev Rena was always, always concerned about the street's children.

I thought a lot about what she said. I was used to collaboration and communication — that was *my* "first line of defense." I would engage and consult and brainstorm with others, fostering a team approach. That was not the code here, and I needed to accept that. But I wrestled: To me it felt dishonest. It felt like hiding. It felt inauthentic and fake when you weren't honest with your neighbors. It didn't feel like the Kingdom of God to me. I really wrestled with this; so did Grant. But we had come to this neighborhood and their code — we were the outsiders, and for outsiders, there is always a learning curve. I asked Miz Janet about the goal; she too disliked the foul language and the trash. We all agreed on that.

After hours of conversation, Handsome and I decided to remove the goal. It was so sad to us. Our intentions had been so good! Gather. Gather and create space for play, for fun, for relationships to build. We did not anticipate the bad language, the trash, the disrespect, the lack of self-awareness, or the offense. We didn't anticipate the silence if we were causing problems.

Handsome's first response was, "I put up that goal and never thought to ask our neighbors. That was wrong and I'll apologize. What a blind spot." I loved his humility ... and realized that my picture of collaboration began *after* the goal was up, not before purchasing the goal. Sigh — it was a blind spot for both of us.

Then he noted, "You know, some of our neighbors never cross the street to come to our house; it's always us going over to them. You go over to their porches to talk. I didn't even realize until now ... they don't cross that invisible line. Ever. Not once. Only Miz Janet, the kids, and Ray-Mee freely come to our house. None of the other adults."

I mused, "I wonder if we've offended them in other ways, and they just haven't said anything? I may never know because if I've offended them they might just 'suck it up and adapt.' Ugh. Is this authentic friendship? What is our relationship to them? Maybe it means far more to me than it does to them."
"You're starting to question everything," Handsome remarked.
"Yes, I am. I don't know what's honest and what's 'suck it up.' I feel my insecurities hammering at what I thought was stable and good. God, help me perceive this rightly. I don't want to be paranoid or reactive ... and I know I'm hurting and questioning right now."

219

So we emptied the goal's base of all the water that stabilized it, envisioning all the dunking and airballs and attempted shots. Memories drained out of us like the water drained out of the base, pouring down the sidewalk and onto our beloved Woodbine.

We knelt in the kitchen and prayed for God to bless our neighbors, to be gentle with our wounds, to help us love and serve our neighbors, and to continue to help us see our blind spots. We professed trust that He would make something good come out of this.

Then Handsome took a shot ... the liquid kind ... and we closed this long, emotional day.

~~~

Once we removed the goal, we noticed — sadly — that the neighborhood boys didn't come by anymore. When we saw them walking on the street or at the Y, we were all glad to see each other, but then nothing further developed. Grant wondered if we did the right thing. There was definite tension between loving the kids at the goal and loving our neighbors.

The "invisible line" was an important concept for me to grasp. Some people — the ones who owned their houses and were not subject to the whims of gentrification — had lived here for decades. I had to remember that Grant and I were outsiders, relatively new to this neighborhood, and we didn't know all the hidden, unspoken rules. And as the neighborhood was gentrifying, the rules were changing.

When we were considering moving to 37917, we interviewed a few Knoxvillians who had done the same. What learning curves did they experience? What advice did they have for us? One man had offered us this: Stay a decade. Stay planted even if you get uncomfortable and want to leave. He said, "It will take up to a decade for you to earn the trust of the people who live around you." Based on his advice, Grant and I had committed ten years minimum.

It was true: It was taking years to earn the trust of some adults. They had good reasons to be reserved in their trust and affection toward us: hard stories mixed with racism, American history, and painful personal experiences. It would be quite arrogant of us to assume we could come in and sweep people off their feet. We needed to consistently love, to kindly serve, to be winsome like Jesus and steady at our house. Perhaps someday our adult neighbors would feel more comfortable in and near our home.

One problem that I observed immediately, though, was the rapid turnover of buyers and renters due to the exploding housing market in Parkridge. I looked up and down the other side of the street: the half-way house was gone. Reyana, Ray-Mee & crew, Thunderbolt and Freddy, Angela and MeLissa and Henry (Misi-ell's dad) were gone. The Loud House kept changing. A few houses were still vacant, a few were being flipped. Our side of the street was similar. All that change in four years. How could we foster trusting relationships in such a quickly changing environment?

The first steps seemed to be to know everyone's name, to intentionally say hello, and — for me — host some gatherings for those who were open to friendship.

Reys and Proximity

A quiet COVID evening of watching Poldark was interrupted by a call from Reys.

"Suzy? Suzy, you home? You got one-uh those slide thingies that can unlock car doors?"

"I'm sorry, Reys, we don't have one of those things." I looked at Grant, whispered the situation to him, and told her I'd call her back. We called a local service. For $54 they would come within 45 minutes. Done.

K'mia got on the phone.
"We called one of those lock service places," I started.
"How much they cost?" she said worriedly.
"We'll pay for it. They'll be there within 45 minutes."
"Oh, okay, thank you. Thank you very much."

About 25 minutes later a tech man met Grant and the Reys women.

We reflected on the simple experience.
"They've never asked anything like that of us," Grant said thoughtfully.
With conviction he stated, "This is all about proximity."
"What do you mean, Handsome?"
"They called because they know us. They know us because we've lived closely enough to them that Reys could walk to our house. This is all about being a neighbor and living on the same block. Proximity. They didn't expect us to pay, but they allowed it because of relationship."

We held the word gently, feeling the firm weight of what proximity had cost us and given us, and how our lives had changed so radically over the past several years. Both of us reflected on the challenge and goodness of being on Woodbine, of being given the honor and privilege of loving Reys and being loved by her.

Proximity. Nearness.

I think of all the kids who have passed through our door … neighbors who have come and gone. Sometimes they've been like feathers in the wind, blowing through long enough for me to admire their colors and patterns and shapes, then moving on with the breeze. Meals together. Cooking together. Basketball games together. Time on the porch, time on the street, time at the park. Meeting family members, dogs, and cats. Knowing names and faces and cars. Knowing the voice of which Mama was yelling for her kids and knowing if she was upset or annoyed or concerned by her tone. And the adults: break-ups and job changes, favorite desserts and swapping books. Ah, Woodbine. Home.

~~~~~

"Hey! Hey y'aw!" It was Freddy — Thunderbolt's Freddy.

He told us he was going to check himself into a Salvation Army program for substance abuse. He saw himself. He saw the beast that longed to wrestle him down and bleed the life out of him: drugs. "Druhs."

Our list of neighbors who had left grew longer: Freddy was gone. I missed seeing him on his very-tall bicycle. I had hope that he would be able to work out his life, to conquer the Goliath of drugs, to again be able to manage his own home.

We need food.

Some garments are well made, with reinforced seams, sturdy fabrics, and durable threading. Others are cheaply made with little quality control, and easily torn. In the fabric of Knoxville's economy, our poor friends quickly felt COVID ripping at the seams of what they barely held together. With the fraying came fear.

In my neighborhood, people had all kinds of jobs: professional, office, manufacturing, fast food, education, stay-at-home mom, nurse practitioner, welfare-at-home. As the nation adjusted to COVID-19 closures and restrictions, lower class jobs were quickly in jeopardy and some middle/upper class jobs were modified. Among my neighbors, closures, furlows, and job availabilities seemed to run along the seams of class. I realized this truth: When someone was in a higher class, they didn't feel or experience the concept of classism as much as those in the lower classes, who felt it every day, exacerbated by COVID.

Ray-Mee lost her job at a local fast food restaurant. Her government-supplied food aid was too low for the family of five, so people filled in the gap until her food stamps were adjusted and the family received their relief check. It was truly a beautiful thing: I asked Beth Biller, a woman in my congregation, to speak with her women's Bible study about helping Ray-Mee. Many of them were stay-at-home moms by choice, to their joy. They all lived in prosperous areas of town and were financially secure. Within days of connecting with Beth, food spilled out over the car seats and onto the floorboards and under the seat belts and on top of the toys in Beth's minivan. We transferred food to my car — literally stuffed it full — and off I raced to East Knox.

At the top of Ray-Mee's steep driveway, I honked and put on my face mask before everyone piled out to help with groceries. The girls instantly spotted some sidewalk chalk, which was a rare commodity for them, and some bubbles. They quickly began driveway masterpieces in pastel chalks. My heart ached: I wished everyone had a Beth Biller.

A rhythm of help requested and help received emerged. Ray-Mee would send me a text: "Hey. We're out of meat." Simple, never demanding, but close enough in friendship to let me know their situation. I appreciated her vulnerability and did what I could to find people who could help. A West Knox woman named Jackie began to send me a letter every month with a $15 Kroger card for any neighbor who might need it, placed with love in an encouraging note. I wished everyone had a Jackie.

Our school system was still making breakfasts and lunches available to students (caveat: if the kids didn't have a way to get to the school, they didn't get the food). My church got involved by packing lunches. We worked for hours in the cool of the morning safely in the outdoor breezeway, talking about what series we were binging, how many times we had heard, "You're on mute," who had rearranged their furniture, who had put up a puzzle, who was baking bread, who had watched cat videos, who had found toilet paper at the store, who had cabin fever, who was ordering take-out from local restaurants, who had mask-ne, who had ordered something off of Amazon that day, what people thought about vaccines, who started a DIY project, who talked to themselves or their pets … all the COVID-related conversations. We packed cans of peas, green beans, and tuna; bags of rice and pasta and powdered milk; boxes of cornbread muffins and pancake mix; jars of peanut butter and spaghetti sauce.

In the 'hood, there was a restlessness and frustration rising. It stayed low, hovering above the streets, tumbling as people slowly walked to the corner store for a Gatorade or a pack of rolling papers, or hit up the gas station on Magnolia for something to eat. It was as if people were wading in limitation, feeling the shock-collar effect again of losing faster than the middle/upper class, being reminded (again) of their lower place in society, swimming in dirty waters of disregard. Gunfire in the dark echoed again across our area, evidence of agitation. Reports of abuse skyrocketed at a local aid agency.

My friends who had white collar jobs were leading life as if not much had changed, but had a heightened sense of anxiety. My medical friends were working at a furious pace with increasing pressures. My friend groups were polarizing around the vaccine, government stimulus checks, and the politicization of the pandemic. Some of my neighbors were quickly laid off or had to quit their jobs because their children were now at home for virtual learning.

The winters were the worst: I knew a few of my neighbors were asking the question, *Do we heat or eat?* Government payments helped them greatly, even as I heard my wealthier friends scoff at the effectiveness of how the money was used. In 2021-2022, The Great Quit became part of everyone's conversation. Businesses everywhere were advertising for workers, including signing bonuses and increased hourly wages. Along with most other business owners we knew, Grant couldn't find enough workers for his company.

People who had reserved times at the Woodbine house began to cancel. No one wanted to come into an environment outside of their own particular bubble. Grant and I found ourselves hosting one of our daughters for a year, which was our most beautiful gift delivered by COVID. But no one else came ... for two solid years.

Time lost its framework, and we had to scramble to keep our footing as time felt boundary-less. Screens helped maintain relationships at one level, but left most of us lonely in our true selves. We began to notice changes: People walked their dogs more often throughout the day, not just at the end of the day. In fact, there were simply more dogs, nicknamed "pandemic pups," to help us cope with our loneliness and unmet feelings of connection.

Time lost its joy. What gathering could we look forward to? A Zoom happy hour? There was no need to do your hair or makeup, no need to buy work clothing — in fact, people began to invest in athleisure outfits as they worked from home (WFH). People became unmoored, anxious, stale, relationally adrift, questioning their purpose, floating through days of work or loss of work. Conversations were centered around who had the virus, how severe were their symptoms, how fast their recovery. Did they regain their sense of smell? How were their lungs? Had they tried to do vigorous exercise yet? Companies raced to produce a vaccine. Society felt scrambled.

George Floyd's Murder

There are events during which you think, "This might change everything." In my lifetime: hearing God say He loved me, and He was enough. The death of my Grandaddy O. The birth of my daughter. My divorce. Awakening to Biology, and the privilege of teaching it. When the Twin Towers fell. Building a new life with Grant Standing. Moving to Woodbine. COVID-19. Cataclysmic times, times of restructuring, of life and death, even if unseen by the world.

46-year-old tall, black George Floyd's murder by white police officers was one of those national moments. I can still feel the outrage well up in me as I heard his cries on video: "I can't breathe." "Mama! They gonna kill me!" (Even now I write in tears.)

For eight minutes and 46 seconds an officer, Derek Chauvin, knelt on George Floyd's neck. Another officer even made suggestions about moving Big George, but Chauvin wouldn't budge from his perch like a vulture on Floyd's neck. Chauvin has since been convicted of murder and is in prison.

It was unfathomable to me, inhumane. Our nation was traumatized by it, rocked, moved to the heart, with protests and marches breaking out throughout the country and spreading to the world, bringing attention to racist police brutality. At this time in history, America was like boiling water.

We added our voices to the conversation, advocating for our black neighbors and friends who lived micro- and macro-aggressions every day. "White privilege is a real thing," I would explain. "If you've never been pulled over because of your skin color, that's white privilege. If you've never been followed around by security in a store, that's white privilege. If you've benefitted from the systems in your community because you are a white person, that's white privilege. Consider banking. Consider traffic stops. Consider food availability. Consider gentrification. It's in the air we breathe in Knoxville (80% white). The problem is it smells like perfume to us white people, although I'm convinced it's a stench in God's nostrils. Factors that propelled whites up and blacks down (such as slavery, redlining, and loan availability) have allowed classes and races to mix shallowly, so many whites do not realize, analyze, acknowledge, apologize, or change their community's systems." Those were hard conversations, and not always well-received.

This reality was blazing from the fire-gutted, looted buildings of our nation, spray-painted on the streets, shouted in every march: "I. Can't. Breathe." "No justice, no peace! Know justice, know peace!" I kept thinking back to Rev Rena's words: "Suck it up and adapt." After so long of sucking it up, people were exploding. And their feelings were valid.

A group of friends at dinner discussed power and racism as a terrifying combination. Bryant was on fire, his compassion and sensitivity to black Americans morphing into near-rage frustration. "Imagine yourself in the persecuted minority… put yourself in another country to really consider it … how would your life change? How would your opportunities change? How would your future look? How would you train your children? And for the men, how would you protect your wife and children in that environment?"

No one had a gripping answer. We were mostly silent.

A quick survey of our group revealed that most had believed American History as they had been taught in school, which was quite incomplete and told with a pro-white bias. If someone had a different perspective on race-based topics, most experienced conflict, though they did not seek it.

"My old man just can't have a thoughtful, calm, open-minded discussion about other ways of looking at history. To this day, he just can't do it. He thinks I'm crazy! I am met with anger, even an accusation of betrayal of family or friendship. *'You think that? Who are you now? What has happened to you?'*" Bryant mimicked.

Good question: What has happened to us?

~elles~

In June of 2020, Grant and I met hundreds of Knoxvillians at the World's Fair Site to express our high value of black lives, our frustration with police brutality, and our solidarity with our black neighbors. I was so glad to be there, so glad to show support publicly and boldly. This was a cultural break from my parents, who were not marchers. They did things through personal contacts, personal time invested, and generous contributions, whereas this time I felt moved to get out into the public square, wear black, and be with people. I needed to yell, to do something with the wave of angry energy sloshing within me. I wanted to feel the power of not being alone as a white woman advocating for black lives.

The rally signs were varied and telling:
Anti-racist mother raising anti-racist children.
No justice, no peace.
I. Can't. Breathe.
8:46
Racists have small dick energy.
Community not cops
#BLM
There comes a time when silence is betrayal.
Breonna Taylor would be 27 today. Say her name.
I understand that I will never understand, but I stand with you.
White silence costs lives. Be an #ally.
I'm here for my black students.
End white silence

One of my favorites:
I am not Black but I see you;
I am not Black but I hear you;
I am not Black but I mourn with you;
I am not Black but I will fight for you.

226

We marched with signs and chants to our cool downtown area, Market Square, which the protestors completely filled. White people who were having drinks or appetizers looked on awkwardly, even apprehensively — would something erupt?

On the march I was taking pictures and spotted an area of steps that would give me a sharp vantage point. As I ran ahead and climbed the steps, I tried to stay socially distanced from a young black guy and his friend who were filming the march. Still, we were close enough for me to hear him marvel: "I had no idea," he murmured as he leaned toward his friend. Through my mask I said gently, "I hope you feel loved and supported." He looked directly at me, eyes wide with awe, and said, "I do ... I do." Seeing his honest, marveling eyes gave me chills.

Notable black speakers and athletes spoke via bullhorn to the crowd, and then we observed 8:46 seconds of silence as an actor represented George Floyd as he died. "I can't breathe!" "Mama! Mama, they gon' kill me!" It was excruciating, emotional, uncomfortable.

People might make assumptions about who the hundreds of marchers were, what they believed, what their motivations were. I can speak generally: The rally was *not* about agreeing with Critical Race Theory or being a committed supporter of the organization Black Lives Matter. It was about caring, and showing it. It was not about political agendas or hot-buttons. It was about being outraged that a captive black man was killed in an illegal power dynamic. It was about all the other black people who have been treated like George Floyd. It was about loving my neighbor ... my black neighbor, my suffering neighbor. This rally was not about grasping for power; it was about letting those with power know we were watching, we were concerned, and we wanted healthy use of power and authority. It was about protesting injustice, speaking up, not wanting that horrific injustice to happen in our city, on my watch. It was about walking with my black neighbors so they would see with their own eyes that they had allies — being a visual testimony. It was about looking in each others' eyes and saying, like Romans 12, if one of us hurts, we all hurt. It was about declaring the diversity of the Kingdom from Revelation 7:9: Every tribe. Every nation. Every language. The honor of being God's people binds us together more than being a citizen of America or a certain city.

In the Name of God, black lives *do* matter! Why is that so important to speak out loud? Because historically for hundreds of years, black lives didn't matter much beyond economics. As a white woman, I needed to yell, *Yes, black lives matter.* I was not speaking from a place of guilt: I was speaking from a place of faith in the God who made His image-bearers of all colors and forms. I was honoring God when I shouted with conviction and hope, *Black lives matter!*

I affirm that all human lives matter. As a former Biology teacher and believer in a Creator, I think all creation matters. Because of the historical harm done to blacks by whites, however, I think it is crucial that white people determine to say and act like *black lives matter*.

～elles～

There's something captivating about how a small stream flows into a larger one, which then flows into a river, which, at some point, cascades violently and majestically toward the ocean.

Figurative streams were converging in my own life:
I was brain-hungry, intellectually alert to my next feast. I was unsettled with the disparities between classes and races I was experiencing daily. I was working with the Knoxville Fellows, a small cohort getting their Masters of Arts in Ethics and Leadership, who were collectively exploring justice, race, Scripture, ethics, spiritual formation, and leadership. I was eager to find the most accurate historical narrative of American history I could find, and, I wanted to know what it felt like to be black in Knoxville.

During turbulent 2020 I joined the Fellows to earn my Masters of Arts in Ethics and Leadership. One engaging professor, Doug Banister, taught us God's view of Biblical justice, classism, wealth gaps, and racism through Exodus, the Torah, Lamentations, Amos, and Paul's books. Each Biblical book was a stream; each stream was flowing into a river describing care for the poor and a national ethic of justice.

Professor Mary Terry, through articles and American history lessons, opened up the uncomfortable world of racism through more modern articles and discussion. I had wrestled with two historical questions on my own: Why did my American History class teach me that Columbus discovered America, when 30 million people already lived here? Why was I taught that the explorers were heroic, when some were guilty of greed-based genocide in the name of their sending country?

In class, I was left astounded, horrified, and confused: Why did some Christians think it was okay to go to church, then walk directly from their pew to a lynching? How did they convince themselves that lynching was Christ-like? Who do we perceive to be "right" Christians and who do we perceive to be "wrong" Christians? How did redlining work, and where was Christian vision and brotherly love when it was implemented? How did city-level governments justify urban renewal? What is Critical Race Theory, not just the harangue surrounding it? How is white nationalism intertwining with Christianity? What is Christian Nationalism, and does it reflect God's heart? Why has the term *woke* shifted, when originally it meant a white person who 'woke up' to the historical facts about racism, was moved in heart, and became an ally, but now is used as a scandalous accusation intertwined with political parties?

One afternoon I let my imagination run. I pictured each American historical people group as a stream flowing toward the ocean of melded humanity, each stream with their own story to tell: European white Americans, colonialists, African slaves, Irish folk, Chinese laborers, Japanese Americans, Black Americans, Native Americans throughout the mountains and plains, different classes of each race ... these and more were converging into one bubbling, roiling river near the mouth of the ocean. Clashes with boulders and barriers splintered the best and the worst of people; undercurrents and eruptions slipped one stream below another, sometimes unseen; eddies swirled in circles for those looking for safety. Waterfalls became moments when all the streams jumbled violently together, forceful and loud and unsafe.

The thing about water is it always seeks the lowest place, then rests. I find that people usually do the opposite.

In my mind's eye I pictured a waterfall tumbling and bumbling toward the ocean so it could find the lowest place and come to a placid state. I imagined the explosion of water on the rocks and the water swirling around itself under the surface, blending all the streams until they emerged at the delta. The muddy, sickening sediments of racism and classism settled in streaks on the way to the ocean of oneness, mere aerial decorations that told an ancient story. And then there was blue ... deep and rich blue, beautiful hues that created a winsome, majestic scene.

I wanted to swim in those waters with my brothers and sisters of humanity. I wanted the healing feeling of seeing them swimming weightless after lamenting over their burdensome, heavy chains. I wanted to see the sun shine on the skin of the darkest Somali and the whitest Finn. I wanted to hear laughter and see children build sand castles together without prejudice.

~elله~

Handsome and I began to hear of people in the Parkridge area who were out to create change, one neighbor or one block at a time. All those nights I had awkwardly prayed for the prostitutes, not knowing how to reach them or love them ... God answered my cries by sending a dynamic yet quiet young couple, Will and Katie Boggs, into Parkridge to serve the street walkers. We had actually walked by their house dozens of times, never realizing who they were or what they were doing for our area of town. They began Likewise Coffee, a small café on Magnolia Avenue, to fund their ministry efforts. The name originated from the parable of the Good Samaritan in Luke 10:25-37:

229

"Which of these three do you think was a neighbor to the man who fell into the hands of robbers?"
The expert in the law replied, "The one who had mercy on him."
Jesus told him, "Go and do likewise." (excerpt, NIV)

I have to listen to Scripture to know who I am. Daughter, beloved, co-heir, warrior, nurturer, even farmer. When I read this parable, I am instructed about my redeemed self:
I cross cultural boundaries with compassion.
I am not afraid to get in the mix of something truly horrible, even life-threatening.
I enter into others' misfortunes. That may mean showing up with money, hospitality, and care.
I am alert to my path.
I am willing to be inconvenienced; I can accept a turn in my schedule for the sake of a person.
I can represent Jesus outside the church among the broken and helpless.
I care. I care at my own expense.

That is the identity behind Likewise.

Our community was rocked during the second spring of COVID-19. 2021 held such promise: People were hopeful about taking off their masks, returning to 'normal,' resuming work and school, and vacationing again. Our Knoxville black community had suffered horribly with sickness and death. I asked two black pastors how they were, and they said, "Busy. Busy with mental health. Busy with funerals. I'm burying too many people." Neither had been paid for almost a year. Their congregations were struggling financially so monetary support of their churches had dropped significantly. Everyone needed the sunshine and hope of spring.

Then the unthinkable began to happen.

Gangs from other cities moved into Knoxville to recruit for membership, trafficking, and drugs. A wave of crime and harm flooded our East Knox community. One by one, six Austin-East (AE) high school students died: shot.

The first child, Justin. January 27th, 2021. Age 15.
The second child, Stanley. February 12th. Age 16.
The third child, Janaria. February 16th, 2021. Age 15.
The fourth child, Jamarion. March 9th. Age 15.
The fifth child, Anthony. April 12, at AE, involving a school officer. Age 17.
The sixth child was shot just as schools were about to begin the fall semester, August 8. John John, age 17.

At first it was shock and horror, tears and wailing, protests and responsive promises by the city government. There was the immeasurable weight of sorrow and loss, boulders in my neighbors' shoes, steel beams shot through their souls, freight trains dumping pain in their heads, stone pyramids in their hearts. For a time, my neighbors couldn't even speak. We were zombies together, functioning and afraid of feeling more pain.

In the aftermath of George Floyd's death and the explosive tension around white authoritarian positions, very few people were training to be the new generation of policemen. The Knoxville police force was stretched to the limit; there were dozens of vacant positions and too few officers of color. Patrols picked up in the school's neighborhood but were inadequate to stop the murders. Athletic opponents began to cancel games scheduled at AE's fields; my Handsome was evacuated one evening at a football game because of a nearby shooting. The kids and community felt bereft.

Knoxville slumped onto a list of dangerous places to live. I read an article to my husband that designated our area as 'threatening.' After listening, he said in a firm and loud voice, "Where are the Christians who will read this article and say, 'Let's move there. *That's* where I want to make a difference. Let's go join all the other Christians who already live there and are suffering through this situation.'" Oh my goodness, I love that man.

For weeks, people came from all over the city to pray for the AE neighborhood, joining the neighbors who call those streets home. They met in large sanctuaries or outdoors in church parking lots so they could socially distance yet be together. I imagine from heaven we looked like a flock of birds landing and lauding with each prayer, hands high or heads bowed.

Flowers and food were sent to the teachers as offerings of kindness and support. People began to quietly meet and walk the circumference of the school grounds, praying and picking up trash as they cried out to God for relief and safety. Likewise Coffee did a t-shirt drive to benefit the school, printing 35 t-shirts for $20 each. They quickly sold out and ordered more, ultimately selling around 400 t-shirts! After one home game, we saw the AE football team gathered outside the stadium, thanking the kids who still played against them. Visionaries booked a prestigious University of Tennessee field so the school's football games could resume safely.

I will never forget sitting in the sanctuary of Overcoming Believers Church when the mic was spontaneously handed to the AE football coach. People had gathered to pray there, an open invitation to all of Knoxville, and it was packed. The coach walked up onto the stage and began praying with all of his heart. It was as if his soul was ripped open for all of us to see: a broken man. A devastated man. Weeping, he half-yelled, half-begged: "My babies are dyin',

Lord, but still I'm gonna praise You! My babies are dyin', Lord!" As he prayed, he paced with long strides. He was a big man, solid, and when he set a foot down, it felt as if he carried the weight of the world in each step. He reminded me of a lion — full, well-maned, powerful — in zoo captivity, pacing at the perimeter, knowing this was not the way it was supposed to be. Everyone's tears flowed freely.

I witnessed breath-taking faith. The immeasurable riches of knowing God deeply. The maturity of being able to hold the tensions of death and love. Truly the Holy Spirit hovered over us, bringing His peace in the midst of incalculable sorrow.

The fall of 2021 came, and it was as if my community was holding its breath. Grant and I still heard gunfire some nights, but no more students were shot. While the rest of the country was eager to rip off their masks, my 'hood was still fully masked up at the Fellini and the utilities payment kiosks. So many black folks still had their people in the hospital. Grant and I, fully vaccinated, hunkered down at home when we experienced COVID, mostly as a mean cold. He still has a very poor sense of smell to this day. Over several months, the majority of our neighbors suffered with the Omicron variant. It felt neighborly to give and receive fresh rolls or chicken noodle soup on the doorstep. All of us healed and returned to work, thanking God for His kindness to us for restoring our health.

Winter came with sporadic gunfire in the wee hours, fewer funerals, and very high utility bills. Food prices rose and my beloved Ray-Mee began asking for help with food again. The Fellini experienced shortages of most goods, off and on, but we all coped. The homeless population continued to increase, populating the interstate exit ramps and Fellini parking lot. Camps and trash sprang up in the weeds and brush. But as the temperatures thawed from 18 degrees up toward the 50s, the birds began to sing in February. Crocuses opened their purple faces. Daffodils pushed toward the sun.

Hope.

I have a secret: I have a wealthy uncle who loves to quietly, generously give money to those who need a boost. He called: "Suzanne, how is your neighborhood? I know this COVID impact is more rough on the poor. How about I give you some money and you help some folks? They don't need to know who it's from — just go do some good with it."

I discovered I like being a sneaky do-gooder. Waiting in the drive-through line at our local McDonald's, over and over, to pay for people's food was so fun! I made an arrangement with the manager and slipped him $100 in bills. Hearing people squeal made me giggle. "What? It's free?" And then there was an electrical bill ... anonymous food from the Fellini ... ah, the joy giving brings!

Reconnecting with Thunderbolt and Freddy

Handsome texted with Freddy as the spring warmed toward summer. We were hoping to share some of a housemate's durable goods with him since Freddy had just gotten a placement in subsidized housing. It turned out that Thunderbolt and Freddy were back together and on the third floor. What a surprise!

Freddy was waiting at the complex's main door for us; Thunderbolt looked very annoyed. They buzzed us in; I was surprised at all the security. "Thih heah i' the quiet buildin'; that theah i' the loud par'," Freddy explained.

They invited us in and we sat on their loveseat. Their small apartment consisted of two rooms: a bedroom/bathroom and a kitchen-closet-living-room-in-one. The kitchen was about the size of my wingspan, flat-handed, from wall to wall. They had a massive TV, the two couches, and nothing else. One wall was an open concrete closet with a single rod at the top. It was such a cold interior. I was reminded of someone who said, "The poor need beauty more than anyone else, because their lives have so much ugliness in them." No artwork, no flowers, no gardens outside; there were benches, however, and large shade trees that caught the breeze. And perhaps the beauty Freddy and Thunderbolt found was in each other, not in their surroundings.

Their cat was a bright spot. I could tell the story of my life in cats: from the time my mother wanted to teach me about babies and birth, cats have been my friends for fifty years. For some reason, I can charm 99% of them into friendship, however brief. Africa, Asia, the US, it has never mattered; I call to them with a trill and they "see" me, and I am invited in.

It took a moment to convince their kitty that I was a friend, but then I had a playmate for the rest of our visit. She had ocelot-patterned fur and wanted to be loved. She was a sweet distraction from the acidic, biting sting of entrenched cigarette smoke.

Thunderbolt warmed up and our conversation was congenial. She was short with Freddy; were they back in old relating habits? I felt my soul sigh. *God, bring them health, and may they be beauty to each other.*

∽‿ℓℓℓℓ‿∾

My final interaction with Thunderbolt was remarkable: she had been in the hospital, died, seen Heaven, looked at the book with names of people who trusted Jesus to get into Heaven, and come back to earth and her body. She spoke with love in her voice, and wonder: "I am a child of God. I saw Him! He

233

loves me. He loves me!" She seemed so much more free, this little pint-sized, big-voiced woman. Restful. There was not a shred of striving or strife about her.

I was dumbfounded, happy for her, and curious. I had so many questions, but she was still recovering and foggy-minded, so I didn't ask them. That was the last time we spoke.

Thunderbolt
Energetic dark crackles across the sky of her soul
Screeches that lit her deeps with fury
Scratching and screaming,
Needs as yawning as canyon lands.
Who was this woman?

Ah, I see her now: look at her eyes.
Child of God.
Relieved lamb.
Throwing light now, not darkness.

You made a way
For the snarls to soften,
the rage to rest,
for the chemicals to give way to clarity.
Ah, Your charity.
Boundless and brave,
touching like a thunderbolt in a storm:
Live!

The first summer of COVID I was frequently on my porch emailing women whom I usually saw in person. We were adapting to the times, doing Zoom meetings and making phone calls, limiting our visits while trying to still care for our people. Suddenly coming up the steps was a tall black lady frequently fingering her silver nose-ring and bountiful braids, dressed only in a bra and shorts, her thickness spilling out everywhere. Her very distracting breasts had a life of their own. At first I was reminded of Jell-o, but that morphed into plate tectonics: you could tell that in a far-away time her breasts were like plump and rounded mountains, but now they were striated with stretch marks striping a pattern which ended in an overflow in the red lace cups, swaying around with her every breath and gesticulation. Her chest was a subduction zone, a plate fluidly overflowing into her lacy red bra. (*"That was lingerie!"* one of my neighbors snorted.)

Her belly brimmed over her waistband in a deluge depending on which direction she was pacing. She spoke rapid-fire, whatever drugs she was on hyper-

234

animating her brain so thoughts tumbled over into each other. She spoke gibberish, but in structured sentences. It was simultaneously disturbing and fascinating.

She ranted against my neighbors at the Loud House, blaming the children for the torn-up books that lay strewn in the street, pages feathering westerly in the wind. "Disrespectful. I'm the adult. That little boy talked back …" and then the tug-of-war between her brain and her mouth sent her spiraling down trails with Eddie Murphy and Bernie Mack and the homeless man who was going to come after her to "clean up [ie, kill] these m*f* idiots and their *** children."

She would stand so close to me it was unnerving, with COVID-19 protocols newly in place. At this time in the COVID learning curve, most people were hyper-vigilant, careful, distant socially by at least six feet. Not her. So I kept walking around the porch trying to keep her mouth, already spewing filth and confusion, from possibly giving me COVID. She had grasped our bottle of disinfectant and thought it was bug spray, spraying here and there at bugs I never saw. I did get that back from her and got concerned when she noticed my outgoing mail, that she might do something with it.

Where was Handsome? How could I end this conversation? The 15 people at the Loud House were yelling at Red Bra Lady every time she looked over at them, both sides threatening to kick the other's ass. The lady who owned the books began sweeping the street, cleaning up Red Bra Lady's volcanic spew.

I broke away by telling her I was going to dinner. "Bye, bitch," she intoned happily, and began careening to my right. There, she kicked my neighbor Kent's gutter drains off, took his garbage can lid, destroyed a hummingbird feeder, and pulled up the reflective fiberglass marking stakes that he kept on either side of his driveway. Kent called the police. The Loud House started filming her as she went back by them, obscenities flying, throwing threats and making aggressive gestures. A few minutes later the police pulled up.

After speaking with the police and Kent, I walked toward the Loud House. I noticed one of the dads said, "Oh Lord," under his breath as he turned away from me. I knew this particular family were not big fans of white people, but I had been trying to bridge that gap slowly with little kindnesses. Leaving them eggs from our chickens. Yelling "Happy Father's Day!" at the top of my lungs when we walked by, huge smile on my face, genuinely celebrating the adult men. One step at a time, in the little things.

As I approached, the matriarch looked directly at me and she was fierce. I walked up to their chain-link fence; she walked up too, with an "I ain't backin' down" look, lips flattened tight and fists balled. About eight kids gathered around her, waiting to see what would happen, looking from her to me, back to her. Her brow gathered in a knot between her dark eyes.

"Are y'all okay?" I asked, grabbing the fence top and leaning in, and her icy attitude immediately softened. As her defenses came down, she started talking.

It was key that I knew the names of some of the children; that let me in as a neighbor. "RJ, she cussed at you? I'm so sorry, she shouldn't've done that. I know you wouldn't tear up books. You know better than that. Are you alright?"

Everyone started talking at once, exclaiming and retelling the story about the Crazy Red Bra Lady. We laughed and wondered and shook our heads — *together. Hallelujah, thank You, God.*

It was July 4th and Woodbine had fire in the sky.

We were from the country; it was illegal to shoot fireworks there, especially if it had been a dry summer. For fireworks celebrations, most people would head into the city and watch, mesmerized, as the fireworks exploded across the sky or descended in brightly-lit waves off the main city bridge or burst in synchronicity to the patriotic soundtrack playing over the speakers. I have heard an entire crowd of tens of thousands singing Lee Greenwood's hit song: "I'm proud to be an American, where at least I know I'm free … God bless the USA!" The majority of the tearful crowd was white, but it reflected our city's black/white ratio.

On Woodbine, the celebration goes on for weeks. One year I counted almost 30 days with various spurts of fireworks (Juneteenth through July 4th).

Around fireworks, I am like a child filled with delight and wonder. I think about the chemistry of the colors: red from lithium and carbonates; orange from calcium combinations; yellow from sodium compounds; and silver from burning aluminum, titanium, or magnesium powders. It's glorious. We are truly burning and bursting man-made stars.

Yelling and running and gleeful, kids clustered in the street as the adults lit boom after boom. The streetlights shrouded in firework fog that moved quickly. Strangely enough, both the bats and the mosquitos still darted about.

Our first year on Woodbine I stood on a stump in the back yard covered by a quilt (I'd been bitten enough!) to enjoy the show, and sang "Proud to be an American" at the top of my lungs (no one could hear me because it was so loud outside). It was amazing out there, magical. I owed a great debt to those who sacrificed to keep America strong and safe. Only later in conversation with neighbors did I realize that our urban celebration had included lots of gunfire, bullets aimed up toward the stars, indistinguishable from the booms and blasts of the other pyrotechnics.

Where did all those bullets land?

~elle~

One of the most consistent ways we have gathered our neighbors is to host a Halloween party. Because I do not like the evil visuals of Halloween, I decorate the front porch with gourds, lanterns, pumpkins, and mums, and keep it light. Fold-out tables get loaded with pretty fall-themed tablecloths, bowls of treats, and whatever we are serving that particular year.

Little brown girls turn into Cat Woman and fairies and Belle. Wonder Woman always makes an appearance, as does a cheerleader or two. They pitch and twirl and hiss and race about, taking on the vocal inflections of their characters. Their makeup is beyond extravagant (usually done by able older sisters or Aunties), and they sparkle like little diamonds. Boys become fearsome heroes, especially Marvel characters. One year I saw at least two dozen boys under 12 who were the Black Panther and could pose to prove it. I love watching the children separate from their day-to-day circumstances and elevate into characters. They do it well.

Mulan, Gekko, Scooby Doo, and Butterflies came with pillows to fill, buckets, or plastic grocery bags. Some who started at our house borrow a bag, greedily eager to fill it with candy.

In our neighborhood, families walk or (mostly) drive together, pile in and out of the car, say, "Trick or Treat," and wait expectantly for goodies. Halloween starts later — dusk, not before — and goes later. Even as we were shutting down around 9 PM, folding up the tables, and turning out the lights, we still had kids stopping by.

Our first year, Grant and I decided to have a bit of fun for the worn-out adults: hot dogs. Well, you can't have a hot dog without condiments. Or chips. Or drinks. And it was cold, so we needed hot cider. It became a big, fun production: Grant was our grillmaster ... on our brand-spankin'-new $18 hibachi-style grill that he assembled at 5:25 PM. With Reyana's and Beels' help, I did candy, drinks, and kept the chip bowls full.

People loved it! They hung out around the chips bowls, talking as their children compared costumes, played chase, or performed like their costume character. The little ones in strollers were the cutest as Star Wars porgs and peanut MnMs. Moms and Dads really appreciated the food. I stayed predictable in my Star Wars' homemade Rey costume; Grant stayed predictable by not wearing a

237

costume at all. (I looked just like an older version of Rey. We could've been Star Wars sisters. Actually, we are, because I love her. *"Be with me. Be with me."* She sees into my very soul.) We saw about 100 kids come by for candy, hot dogs, hot cider, or s'mores. The kids' favorite, hands down: SourPatch Kids. We ran out of candy! I had bought five bags of Milk Duds, SourPatch Kids, Peanut MnMs, and Skittles.

The second year we had two grills but got smacked by high winds and inclement weather; one of the mini-grills blew off the table and scorched our front porch. Kids tracked the ashes down the street for days. The third year we asked a team of neighbors to help spread the love. Dozens of adults and children were sitting and standing all around the front of the house eating and drinking hot cider. Every step was full of people; adults in jeans and costumes were out in the street talking and kids were roaring around being happy. It filled my soul! We had a station where kids could roast marshmallows and smush them into s'mores. Several of the kids who were close to us had stepped in to offer water refills and keep the chips bowls full. I took a moment to relish the scene and just thanked God for all the neighborly fun.

All of the sudden a newborn in a stroller started to fuss and cry, and the new dad got really nervous, trying to help his Baby Mama breast-feed on the porch swing. We offered some privacy inside, but she didn't want to miss out on all the fun and conversation. He disappeared for several minutes, allegedly looking for apple juice for Baby Mama. When he returned, the distinctive smell of pot filled the porch. He had already had a bit too much to drink before he ever landed on our porch, and now he was *rolling*. He started to relax and entertain half the porch with his stories and antics. They stayed at least an hour and a half, and we suspect his munchies were why we ran out of hot dogs that year.

Halloween during COVID was like going on a rainy vacation compared to the sunny, fun, playful experience of other years. But Grant would not be thwarted. He bought a large PVC pipe that was 6 feet long (for social distancing), then came home, angled it to fit our porch step railing, and affixed it to our rail with zip ties. We did a test run: yes, the Baby Ruths went straight down the tube. We did not have many treaters, so they got lots of candy, "catching" the candy in their bags at their end of the PVC pipe.

2021 was back to hot dogs on grills, chili, bags of chips, hot cider, hot chocolate, and candy. Our numbers of visitors crept up to around 50, but the fun was how many people just stayed, talked, rested, and had conversation with each other. Our DropBy people came; neighbors walked over and stayed, some for two hours. It was sweet redemption after the loneliness of 2020. In 2022 we grilled about 100 'dogs and could've kept going.

Halloween turned out to be more about community than I realized it would be. The kids who knew us seemed genuinely happy to see us, be at our house, then move on to the next place. They were like colorful butterflies going from flower to flower, house to house, filled with delight and seeking treasure. They were high with energy and sugar and anticipation.

At one point Beels and Reyana were with me as I was setting up the front porch. Ninja Bear, our fat feline, strolled next door, alarming the girls. "Where Ninja? Where Ninja?" Reyana (CatWoman) kept asking. Suddenly Beels (a combination of SuperGirl and flapper dancer) put her fists out in front of her and pretended to fly to Ninja's rescue. She became a one-girl search and rescue, superhero voice intoning, "I'll find him! I'll bring Ninja back to you, Suzanne!" Then off she dashed, looking under every car and the broken-down boat and over the fence with missing boards and behind the disintegrating barrels. Eventually she closed him inside the house for the night.

It was delightful to see her feel so empowered. Here she was, not even ten, still wetting the bed, bounced from foster home to another home, working hard on relational skills, a wonderful work-mate when it was just the two of us, picked on at school, lazy eye wandering, awkward and defensive and always food dried on her face and snot dried around her nose … but she fully embraced being a heroine, flying about with her fists in the air, ready to do justice and love mercy and find my wayward kitty. I fell in love with her all over again. She was one of God's lambs, and I saw His reflection in her. How charming she was, how enchanting. I found myself watching her with a smile on my face, motherly delight welling up within my heart.

The world often batters little girls. I whispered a prayer:
May she find her identity in You, dear Father, as a treasured, empowered, kind worker of justice and mercy in the real world, in real time. These girls: God! Don't let them die with their songs still unsung, their dreams small and unrealized. That would completely break my heart … and Yours too.

We knew it was a good routine to keep when we'd be outside working in the yard and someone walking by would say, "Y'all's the ones who had the Halloween party, right? That was so fun. You gonna do it this year?" Yes, absolutely. Why? Because it's a simple way to love our neighbors. No cap.

Edna and the Couch on the Grocery Buggy, 2021

Handsome and I were walking Wiley to the park, and for some inexplicable reason, Wiley wanted to walk down Magnolia Avenue on the way home. It's a busy five-lane artery leading east out of Knoxville. We usually would not have walked him on such a busy road, but since it was our Sunday stroll, we followed him.

As we were heading toward home, we saw a woman on the other side of Magnolia pushing a medium-sized floral couch on a grocery cart. She was struggling! We looked at each other, kept walking a bit, then both stopped and looked at her again. There was no way we could not help. We crossed the five lanes, Wiley in tow, and met Edna.

Edna was short, dressed in baggy clothing, and had one semi-closed, gray eye. It looked like she'd met a fist on that orbit too many times. Her hoodie was up, covering a mass of wild hair. She had bright blue eyeshadow, red cheeks, and shapely lips. Her Sketchers were worn but white.

We helped her re-position the couch and offered to help push, and she was grateful. Handsome pushed from behind and she steered from the side while I held onto Wiley and my fall leaf collection.

Magnolia is a worn street with many stories to tell in its uneven, cracked concrete sidewalks. Every uneven sidewalk section jarred and jolted the cart, forcing the couch forward in a lurch and the back wheels lifted off the concrete. Handsome would patiently reorient the couch, use his feet for leverage, and keep going. I tried to kick aside any branches or empty liquor bottles that would get in their way.

At first Edna pointed to a steeple and said she was on Fifth Avenue, one street over from Woodbine.
"Oh, at East Fifth Baptist?"
"Yes, that's the one, we turn left and then my brother's house is just right there."
Okay. We can do this.

We precariously bumped along Magnolia, chatting with Edna about the couch she'd rescued from a dumpster. "My brother will love this on his porch. I've already made two trips with just the cushions. Can you believe someone just threw this away? These are my mother's colors."

To reconstruct Edna pushing the cushions and couch by herself that far was unimaginable.

The couch was falling apart, the fabric ripped off at the upper edge of the back seat. The red floral was stapled over the original neutral color; the edging looked like it had been torn off. The underside was open and stuffing was falling out. We would have put it in the dumpster too.

We crossed to the church, and Handsome asked, "Okay, so where exactly are we going?"

"It's just down there, just down the street, down toward Cherry Street."

"Wait … all the way to Cherry Street?"

We were both thinking, *What did I sign up for here? Am I willing to keep going? This is way farther than she said.* "When your enemy forces you to walk one mile, walk with him two" came to mind; and Edna was no enemy. She just needed help, even if her sense of distance was badly impaired — or, if she was afraid we would turn away, she could deceptively lead us on one block or one lie at a time.

Crossing Cherry Street was epic. Cherry Street is a main boulevard from the interstate to Magnolia Avenue — four lanes plus turn lanes and a median with struggling trees. I had the front of the couch up on my back, Grant had the back of the couch at his shoulder and Wiley on the leash, and Edna strolled right into traffic with her empty grocery cart. Everyone stopped for us, telling us to go right on ahead. We even had to cross a raised grassy median.

Once on the other side of Cherry Street, we put the couch back on the grocery cart — which we'd been rolling now for almost a mile — and a guy in a big white truck asked if we needed help. Again Handsome asked Edna, "Now, where are we going exactly?" "#2715, just right there." "Just right there" was actually two more blocks down the street!

The guy in the passenger seat loaded the couch with Handsome. Not even quite half of the couch would fit, as they had a bunch of stuff in the back, so the guy jumped in the truck bed to weigh the couch down, and Grant jumped on the bumper to keep it steady. The driver kept popping Now & Laters; his mouth was red from the candy. No mask, no worries.

Edna and I walked down Fifth Avenue, she still pushing her cart. We chatted, but because of the noise of the cart on the street, I did not catch everything she said. She was talking about her family. With sadness she explained that the man she was with did not love her. Her step-daughter lived in *that* house there, her uncle had once lived in *that* gray house; she pointed and explained as we rolled. She seemed to know the history of this street quite well.

The guys arrived at #2715 and off-loaded the couch. As Grant was waiting on us to arrive, he struck up a conversation with an elderly man with a long, scraggly white beard and uneven teeth. I noticed his slim frame and slightly bent posture as we got closer. His hat framed the rest of this white hair and images of Appalachia flashed in my mind.

Edna said, "Where are the two guys who live here?" to the older man. He looked at her quizzically. She looked confused by his lack of an answer.

We said our goodbyes and turned to go. Handsome said in a low voice, "That old man said no one had lived in #2715 for years. Nobody lives there." Wait. What?

"I think Edna needs psychological help. That old man had a blank look on his face when we said we were delivering the couch because *no one lives there*."

I was stupefied.

Handsome went on:
"Why do you think this happened?
We just spent an hour and a half
rolling a couch
on a grocery cart
for a woman we don't know
to a house that's unoccupied.
Is the moral of the story, *Stay away from people rolling grocery carts unless you are at a grocery store*?"

We both laughed, baffled and bewildered.

"Have we just been had? Was this a test and she was an angel? You know, I didn't see any of the cushions she said she'd put on her brother's porch. I don't think Edna's okay. What in the world?"

Perplexed, we just half-laughed incomprehensibly and stared at each other. We had no clue.

Update: We've never seen Edna again, and the house is unoccupied to this day. And the couch? There is no couch — or cushions — within sight.

Roses

In 2021, with permission, Handsome planted a climbing rose on the fence between us and Miz Janet. He wound it through the chain-link fence and, green and growing, it expanded quickly, reaching for three feet in each direction. In 2022, as April eased our temperatures upward, the rose began again to branch and stretch. By the end of May, the rose had grown eight feet in each direction, even turning a corner onto Miz Janet's front side. We admired the rose greatly; it was loaded with blossoms the color of a healthy piglet.

One evening we were remarking about how beautifully it was branching, and I complemented Handsome on the care he took in digging the hole, fertilizing,

242

and pruning it. It was magnificent! Miz Janet ambled out and said, "You know why this rose is so beautiful? I prayed for it every time I watered it. *Every* time. This is aaaaaaaaall prayer," she said, waving her arms the length of the plant.

I smiled at Handsome, and we shifted the credit upwards, schooled by Miz Janet.

In 2021, I resigned from my job. For 12 years I had endeavored to nourish the 1,000 women of my church community in all things spiritual, maternal, vocational, and feminine. The invitation I offered women was to be real about life and talk it out. Questions were welcome: Does God see us? Does He care? Can you help me make sense of the Bible? What do I do with my shame, my unforgiveness, my wildness? Does God celebrate me? How do I live in conversation with Him, empowered by Him? What is the bigger picture?

I took a month to debrief this chapter in my work life:
Did I stay too long?
Did I serve my women well?
Did I steward the gifts God has given me, giving Him glory?
What were my highs and lows? My joys and sorrows?
How can I be a good steward of all they invested into me?
Am I free and clear of all rancor or frustration? Am I completely clear to move forward?
How can I freshly energize mentally, spiritually, emotionally for my next phase of life?
What do I want to create?
What are the projects I want to tackle at home, in my mind, in my body?
What do I do with my time and energy now?
As I pondered these questions, I walked around my back yard each morning, meandering with the hens: Midnight off and independent; Dotty, always talking; Alpha at my feet; and Vanilla waiting for me to turn over rocks.

Since our hens first molted in the fall of 2019, I have been obsessed with feathers. Their feathers are stunning works of artistry — and these are simple hens! The symmetry, design, color, and purpose embodied in each feather are astonishing. I feel rich when I find one. The simple marvel of whispering feathers found at my feet transports me to God.

Once I resigned, I began to find feathers on walks, in our yard, or floating toward me from the sky. Every single day. This went on for months. It became comical; Grant rolled his eyes at first, but then gave in to the marvel. Consistently I was given feathers, daily. It was as if God was saying, "I am with you. I see you. I love you. You are safe and treasured in the shadow of My wings" (see Psalm 63:7). Once I was even in an (enclosed) airport when a feather floated down in front of me. What?

I began finding dove feathers in my backyard. *Here* was one held by the dew on the grass, *there* was one with distinctive, darkly dotted markings; *here* was a small pin feather that was gray-blue, *there* was a bit of fluff with a curved, manicured edge at the top tip. I pondered the meaning of this scattering of beauty and glory. Why me? Why now? Was it to remind me to be at peace during this transition? In Scripture, doves were used as offerings. I definitely felt like I was on God's altar, surrendering the next phase of my life, offering all I was and had been to my King.

"I am with You, Lord God Almighty. Be with me. Thank You for how extravagant Your love is, how faithful, how demonstrative. Please, Lord, keep sending me feathers. I love Your love."

Chapter Thirteen: Epilogue, 2022

Behind, Summer 2022

BECAUSE OF THE PANDEMIC, Cinco was sorely behind academically. He had not been in in-person school for two years. Now entering high school, he felt prepared but was also nervous. He drew from a small pool of confidence that came from team sport, often the life raft of lowly freshmen. He had made some friends during summer football practices where he was slotted as a corner and wide receiver.

"Cinco, what to you want to do when you are a man?"
"I want to play football for a professional team."
"Do you want to get married and have kids someday?"
"Affirmative."
"Okay, Sync, then after your career on the field, what do you want to do? Football is rough on your body. You can't play forever. If you played till you were 30 years old, you'd probably still live another 50 years, so you need a profession. Something that will earn you money and equip you to support a family."
"I want to be a businessman. Earn alllllllll the cash. Have nice cars and buy a house for my Mama. Get gold on my teeth."
"Okay, so put your right arm up and out to the right. Your fingertips are where you're headed, your future. Now put your left arm out. Your fingertips are where you are now. Get it? Your wingspan is your life. It's a timeline."
"Got it, Suzy."
"Begin with the end in mind. So where are we going to start?"
"Uh, my right hand?"
"Yes, where you're a businessman, good. You're older, say, 50."
Cinco snorted. "Fifty? That's *old*. Ain't you 50, Grant?"
Grant just smiled and punched his right hand playfully.

"Cinco, to be a successful businessman, you've got to have skills. Just like in football — skills in handling the ball, protecting it, taking it to the field. Without skills, you can't compete. Same in business. You've got to gain those skills. Where do you learn how to be a businessman?"
"School?"
"Yes, school, and from mentors who are older than you and are in the same type of business you are getting into. People who can give you wisdom, pass on what

they've learned. You find those people in the community. But they aren't gonna waste their time on someone who isn't serious about being successful."
"I'm serious, I'm serious! I want those teeth and the house for my Mama!"

"So back to your arms." I grabbed his scrawny, ninth-grade right bicep. Here's college. You need to be in business classes. To be prepared for college classes" — here I thumped him on the left shoulder — "you've got to have a strong senior year in high school. Math. Science. Language. Writing. To have a strong senior year, you need a solid junior year, sophomore year ... and here we are, at your freshman year in high school, current day." I wrestled his left hand's fingertips. "More than just passing grades, or average grades. You've got to compete with your mind. You've got to put in the time, the effort, to get those skills, so Old Cinco, big-bicep Business Man Cinco, can buy that house for his Mama and get the gold on his teeth."

It clicked, and Cinco looked crestfallen.

"I can't do it, Suzy. I hate math. I don't write good. Science is ... I just don't care. I hate school. I'm not like you, smart and stuff. I'm an athlete."

He paused for a minute, pondering. I was struck with the image of bald, beloved Cinco geared up in a classic spacesuit and helmet, floating away from the space station still with the tether in place, but feeling lost and weightless.
"May I tutor you?"
It felt like an innocent question, yet still a leap off a cliff. Why did I feel so vulnerable? Why was I holding my breath?
"Seriously, Suzy?"
"Yes. Maybe two days a week? I'm a good writer, and I used to teach science. I don't remember advanced math, but I'm sure we could figure it out. What do you think?"

I felt a visceral reaction in my gut: the familiar thrill of the classroom, of teaching my students so long ago, mixed with the fear that I might not be enough for Cinco's benefit. Oil and water, mixing together to create a tension inside my body. Could I help him learn? How far behind was he? Could he be still long enough when he needed to concentrate? Would he engage some of my crazy schemes of learning? I would use the basketball ... I would get him moving ... I would .... Wow, I was already in lesson planning mode.

Still looking down, he agreed: "I'll try, Suzy." Seeing my smile, he perked up. "We'll have some fun, Cinco, but I'm going to ask a lot of you. You're becoming a man. No crazy kid excuses. We're gonna do this!"

We fist-bumped. I felt an eager excitement fill me. Ah, teaching and learning. Familiar, beloved ground.

He cancelled our lessons before the fourth session. "I'm an athlete, not an academic, Suzy," he explained. "An athlete," he said emphatically.

"You don't have to choose, Cinco. You can be both. You can do this!" But he chose not to.

I was reminded that I can't make anyone do anything. I can't force someone to love me. I can't force beautiful things to sprout within someone else's soul, even in the midst of loving them. I can't *make* someone believe that I genuinely care for them. I can't control another's free will. I can't control others' choices or their futures. I'm simply here as a learner to love my neighbor, and sometimes, that feels like a gut punch. Like finding out Njalla and Atticus were in jail for a time. Like waving goodbye to another neighbor moving off the street in search of a lower rent. Like Miz Janet's stroke. Like flat-out rejection or suspicion.

But there was also much encouragement. Seeing one of our young basketballers working in a local Walmart. (I spied on him for a minute before walking up and giving him a hug; he was diligent and focused. Yay!) Sharing figs. Genevieve bringing over hundreds of worms for our hens. Setting up watercolor paints, brushes, and water on the front porch for painting with whomever walks by. Hosting a block dessert party and meeting new faces. Drawing out the organelles of a cell with a middle schooler before her big test. Leaving Valentine's Day brownies in red aluminum heart-shaped pans at neighbors' doorsteps. Dreaming of starting a neighborhood bakery. Still sharing bread and cookies, still finding feathers daily: yes, God is with me.

Forgiveness

One evening, alone on the back porch, I wondered: Wounding and healing. Darkness and light. Injustice and justice. Fear and courage. These are powerful dyads, and sometimes humanity fails to reach the shalom side. Why?

Like a scientist, I examined a phrase from my class with Mary Terry, turning it in the light of Scripture, trying to see it from every angle, placing it on a mental microscope slide: *power over, power with, and power to.* Historically white people had pursued 'power over,' but I did not see that permission given by Jesus. Rather, I read Him calling me to share my 'power with' others, to not claim a special status, to be inclusive and have a *doulos* attitude; to enter into a dynamic of sharing power, of validating another person's abilities and trustworthiness. In Scripture, I was being asked to help others rise, not suppress, control, and use them, particularly for some type of economic benefit to myself. 'Power to.' Verses flooded my mind about training others, entrusting God's truth to them, thinking better of them than myself, carrying others' burdens, being someone who reflected Jesus' own attitude of coming to serve, not to be served.

My rumination led to the radical, revolutionary power of forgiveness and reconciliation: first, humans forgiven and reconciled with God through Jesus' cross and resurrection. Then, humans with each other and within our own selves, through the power of the cross and the Holy Spirit.

As quickly as I could, I wrote down all of the conflicts I could think of:

Russians vs Ukrainians
Tutsis vs Hutus in Rwanda
Black vs Whites
Native Americans vs Whites
Whites putting Japanese Americans into camps during the World War
Colonialists vs Native Peoples
South Sudan vs North Sudan
Tribal conflicts in Africa
Arabs vs Israelis vs Palestinians
Afghanis vs Taliban vs US troops
Somalis vs other East African nations and coastal ships; Al Shabab
Kurds and Turks
Boko Haram kidnappings in Nigeria
Iran vs US
US vs Russia
Being a woman in the Congo (shudder — so violent)
North Korea vs South Korea
Libya's terrorists and civil war
ISIL, Syria, Lebanon
Rohingya people in Myanmar
India vs Pakistan
Yemen's civil war
Militant terrorists of all kinds
Political instability in many nations
Catholics vs Christians vs Muslims vs [religious conflicts]
Cyber security
Gender violence (honor killings and female genital mutilation)
Social media furies
Political Right vs political Left
Mass shootings
Sex and labor trafficking vs peace and flourishing

My question evolved: What stops conflict?

It seems historically that very little actually does. There are cease-fires, agreements, pay-offs, and treaties. There are heroes and legislators and summits. There is force, oppression, silence. But what actually changes hearts, not just boundary lines or power plays or egos or weapon stockpiles or resentments?

Forgiveness. Reconciliation. These two separate-but-related, radical notions: forgiveness, something I can do between me and God. Reconciliation, all parties agreeing to walk together in truth, owning their part, moving forward, committed, truly seeing themselves and each other.

What is necessary to forgive someone? I asked my therapist friend Marla Delong for her wisdom.

She said, "Suzanne, you must recognize and name the offense against you and feel the pain and cost of it. We can't avoid the emotional impact (despair, bitterness, anger, rage, helplessness, horror). Christians aren't good at owning the darker, more negative emotions, but it's got to be done. They're part of being human.

"Then we've got to shift, and be brave. We make the serious, sober choice to forgive him or her or *it*, if it's an organization, or government, or group of some kind. *Actively forgive*, which means holding the other up to God and releasing them and all consequences up to His sovereign, knowing care. We see the humanity of the offender. In doing this, you absorb the cost of their actions; the harm stops with you and travels no further through bitter slander, retaliation, or harm."

My mind trailed off to Haiti, to the dump called Jubilee in Gonaives, a dusty, sunburnt truck-ride north of Port au Prince. Kathy, an American who lives there, was translating for me. I was explaining to the Haitian women who lived in the dump how I knew Jesus forgave me.

"Wait, wait, Suzanne, they don't understand the concept of forgiveness. It's not a part of their culture. Hang on a sec. Okay. Stand over there, and haha, I'm going to throw rocks at you. Just go with it."

Wide-eyed, I stood on the other side of the small gravel area where women had gathered to sit on benches and listen to Kathy. When Kathy picked up a stone and threw it at me, their brown eyes got big, and they drew back, shocked. They began to whisper behind cupped hands.

"Throw one back at me, Suzanne, sorta gently and toward my legs. Just do it." I did.
The women, titillated, couldn't believe I did that, and began to *tsk* and cluck with their tongues.
Kathy threw more rocks at my knees, then gathered a few women to help her. She instructed me to do the same.
Soon, we were all throwing rocks, divided into two groups, women laughing but playfully fierce, still not understanding what was happening.

"Okay, sit back down on the benches and let me explain. I got mad at Suzanne and threw a rock at her; she responded by throwing one back at me. I got a few friends on my side, slandering Suzanne and getting them mad at her. Then she did the same. Soon, we were all at war, do you see?"

The women nodded.

"Here is what forgiveness is."

She directed a woman to throw rocks at her. Kathy put her arms outward so her body was the shape of a cross. As the woman threw rocks at her, she loudly proclaimed,
"I will not harm you.
I will not curse you.
I will bless you in Jesus' Name.
I will be kind to your children.
I will not retaliate.
I will not harm you or gossip about you or mistreat you.
I will not spread this hurt; it stops with me, here, now.
I will absorb this pain, the cost, the hurt, in the mighty Name of Jesus.
I will bless and not curse, love and not hate.
I will look you in the eye and know
and choose to forgive you."

During Kathy's words, the woman stopped throwing the rocks; she just couldn't do it in the face of such brave kindness. Tears flowed down her cheeks, something rarely seen among the tough women of the dump.

Kathy put her hand on her friend's shoulder. "Forgiveness is a choice to *not* retaliate, to *not* make them pay their debt to you. You cancel what they owe you in the Name of Jesus, knowing He has paid the debt in full on the cross … for both of you."

Anne Lamott calls earth "forgiveness school." True dat. No cap.

I snapped my attention back to my friend. She was saying, "Get free within, trusting God to do as He deems best. **'Vengeance is Mine, says the LORD.'** You can say to yourself, 'I don't have to hate anymore; God's gonna do what He knows is right for me and my offender. I don't carry that weight anymore. He is their judge.'

"If possible, speak to your offender; you might even be able to clear the air and come to mutual agreement. If possible, pursue reconciliation, which is different from forgiveness. If you both want to be reconciled, create opportunities for renewed trust; trust is earned in the small things, over time. Practice good relational skills as you move forward, whether or not you are reconciled with your offender: boundaries, listening, conflict resolution, win-win solutions, that kind of thing."

"Oh thank you, my friend. One final question: *Why is this so hard?*"
She laughed, but seriously. "Because it feels like you're dying."
I agreed.

I mused: Forgiveness and reconciliation require humility; honesty; integrity. Are we willing to enter into this process with each other? Could black folks forgive white folks for hundreds of years of harm? Could our races be reconciled? Could that be the truth of my block on Woodbine Avenue? Our forgiveness and reconciliation processes may not make headlines. I may not hear encouraging applause or cynical criticism. Was I willing to be unknown, to be quietly engaged, to simply know and love my neighbor, to be an agent of reconciliation on my block? Was I willing to patiently stay, to be a consistent loving presence in the Name of Jesus?

~elles

Knoxville, my beloved hometown, is growing and evergreen, expanding in every direction around our sinuous river. It seems to me that over the decades, racism within the government and social structures is lessening, to my joy, but I know this foe better by now: Racism adapts. In what new form would it arise to harm my friends? I felt myself steel against it. I prayed a blessing over the city:

God, may our leaders rise up to do what is right and good in Your eyes! When You call them, may they eagerly cooperate with You. Grant them a spirit of ferocity and humility as they serve. May they be good listeners. People of vision. People who honor others.

May You give people longing for a diverse, engaged, vibrant life. Defenses down. May we be for *each other. May we see each other with love.*
May classism fade in the bright light of learning from each other. May the rich be generous and humble stewards of Your wealth, and may the poor industriously move out of poverty. May these partnerships be healthy, neither taking advantage of the other.

Protect the innocent, Lord: the children, so vulnerable. Shower them with delight, curiosity, wonder, and nurturing. The animals, who knew You before humanity was created, who need human tenderness and provision, who are the most loyal companions when well-treated. May You bring joy into every heart.

251

May we not tire of 'forgiveness school.'
May You show Your people how to truly act and breathe as a body.
Jesus, breathing, here. Jesus, standing in the path of evil and
welcoming the good and beautiful, here.
May You gain glory from Knoxville, Tennessee, God. You know this is
my heart.

～elles

As I write, there are now only four black families on my block, almost the complete reverse of what it was when we moved onto Woodbine. Development up through our block is visible, definable, and measurable.

Again I find myself disoriented and adjusting to a new normal. The people who buy into our neighborhood currently are often young, white, single, professional women or young white couples. Their hearts for the neighborhood are beautiful … it's just different.

Renting has decreased and owning has increased. Some larger homes have been listed in the upper $500,000 range, unthinkable just a handful of years ago. Many of our former neighbors have moved not just once, but twice. Tracing gentrification's aftermath feels like tracing the path of the tornado, but the damage was done to relationships rather than real estate. Although friendships were torn apart, the outside looks better. But the paint and nicer yards don't soothe my ache for our first people.

In Closing: Beyond Woodbine
Book Club Topics for Discussion

DEAR READER, AS YOU MOVE FORWARD from this book, I encourage you to review some experiences within the accounts from Woodbine. Use these brief paragraphs as suggestions for your discussions, prayers, and wonderings.

Proximity: With a strategic eye toward gentrification, I challenge you to humbly, courageously move to hard places in your town. Do your research. Simply and consistently spread the love of God on your block. As we found, you may see that there are lots of Christians already about, hearty souls from whom you can learn. Get to know your neighbors.

Actively open your home. It will help you live what you say you believe. Practice Acts hospitality by serving others through sharing your space. Remember the beauty and mystery of "the love of strangers." Walk humbly; be willing to learn from your mistakes. Learn to laugh at yourself, roll your eyes at your mistakes, hit your knees and ask for forgiveness and help, and then get up and try again. We're still doing that.

What was your first context (likely, your family of origin) for comprehending life? How is a different context disorienting or disrupting your understanding of systems you had in your first context? How is God requiring you to grow and expand your understanding through **disorientation**? What are you being challenged to unlearn?

Starting at the GI Bill, **trace your family's financial situation** through our current day. Who or what helped your family gain or lose financial ground? I know it was a helpful exercise to trace in my family's rise from pockets-turned-inside-out-broke orphan (my grandfather) to my father's financial strength. Use this exercise to both humble yourself ("We all need help") and encourage yourself ("I can add to this story of financial stability").

Create a safe space for people who are either unchurched or de-churched to know and experience the love of God through you.

Follow Jesus closely! **Say no to lesser loves** of safety, security, education, etc. Be less in control, less afraid, less about American idols. Watch what remarkable work God does in you and through you, and feel His nearness.

Learn from minority communities, authors, artists, and singers. They have much to teach us and we have much to learn from them. Go tenderly; many minority communities have suffered greatly. It costs them to recount their experiences. Diversify your reading list, your music, your podcast content.

Don't have a savior mentality; be humble. There are people who are already present in challenging spaces you might just now be considering. Join up with those who have gone before you and learn from them. Join John the Baptist in saying, **"I am not the Christ"** (John 1:19-26). Remember the theophany, Christ appearing to Gideon, saying, **"Go now in this strength of yours"** (Judges 6:14). Remember Jehoshaphat: **"We do not know what to do, but our eyes are on you"** (2 Chronicles 20:12).

Cross classes. Class and race are powerful separators. To learn practically about class, take a course like *Bridges Out of Poverty*. Instead of going with the flow and staying in your own class, shake it up — with love, grace, and truth, and maybe a simple meal with a new friend. Who is in your life who is in a different class? How can you broaden your range of relationships?

Invite others into power. Share privileges, make a way for others to succeed, advocate for the advancement of the marginalized and capable people in other classes. Hire diversely. Give; stop protecting yourself and your family and your advancement. God's got you; don't be afraid. Choose to share: not 'power over' someone but 'power to' them or 'power with' them. It's an entirely different mindset. Network with minorities in mind.

Recognize **class and race** are *massive* structures that thrive *now*, on our watch. Pay attention. What do you notice?

We may not lynch people now, but it can feel like a noose around someone's neck when they can't get a loan or are denied the option to start a business or cannot advance into a higher position. When another injustice is done to their people. When they feel another disappointment in a fellow believer who does not stand up against injustice. When they are excluded again, reviled again, forgotten again. Do all you can to **throw away the rope!**

Learn to disagree well. Gain skills necessary to dialogue and engage with a variety of views. Set down your preconceived ideas and perceptions so you can listen openly and honestly. Learn to ask questions to clarify thoughts. Practice reflective listening rather than accusation, criticism, or stonewalling (shutting down). Take turns explaining why you think what you think. You can disagree and still be friends, particularly with followers of Jesus. Don't assign Jesus to a political party; He is far above our temporary politics.

Be generous like the Good Samaritan. Who is your neighbor? Who is crossing your path lately? Do you see them? How can you lift them up and show them the care of God?

See history from a minority or native perspective. This may take a bit of digging but it is worth it. Start with Phil Vischer's YouTube on Racism. It's only 17 minutes long and *packed*. Excellent. It will give you a helpful foundation before you speak with an actual person. **History is best told in relationship**, but if you don't know a person who can speak up for a minority, through friends, find a perspective that is different than yours.

Learn about your city's racial history. Honor what other minorities and classes have experienced in your city. Own it and be tender-hearted in response.

Explore Jesus' life with a cultural map in your mind. Ponder this quote by Christena Cleveland: "We can meet Jesus in our own cultural context, but to follow Him we must cross cultural boundaries." Do you agree? In what ways are you open to and experiencing other cultures, classes, and races? How are you loving others who are different from you?

Jesus was excellent at **connection**. When I read the Scriptures I see that Jesus invited connection even if there wasn't agreement. This is something I believe Christians could do better. Proverbs 27:17: "Iron sharpens iron; so one person sharpens another." Who in your world is unlike you, and sharpens you? Are you surrounding yourself with people who only agree with you, look like you, and have your historical perspective on racism? Are your news and information sources all from like perspectives? Ultimately, that's not helpful, because the Kingdom of God will be every tribe, every nation, every language (Revelation 7:9). Expand your connections and learn to disagree without cutting off relationships.

The Bible Project's video on *mishpat*, justice, is excellent. It gives the viewer a powerful visual image of injustice as well as justice. It's worth your time. Search for it at https://bibleproject.com/explore/video/justice/

Yes, you: all those things and places you own? Lay them at God's feet, and ask Him what to do with them. Literally write it down and put it on the floor, figuratively letting go of it all. He is the Owner of all you steward; your stuff is not yours. *It's all His.* Stop using ownership language and begin to **use stewardship language.**

Find minority individuals in whom to invest. Look for the strivers! Get to know them, encourage them, and then use all of your power and privilege to help them succeed. Help them make their dreams come true, and then refuse to take any credit; give the glory to God, who loves the poor and the meek and gives power to earn (see David's brief prayer in 1 Chronicles 29:10-12 and Deuteronomy 8:17,18). Your Father, who sees what is done in secret, will reward you. It's fun to do good things that only God knows!

Help your church or friend group talk about these things. Read *Waking Up White* as a group or staff, then have discussions. How can you move toward Revelation 7:9?

Disrupt chronic racist and classist systems through your own expertise, capacities, vocations, and skills. **Make your career about humanity.** Leverage your skills to disrupt biased, unjust systems. Lift others up! And remember Jesus' caution: it may cost you. It certainly cost Him (see Luke 6:40).

Create an inclusive collective, a partnership, to address community challenges, or join one that already exists. For the first few meetings, consider just listening as a learner, a watcher, a listener. Ask God to help you hear and see from His perspective, not the perspective of a political party or other grouping system. Simply, kindly see who you are listening to without your armor, cynicism, defensiveness, or past disappointments. This calls for great maturity. Look for the innocent child within them if they complain or threaten. Many people carry unfathomable wounds; I pray you can be part of their healing.

Gain awareness. Read from various perspectives (even if they confirm your opposition). Watch movies, listen in relationships, take notes, and be willing to change. It can be frustrating when each view, though differing, can back their position with statistics, which is typical today. *You must be wiser than metrics.*

Get outside and walk your street. Say hello with a smile, engage naturally as you are able, and pray for each house according to how the Holy Spirit prompts you.

Share what you know about **"forgiveness school."**

~elles~

The Blessing

Cheers to You, Lord God Almighty, Maker of Heaven and earth! All honor and glory to You. And now I pray, Good Trinity, deploy more of Your people to the difficult parts of their cities.

Where there is danger, guard them.

Where there is fear, send courage.

Where there is discord, help them carry peace.

Where there is suspicion, may it crumble quickly in light of their proven integrity.

Where there is hopelessness, may they bring You and Your resourceful people to affect change.

Where there is depression, I pray You send Your joy.

Where there is mental illness, I pray You bring sound minds and compassion.

May Your people be 100% grace and 100% truth, like Jesus.

May the earth be filled with signs of Your love as Your people move into new places.

Amen.

Appendices

A: The Woodbine Confession
B: Scriptures that Smacked Us Around
C: Tell Yourself the Gospel

Appendix A

The Woodbine Confession

Here in the Scriptures I find relief and direction and counsel as I remind myself of the truth (Scriptures are compiled below):

In Christ, I have been given the ministry of reconciliation.
Like Christ, I value the reconciliation of humanity with God, others, and self.
When I wade into conflict with humility, love, and wisdom from the Spirit, the Kingdom becomes tangible.
Like John the Baptist, I confess: I am not the Savior.
I am God's daughter. Beloved, treasured, redeemed, and empowered by the Holy Spirit.
I am about God's Kingdom. My treasure is not here; it is in heaven.
I will love and not harm.
I will bless and not curse.
I will pray in the Name of Jesus and mountains will move.
I will put my hope in God and do what He tells me to do in the issues of racism, class, and work.
I will see my neighbor and be gracious and empowering to them.
I will speak words of repentance out loud, and ask for forgiveness, just like the prophets of old. I will be quick to say *I'm sorry* and choose humility over pride.
I will remind myself that in Christ I am forgiven and "all glorious within," with *His* glory. This is what being a redeemed and free child of God looks like: being transformed into His image with ever-increasing glory.
God welcomes my laments and celebrations.
His glory and light shine in the darkness, and the darkness cannot overcome it.
God wins, and He and heaven are my home.

2 Corinthians 5:18-20, Romans 5:10; Philemon 8, 9a; John 17, 2 Chronicles 20:12, Philippians 2:5, Acts 6:10, 1 Corinthians 2:13; John 1:20; SS 2:16, John 1:12, 1 John 3:1, Acts 1:8; Matthew 6:19-21; Matthew 5:44; Mark 11:23; John

258

5:17, 1 Thessalonians 1:3; Romans 15:13; Romans 12:5; 1 Corinthians 12:13,27; Ephesians 2:11-22; Daniel 9:4,5,13,18; Luke 10:25-37; Proverbs 1:23, Psalm 51:1,2; Isaiah 30:15, Ezekiel 18:30-32, Matthew 3:8, Philippians 2:1-11; Psalm 45:13; 2 Corinthians 3:18; many psalms of lament and praise; John 1:5; Revelation 21 and 22.

~ellee~

Use these Scriptures below to help you be lovingly present in your neighborhood. Choose those that resonate with you and pray them aloud, slowly and thoughtfully.

"'Love the Lord your God with all your heart and with all your soul and with all your mind.' This is the first and greatest commandment. And the second is like it: 'Love your neighbor as yourself.'" Jesus speaking, Matthew 22:37-39, NIV.

Anyone who claims to be in the light but hates a brother or sister is still in the darkness. Anyone who loves their brother and sister lives in the light, and there is nothing in them to make them stumble. 1 John 2:9-10, NIV. Whoever claims to love God yet hates a brother or sister is a liar. For whoever does not love their brother and sister, whom they have seen, cannot love God, whom they have not seen. 1 John 4:20, NIV. My brothers and sisters, believers in our glorious Lord Jesus Christ must not show favoritism. James 2:1, NIV. Whoever claims to live in him must live as Jesus did. 1 John 2:6, NIV. The Lord is good and upright; therefore He instructs sinners in the way. Psalm 25:8, NASB.

Now the works of the flesh are evident: ... enmity, strife, jealousy, fits of anger, rivalries, dissensions, divisions ... things like these. I warn you, as I warned you before, that those who do such things will not inherit the kingdom of God. But the fruit of the Spirit is love, joy, peace, patience, kindness, goodness, faithfulness, gentleness, self-control; against such things there is no law. And those who belong to Christ Jesus have crucified the flesh with its passions and desires. Galatians 5:19-24, ESV.

Out of the depths I cry to you, Lord; Lord, hear my voice. Let your ears be attentive to my cry for mercy. If you, Lord, kept a record of sins, Lord, who could stand? But with you there is forgiveness, so that we can, with reverence, serve you. Psalm 130:1-4, NIV. You were washed ... you were sanctified ... you were justified in the Name of the Lord Jesus and by the Spirit of our God. 1 Corinthians 6:11, NIV. Keep in step with the Spirit. Galatians 5:25, ESV. And do not grieve the Holy Spirit of God. Ephesians 4:30, ESV.

The Lord is compassionate and gracious,
    slow to anger, abounding in love.

He will not always accuse,
    nor will he harbor his anger forever;
he does not treat us as our sins deserve
    or repay us according to our iniquities.
For as high as the heavens are above the earth,
    so great is his love for those who fear him;
as far as the east is from the west,
    so far has he removed our transgressions from us. Psalm 103:8-12, NIV

He has told you, O mortal, what is good;
    and what does the Lord require of you
but to do justice, and to love kindness,
    and to walk humbly with your God? Micah 6:8, NRSV

For thus says the LORD of hosts: "… These are the things that you shall do:
Speak the truth to one another; render in your gates judgments that are true and
make for peace; do not devise evil in your hearts against one another, and love
no false oath, for all these things I hate, declares the LORD." Zechariah 8:16-17,
ESV.

Let the beauty of the LORD our God be upon us. Psalm 90:17, KJV. A glorious
church, not having spot or wrinkle or any such thing, but … holy and without
blemish. Ephesians 5:27, KJV. And your renown went forth among the nations
because of your beauty, for it was perfect through the splendor that I had
bestowed on you, declares the Lord GOD. Ezekiel 16:14, ESV.

[Jesus praying] I do not ask that you take them out of the world, but that you
keep them from the evil one. They are not of the world, just as I am not of the
world. Sanctify them in the truth; your word is truth. As you sent me into the
world, so I have sent them into the world … that they may all be one, just as
you, Father, are in me, and I in you, that they also may be in us, so that the world
may believe that you have sent me. The glory that you have given me I have
given to them, that they may be one even as we are one, I in them and you in
me, that they may become perfectly one, so that the world may know that you
sent me and loved them even as you loved me. John 17:15-18, 21-23, ESV.

Love one another earnestly from a pure heart. 1 Peter 1:22, ESV

Now there were in the church at Antioch prophets and teachers, Barnabas,
Simeon who was called Niger, Lucius of Cyrene, Manaen a lifelong friend of
Herod the tetrarch, and Saul. Acts 31:1, ESV. After this I looked, and there
before me was a great multitude that no one could count, from every nation,
tribe, people and language, standing before the throne and before the Lamb.
They were wearing white robes and were holding palm branches in their hands.
And they cried out in a loud voice:

"Salvation belongs to our God, who sits on the throne, and to the Lamb."
All the angels were standing around the throne and around the elders and the
four living creatures. They fell down on their faces before the throne and
worshiped God, saying:
"Amen! Praise and glory and wisdom and thanks and honor and power and
strength be to our God for ever and ever. Amen!" Revelation 7:9,10, NIV

Appendix B

Scriptures that Smacked Us Around

**...He died for all, that those who live should live no longer for themselves,
but for Him who died for them and rose again. 2 Corinthians 5:15**
We had created a beautiful kingdom of our own for our family, our people, but
in all honestly that was living for ourselves.

**"Then the King will say to those on his right, 'Come, you who are blessed
by my Father; take your inheritance, the kingdom prepared for you since
the creation of the world. For I was hungry and you gave me something to
eat, I was thirsty and you gave me something to drink, I was a stranger and
you invited me in, I needed clothes and you clothed me, I was sick and you
looked after me, I was in prison and you came to visit me.'" Matthew
25:34-36**
Bottom line: In West Knox, we weren't often around those who were hungry,
thirsty, strangers, needy, sick, or jailed. Everyone around us had their basic
needs fulfilled. I often it felt like it was a competition about who was
progressing in wealth and beauty rather than who was progressing in service and
humility. I speak as one who knows when I say it's easy to lose our way from
the narrow road of Christ. Examine Jesus' life: What did He do? Where did He
go? What is He asking of His followers? Then free yourself of distractions and
go do it.

**"Because the poor are plundered and the needy groan, I will now arise,"
says the Lord. "I will protect them from those who malign them." Psalm
12:5 "[The wicked's] evil deeds have no limit; they do not seek justice. They
do not promote the case of the fatherless; they do not defend the just cause
of the poor. Should I not punish them for this?" declares the Lord. "Should
I not avenge myself on such a nation as this?" Jeremiah 5:28,29**
If I am involved in any way with injustice toward the poor, God is angry. I
explored this. How were the poor being plundered in my city? When the needy
groaned, what were they lamenting? I have definitely heard financially stable
people dismiss the poor, simplifying complex lives with, "Oh, they just need to

get a job." I do not think God appreciates that attitude because it does not reflect His heart toward us — like getting a job will solve all the inner strife, any trauma, the confusion, the messages we've implanted about ourselves, the need for rest and love, the various forms of lack. In His eyes, we are all poor and needy. He intervened through Jesus to help, to lift up, to redeem. How can you do that in your city? What radical, crazy, audacious thing could you begin praying about right now?

Defend the weak and the fatherless; uphold the cause of the poor and the oppressed. Psalm 82:3
Investigate what causes the weakness and fatherlessness and poverty and oppression in your area. I had no idea how difficult it was to get safe housing; to access mental health care; to get basic identification; to deal with trauma. Reflect on God as a *father*, not just a sovereign, and see His people (and yourself) like lost lambs, needing a good shepherd.

Whoever is kind to the poor lends to the Lord, and he will reward them for what they have done. Proverbs 19:17
Kindness = "shows grace and favor as to one in an inferior position; leans down toward them."
Lends = "to become one with, intertwine, abide with, cleave, join."
He will reward = "make amends, finish, full, give again; to be safe in mind, body, or estate; to be completed, to be friendly; to recompense, restore." This information is on Biblehub.com, the Interlinear tab for Proverbs 19:17. Whew. I want to be intertwined with God. As He has leaned toward *me*, His inferior, with great grace and favor, so should I keep pouring out grace and favor like a river onto others. He sees; He knows; He's got us; it's okay.

She opens her arms to the poor and extends her hands to the needy. Proverbs 31:20
This is part of the *Eschet Chayil,* Proverbs 31's tribute to the godly woman. She is industrious and strong, a working woman with a staff of servants. She buys and sells of her own accord, anticipates the needs of her household, and is wise with her words. I want to be like her.

She opens her arms to the poor: That's a welcoming posture. Come in, let me love you.
She extends her hands to the needy: That's a connecting posture. Need this (love, food, garment, care)? Allow me to give it to you. Need a hand? I'm here. Let's act. I'm willing to be in relationship with you, to connect with you.

The godly woman *sees* the poor, and is moved to interact with them personally. She, like her good Father, leans toward them in loving-kindness.

You have been a refuge for the poor, a refuge for the needy in their distress, a shelter from the storm and a shade from the heat. Isaiah 25:4
What does being a refuge for the poor look like? I really had no idea how to personally, daily be a sweet place of respite and care for the poor. How can you and I be shelters from the oppressive storms and heat of this world?

"Is not this the kind of fasting I have chosen:
to loose the chains of injustice
  and untie the cords of the yoke,
to set the oppressed free
  and break every yoke?
Is it not to share your food with the hungry
  and to provide the poor wanderer with shelter—
when you see the naked, to clothe them,
  and not to turn away from your own flesh and blood?
Then your light will break forth like the dawn,
  and your healing will quickly appear;
then your righteousness will go before you,
  and the glory of the Lord will be your rear guard. Isaiah 58:6-8

How can you help loose the chains of injustice?
How can you help set the oppressed free?
How can you break the yokes of bondage around the necks of God's image-bearers?
Are you sharing your food with the hungry?
Are you providing the poor wanderer with shelter?
Are you clothing the naked, staying open-hearted toward your own family?

How is God calling you to move toward the poor, to have a heart for the suffering? This is not about using this Scripture as a checklist, then you're done. This is a life-long, cultivated attitude of serving the poor and the disenfranchised, those hidden on the margins of mainstream society.

The Spirit of the Sovereign Lord is on me, because the Lord has anointed me to proclaim good news to the poor. He has sent me to bind up the brokenhearted, to proclaim freedom for the captives and release from darkness for the prisoners, to proclaim the year of the Lord's favor and the day of vengeance of our God, to comfort all who mourn, and provide for those who grieve in Zion — to bestow on them a crown of beauty instead of ashes, the oil of joy instead of mourning, and a garment of praise instead of a spirit of despair. They will be called oaks of righteousness, a planting of the Lord for the display of his splendor. Isaiah 61:1-3 The blind receive sight, the lame walk, those who have leprosy are cleansed, the deaf hear, the dead are raised, and the good news is proclaimed to the poor. Matthew 11:5

This is what Jesus did, His mission; this is who He was, His character. As a follower, I should look like Him in passion and mission. Do I?

Jesus answered, "If you want to be perfect, go, sell your possessions and give to the poor, and you will have treasure in heaven. Then come, follow me." Matthew 19:21
Jesus looked at him and loved him. "One thing you lack," he said. "Go, sell everything you have and give to the poor, and you will have treasure in heaven. Then come, follow me." Mark 10:21
When Jesus looks deeply into me, what is that *one thing* I need to let go of? Possessions, or a standard of living, like this young ruler? My idea of how I would live out what "success" means to my family? A certain profile? The perfect house, the best schools? Illusions of safety? My way, my intentions? What's your *one thing*?

Looking at his disciples, he said: "Blessed are you who are poor, for yours is the kingdom of God." Luke 6:20 Then Jesus said to his host, "When you give a luncheon or dinner, do not invite your friends, your brothers or sisters, your relatives, or your rich neighbors; if you do, they may invite you back and so you will be repaid. But when you give a banquet, invite the poor, the crippled, the lame, the blind, and you will be blessed. Although they cannot repay you, you will be repaid at the resurrection of the righteous." Luke 14:12-14
If I'm His follower, I'm doing those things. Am I doing those things?

But Zacchaeus stood up and said to the Lord, "Look, Lord! Here and now I give half of my possessions to the poor, and if I have cheated anybody out of anything, I will pay back four times the amount." Jesus said to him, "Today salvation has come to this house...." Luke 19:8,9
Oh, so beautiful! Following Jesus makes a transformational difference. It costs … but there is so much joy! Is your brand of Christianity boring and costless? Are you fidgeting with your faith? Are you just so-so, lukewarm, tepid, *fine*? Are you ready to risk and do something crazy like Zacchaeus, letting go of all you've schemed so hard for, ready to change, different in heart? Are you like him, climbing up in a tree hoping with all your might to see Jesus, and there's nothing that can make you miss Him? Well, here's a chance: Let go and do something wild for Him. Feel your faith as you go up to the edge. Go ahead, look foolish to others. Do something that may not make sense, but you feel it in your bones, in your spirit. Sometimes that's what faith looks like. For Zacchaeus, it was letting go of money and riches. What is it for you?

For you know the grace of our Lord Jesus Christ, that though he was rich, yet for your sake he became poor, so that you through his poverty might become rich. 2 Corinthians 8:9. In fact, just read all of 2 Corinthians 8 & 9.

Such a challenging example for us. I do tend to love our wealth. It's outrageous, provocative, even staggering to open our hands and let what we've worked for … go. Can't I just be a generous giver out of my abundance? Do I really need to release *everything* to You? Hear Him say this: "Child, *it's all Mine*. You are My *steward*. I've given you this money and these abilities, so you will put it back in My hands to do with it as I will. Beware: Your worth is not in your wealth. Your position is not in your possessions. Take care not to let your possessions possess you. I lift up the humble and oppose the proud. Don't forget whose truth you are building upon."

It's all so counter-cultural, so un-American, to go low, to give away your fortune, to be willing to be UN-known for Christ. But His poverty made you wealthy in all the right ways: You have heaven in your future. You know God! You are in the family of the King. You are free from your sin and all its horrible, heavy guilt. Oh, praise God, you are so deeply and dearly loved. You are already rich, Dear Reader. Rich in Christ. Your earthly riches are not yours. Make sure you are following His orders. The love of money is a root of evil, and that tree has branches of selfishness, brutality, and dehumanization. The Holy Spirit opposes all of those characteristics. Do you actually want the Holy Spirit to oppose you? Of course not. So be generous, even if it seems crazy.

All they asked was that we should continue to remember the poor, the very thing I had been eager to do all along. Galatians 2:10
How are you remembering the poor? List some concrete actions you are taking or can begin.

Suppose a man comes into your meeting wearing a gold ring and fine clothes, and a poor man in filthy old clothes also comes in. If you show special attention to the man wearing fine clothes and say, "Here's a good seat for you," but say to the poor man, "You stand there" or "Sit on the floor by my feet," have you not discriminated among yourselves and become judges with evil thoughts? Listen, my dear brothers and sisters: Has not God chosen those who are poor in the eyes of the world to be rich in faith and to inherit the kingdom he promised those who love him? 6 But you have dishonored the poor. Is it not the rich who are exploiting you? Are they not the ones who are dragging you into court? James 2:2-6
James is helping us *see*, because wealth carries a deceitfulness with it. Are we showing preference to a certain class of people? There is an entire world out there of other classes, hurts, anguishes, gifts, talents, humor, and power. Am I exploiting workers or a certain group of people just to make a buck? Shame. God, open our eyes.

Suppose a brother or a sister is without clothes and daily food. If one of you says to them, "Go in peace; keep warm and well fed," but does nothing

about their physical needs, what good is it? In the same way, faith by itself, if it is not accompanied by action, is dead. James 2:15-17
How are your actions confirming your faith? How are you caring for fellow Christians who are in need?

July 5th "Daily Light" devotional (my favorite devotional of all time)

Do not set your mind on high things, but associate with the humble. Romans 12:16

Has God not chosen the poor of the world to be rich in faith and heirs of the kingdom which He promised to those who love Him? James 2:5

Let no one seek his own, but each one the other's well-being. 1 Corinthians 10:24

Having food and clothing, with these we shall be content. But those who desire to be rich fall into temptation and a snare and drown men in destruction and perdition. 1 Timothy 6:8-9

God has chosen the foolish things of the world to put to shame the wise, and God has chosen the weak things of the world to put to shame the things that are mighty; and the base things of the world and the things which are despised God has chosen, and the things that are not, to bring to nothing the things that are, that no flesh should glory in His Presence. 1 Corinthians 1:27-29

A favorite way to explore the Scriptures is using Biblehub.com. Type a verse into the Search box, click the Interlinear tab, and click on the Strong's Concordance number. Once there, there is a wealth of information to explore. Maybe try the verses above.

Appendix C
Tell Yourself the Gospel

I started doing this at the end of every day and it changed me forever. I invite you to do it too. It's straight Scripture, compiled with an ear to confession, truth, forgiveness, restoration, and flourishing. Enjoy.

For the sake of Your Name, O LORD,
forgive my iniquity, though it is great. Psalm 25:11

"Lord, save me!"
Immediately, Jesus reached out His hand and caught [Peter].
"Why did you doubt?" Matthew 14:30,31

If we confess our sins, He is faithful and just
and will forgive us our sins and cleanse us from all unrighteousness. 1 John 1:9
Then I acknowledged my sin to You and did not cover up my iniquity …
and You forgave the guilt of my sin. Psalm 32:5

You see, at just the right time, when we were still powerless,
Christ died for the ungodly. God demonstrates His own love for us in this:
while we were still sinners, Christ died for us. Romans 5:6,8
One Mediator between God and men, the Man Jesus Christ. 1 Tim 2:5

The blood of Jesus Christ His Son cleanses us from all sin. 1 John 1:7
I will forgive their iniquity and their sin I will remember no more.
Jeremiah 31:34
Brought near by the blood of Christ. Ephesians 2:13,14

"Your sins are forgiven you." Mark 2:5
You have cast my sins behind Your back. Isaiah 38:17
Who can forgive sins but God alone? Mark 2:7

All beautiful you are, My darling; there is no flaw in you. Song of Songs 4:7
In Christ, I am free. Galatians 5:13

To Him who loves us and has freed us from our sins by His blood,
and has made us to be a kingdom of priests to serve His God and Father,
to Him be glory and power for ever and ever! Amen! Revelation 1:5,6

My soul finds rest in God alone; my salvation comes from Him. Psalm 62:1

But I am like an olive tree flourishing in the house of God;
I trust in God's unfailing love for ever and ever. Psalm 52:8

Blessed is the person whose transgressions are forgiven,
whose sins are covered …
whose sin the LORD does not count against him. Psalm 32:1,2

About the Author

Suzanne Stelling values living simply and artfully with her beloved husband, house guests, and their urban menagerie as she explores what it means to love her neighbor in East Knoxville. She authentically wants to be intimate with God the Father, Jesus the Son, and the Holy Spirit. Suzanne appreciates a rich and nutty frosted brownie, a hearty loaf of bread, world travel, photography, and lively friendship. She really does get a feather almost every day. It's remarkable, truly inexplicable apart from the lavish love of God.

During her job as director of Women's Ministries (2009-2020) in a West Knoxville church, she cared for women by writing Bible studies, offering leadership development, and providing a listening ear. She is a frequent teacher and speaker in her hometown but treasures her regional and international opportunities as well. Her passions and curiosities include Christian maturity, racial and class divides, photography, watercolor painting, learning new vocabulary, baking, and being a good neighbor in her 'hood.

Although Suzanne attended Vanderbilt University for undergraduate studies and holds two Masters Degrees (Education; Ethics and Leadership), she considers her most important learning these days to occur around a plate of warm cookies with the people in her neighborhood.

Other Books by Suzanne Stelling

Suzanne has written two photography-based books to help women pause, take a deep breath, and pursue the God who loves them so dearly. They are available on Amazon.com and barnesandnoble.com.

In *Snapshots*, Suzanne artfully explains the Biblical narrative using carefully curated modern-day snapshots. Touring Genesis to Job, meet God and humanity with Adam, Eve, and Noah; travel with forefathers Abraham, Isaac, Jacob, and Joseph; lead with Moses, Joshua, and the Judges; analyze the rise and fall of the Kings of Judah, Israel, and the region; rebuild with Ruth, Ezra, Nehemiah, and Esther; and peek behind the curtain of suffering with Job.

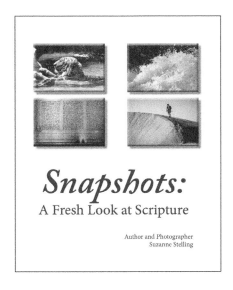

Copies are obtained exclusively through Suzanne at abrightbulb@gmail.com or at Backroads Market, Knoxville, TN.

For speaking engagements, contact Suzanne at abrightbulb@gmail.com.

Made in the USA
Middletown, DE
31 October 2023

41714386R00156